'This biography of a beloved Australian writer and cultural figure who campaigned to create just copyright for fellow writers, and bestrode the Australian cultural scene, is wonderfully lively and, like the subject himself, charming. It is both an engaging tale and a great work of research.' —**Tom Keneally**

Catharine Lumby is a Professor of Media at the University of Sydney where she was founding Chair of the Media and Communications Department. Prior to entering academia, she worked for two decades as a print and TV journalist for *The Sydney Morning Herald*, the ABC and *The Bulletin* magazine. She has written and co-authored ten books including *Bad Girls* and *Gotcha*, and numerous book chapters and journal articles.

FRANK MOORHOUSE

A LIFE

Darling Anne Marie,

CATHARINE LUMBY

*What a friendship!
I am so lucky to
have you in my life.
Enjoy!   Cxx*

ALLEN&UNWIN
SYDNEY · MELBOURNE · AUCKLAND · LONDON

First published in 2023

This project has been assisted by the Australian Government through the Australia Council, its arts funding and advisory board.

Allen & Unwin
Cammeraygal Country
83 Alexander Street
Crows Nest NSW 2065
Australia
Phone: (61 2) 8425 0100
Email: info@allenandunwin.com
Web: www.allenandunwin.com

Allen & Unwin acknowledges the Traditional Owners of the Country on which we live and work. We pay our respects to all Aboriginal and Torres Strait Islander Elders, past and present.

 A catalogue record for this book is available from the National Library of Australia

ISBN 978 1 74237 224 2

Index by Garry Cousins
Set in 12.5/17 pt Adobe Garamond Pro by Midland Typesetters, Australia

Printed and bound in Australia by the Opus Group

10 9 8 7 6 5 4 3 2 1

 The paper in this book is FSC® certified. FSC® promotes environmentally responsible, socially beneficial and economically viable management of the world's forests.

This book is dedicated to five people. All of them knew Frank,
understood him and helped me understand him.
Chef Tony Bilson, writer Meaghan Morris, writer Fiona Giles,
archivist Nicholas Pounder and publisher Jane Palfreyman.
In different and important ways, they helped shape this book for
the better and all of them have been influential for me as a writer.
I thank them for their insights, their generosity, their mentorship
and their belief in this project.

CONTENTS

INTRODUCTION

Frank Moorhouse was one of Australia's most prolific writers and public intellectuals. He wrote eighteen fiction and non-fiction books. He was a journalist who also wrote essays and screen plays. Born in Nowra in 1938, he decided very young he wanted to be a writer. This is my version of his story: of his stories and the storeys within the multilayered, brilliant and complicated person who was home to his writing and his extraordinarily adventurous life.

Moorhouse was first and foremost a contradiction in terms. A man who was wedded to and fascinated by rules and rituals while equally prepared to rail against the overreach of the state and bourgeois morality. His major works of fiction are grounded in this productive tension, in the question of: How many rules do we need to live well? How many rules are too many? Or more existentially as he put it in an email to me once: 'How did we all get ourselves into this mess? And how the hell do we get out of it?'

The rules of social engagement—or etiquette, to truck a bourgeois phrase into the ethical frame—is a subject that recurs throughout Moorhouse's oeuvre: from his early interrogation of social conventions in *Futility and Other Animals* to the full-blown dissection of the limits of the international rule of law in his League of Nations trilogy.

I think rules fascinated him precisely because he liked toying with their boundaries. He was interested in worrying, rather than exceeding, their limits. He enjoyed martinis, but as he made clear—perhaps excessively clear—in his memoir, there are rules. Martinis, like all other aspects of living well, must be prepared and imbibed with care. There are rituals to be observed—rituals designed to keep the wilder beasts of hedonism at bay. Not that Moorhouse was a rigid person. I saw him, rather, as our man at the cultural cliff edge—perpetually running his hand along the railing and staring down with alarmed fascination at the jagged rocks below.

He was also a very courageous man who was prepared to speak out, protest and participate in legal battles for causes he believed in. He was an early crusader against Australia's repressive (and frankly ridiculous) censorship laws in the 1960s, he was central to a series of court cases that resulted in universities and schools paying a fee for reproducing creative works and he was a supporter of the gay liberation, feminist and Aboriginal rights movements throughout his life. He wrote about and scrutinised government overreach when it came to the surveillance of citizens. And ultimately he was a public intellectual who eschewed ideological dogma and was prepared to take unfashionable stances when he deemed it necessary. He frequently employed irony to make his point, leaving some of his critics confused. Above all, he championed the importance of writing and all the creative arts and was a generous mentor to emerging writers.

When I embarked on the biography, Moorhouse had already written a semi-fictional memoir—*Martini*, published in 2006—and in that book he explains the relationship between autobiography and fiction this way:

> This memoir is not a comprehensive overview of my life or my relationships and is not meant, therefore, as a complete diagram of my life now or in the past . . . It is, in passing, also a consideration of the relationship of fiction to memory and to the writer's life and it begins with the unpacking of an earlier story of mine entitled 'Martini'—the making of stories from stories, I suppose, and how stories can bubble out from other stories.

His response raises, as he acknowledged himself, ethical questions about the relationship between writers and their subjects when they draw directly on material from their own lives, a subject that will be explored in detail in this book. It is also clear from his archive not only that he consciously documented his relationships with others, but that he was documenting himself, as a writer who started out as a writer in the 1970s, a period of immense social, cultural and political change.

Moorhouse never set out to live a life of unblemished bourgeois domesticity. He never owned a house or even a car after his twenties. He ate most of his meals in restaurants. Some of his intimate relationships were often unconventional, at least if judged by the middle-class norms of the time— the publicly accepted ones, anyway. That is not to say that Moorhouse did not have significant, long-lasting relationships with women and men. Indeed, he remained close to many of his former partners; Sandra Levy was, until his death, a close friend and confidante. In researching this biography, it has often struck me that stepping outside some of the bourgeois norms involved Moorhouse in thinking far more deeply about ethics than some of those who live a more conformist life.

Moorhouse's work was frequently and transparently entangled with his life. It's not that he directly translated people and events—no writer does. But, more than most, he openly drew on the milieu in which he was embedded. He drew lovers, friends and colleagues into his fiction with sometimes slight disguise and did so repeatedly. The same characters recur in his work.

The Intentional Fallacy test simply doesn't stand with a writer like Moorhouse. His work and his life were, in some of his stories, clearly entangled. Which poses a secondary dilemma for the biographer: when is it relevant to draw parallels between people and events in the life of the author and the narratives, characters and themes in their work? I'm not suggesting that I intend to engage in a banal guessing game about who various characters might be based on, but at a deeper level, it seems to me that there are valid reasons to, at times, juxtapose Moorhouse's life and work—if only because the author did so himself at times. *Martini* and *Forty-Seventeen* are two obvious cases in point.

This biography is not a comprehensive guide to Moorhouse's life and work. And it's not a work of literary criticism. It's an attempt to connect the life and the work of an important Australian writer, and to show how the two were inextricably linked. I want to explore Moorhouse's complex legacy as a writer, an activist and a person, and to explore how the social, political and cultural shifts he lived through influenced his writing—and how, in turn, his writing influenced those shifts.

Many writers fashion a career out of their writing. Some fashion brilliant careers. Very few, however, commit to their art in a manner that inflects every aspect of their own daily life. Frank Moorhouse was one of the rare writers who actively chose to live a life that was as grounded in conscious aesthetic and ethical choices as was his writing.

This biography doesn't follow a timeline—we won't be starting with the no doubt dark and stormy night Moorhouse was born. Sadly, however, the final chapter does end with a reflection by others on his legacy following his death, which occurred as I was writing the conclusion to the book in 2022.

This is a selective biography. It's written from a subjective viewpoint. I've written it with an eye to exploring the relationship between Moorhouse's life and writing, and to offering a literary, political and social framework for understanding the importance of the man and his oeuvre.

My affection for Moorhouse's writing began when I was a teenager in Newcastle, living in a working-class beach town in Australia. His writing gave me a glimpse of a different world—a bohemian and cosmopolitan world that was foreign to the town I grew up in. I used to joke with friends that when I grew up I wanted to be Frank Moorhouse. This book is an analysis of why I think his writing matters. It is an argument, if you like, for the importance of not only the work itself but the difference Moorhouse made through his activism and his role as a public intellectual. It is, equally, a thesis about how his early and later works have many things in common.

While I was writing this biography, many people told me they couldn't understand the relationship between the genres that Moorhouse worked across: short stories, essays, comic essays, historical novels, journalism. This biography is also my attempt to answer that compelling question.

1

LEAVING NOWRA

Frank Moorhouse stood at a sink shucking oysters with his well-used oyster knife while two martini glasses chilled in the freezer. Outside the cabin, the sun was setting over the Crookhaven River. Pelicans glided over the water and roosted on the jetty outside. We were at Greenwell Point, a small village 15 kilometres east of the New South Wales South Coast town of Nowra. It's a seafood port known for its oyster farms, and I had just driven Moorhouse down to the oyster leases to get a sack of three dozen oysters. Dinner would be at the local bowling club—old-school Chinese food. When Moorhouse returned to his hometown of Nowra, he liked to stay at Greenwell Point. Close but not too close.

Moorhouse was visibly agitated after a day visiting his old high school, Nowra High, where, in 1955 and '56, he was school captain. We were welcomed by the principal and two senior students wearing blazers, who looked politely confused when informed that the man standing before them was a Literary Icon who had once attended their school. Afterwards, Moorhouse sat on a bench in the playground and stared thoughtfully into space, remarking: 'There are some odd tunings coming in from the past.' We drove back to Greenwell Point in relative silence.

We were in Nowra to interview his younger brother, Arthur, and his sister-in-law, Rhonda, and to see significant places from his childhood. Moorhouse had a complicated relationship with his past and his family. His mother and father, both highly regarded Nowra citizens, form the basis of two of the most important characters in his books: Edith Campbell Berry and T. George McDowell, respectively. Of the two, Moorhouse was very clear that his mother exerted the stronger influence. He said in 2011 that she had provided the dominant part of his personality:

> Writers sometimes talk of the mother novel and the father novel that lots have. I think my therapist pointed out to me that *The Electrical Experience* is the father novel—about two centimetres thick—and the three volumes [the trilogy completed by *Cold Light*] that constitute my mother are half a metre thick. That's who's won the control, in so far as our personality is a struggle between the parents, for control of the personality of the child. As my therapist pointed out, we can see who won.

Asked how his early life influenced his writing, Moorhouse once quipped to me: 'I'm always writing about Nowra. You could say everything I've written is really about Nowra.' How much of that comment was ironic close readers of Moorhouse can judge for themselves.

Moorhouse certainly had a complicated relationship with his past. He was keenly aware that his parents were somewhat mystified, or perhaps even shocked, by his early work. His first book, *Futility and Other Animals*, published in 1969, was, after all, banned, and other early books were the subject of public controversy. Yet in his work he returned on many occasions to reflections on life in a South Coast country town and his straining against the expectations of his respected middle-class parents.

Nowra is a small town, population 22,000, located on the South Coast of New South Wales, around 160 kilometres from Sydney. It sits on the Shoalhaven River, and when rain has been plentiful the surrounding land is lush and green. Nowra is a farming community with a still thriving dairy industry, surrounded by state forest. The population of Nowra remains overwhelmingly Anglo-Australian, with one exception to the demographic norm: 10 per cent of the population identify as Indigenous.

Born in 1938, Frank Moorhouse was the third of three brothers. Owen is the eldest and Arthur the middle child. There were ten years between Frank and Owen and six years separating Arthur and Frank. Their father was an inventor and the owner of a very successful farming equipment business with a wonder-ful name—Moorhouse: The Machinery Man. Frank Osborne Moorhouse was born in 1904 in Wanganui, New Zealand, into a dairy farming family. His father, Frederick Curtis Moorhouse, died when he was four years old. Moorhouse Snr left school at an early age and trained as an electrical engineer, becoming one of the first licensed electricians in the country.

After moving to Australia from New Zealand, Frank Snr married Purthanry Thanes Mary Cutts in 1928. Their first meeting was at a ferry wharf in North Sydney, where he was approached by Girl Guides selling tickets to their annual ball.

When Moorhouse protested that he didn't have a partner to take, they solved his problem by pointing out that their Girl Guides captain didn't have one either. Moorhouse and his new bride Purth moved from Sydney to Nowra. It was the start of the Great Depression. Nonetheless, Moorhouse thrived. He had a strong work ethic and a talent for innovation.

A reference for Moorhouse Snr provided by Alan D. Cuffe in 1936 gives a snapshot of his character. Cuffe, who was the general manager of a dairy farming manufacturing company, wrote:

> I think Mr Moorhouse is one of the most satisfactory District Representatives that I have ever handled. His mechanical and electrical knowledge is very sound, and his sales figures prove his selling ability . . . He was absolutely honest and loyal in his attitude to employers and customers and I have no reservations whatsoever in warmly recommending him for any similar position.

Frank Thomas Moorhouse was born in a small private hospital in Junction Street, Nowra, and lived in the second family home, which his parents named Rangimarie, a Māori word meaning 'peace'. It was built on the corner of Kinghorne and Worrigee streets, near the town centre. The adjoining terrace houses were converted into a workshop, where Moorhouse Snr designed, built and displayed an invention which revolutionised the dairy industry: the Moorhouse Dairy Boiler. It was integral to the move to sterilise milk in Australia. (One can only imagine what Moorhouse Snr would make of the turn back to 'raw milk' in Australia's hipper suburbs today.) He capitalised on this invention by adding other innovations such as engines, pumps and other agricultural equipment, and was later assisted by his sons Owen and Arthur.

In a speech to the Australian Senate in 1994, following Frank Moorhouse Snr's death at the age of 90, Senator Michael Baume recalled the importance of his primary invention:

> In those days, the problem in the dairying industry was with boiling water for sterilising dairy utensils. With his engineering ability, he invented and manufactured a very efficient device that would boil water very rapidly with a minimum amount of fuel. Approximately 20,000 of these were manufactured and distributed throughout the three eastern states . . . The name Moorhouse the Machinery Man became synonymous throughout Eastern Australia with the dairy industry and with a high-quality product.

When Jack Ferguson was chairman of the New South Wales Milk Board in 1952, he described the Moorhouse Dairy Boiler as 'the greatest contribution to good quality milk for Sydney'.

The 1950s was a time when mechanisation of farming equipment was becoming standard and there was a growing demand for electrical appliances. *The Electrical Experience* undoubtedly drew on Moorhouse's observations of the key role his father played in this trend. The fact that the central character of the book, T. George McDowell, was an inventor and a salesman reflects and refracts this aspect of Moorhouse's father. But McDowell also embodied the values of citizenship and service that were so important to both Moorhouse Snr and his wife, Purth.

The Moorhouses were regarded as upstanding and prominent citizens in Nowra. Moorhouse Snr was a dedicated member of the local Masonic club, a founding secretary of Rotary, a Shire councillor and the Scouts' district commissioner. Purth, a devoted Anglican, was the district commissioner for the Girl Guides and leader of the Country Women's Association (CWA). Moorhouse Park, by the banks of the Shoalhaven River, in Nowra is dedicated to them by the local council. Both Frank Snr and Purth were awarded the Medal of the Order of Australia for services to the community and to industry.

Moorhouse's childhood friend, Fay Martin, recalls the Moorhouse family as the 'apex of the social structure of Nowra, I guess. [The Moorhouse parents had] travelled overseas, and nobody we knew had ever travelled overseas in that era, in the 1950s. Plus the fact that they used to write diaries of what they'd done in the local paper.' Fay's husband, Peter, went to primary school with Moorhouse and, along with his wife, maintained a lifelong friendship with the writer. He remembers his friend's parents as both 'very, very strong', and Moorhouse Snr as 'a big, tall six-foot-two man with dark greyish hair—a very imposing person'.

For Moorhouse Snr, a knowledge of the practical and technical aspects of labour was foundational and was married to his belief in the virtue of industry. His view of the relationship between hard work and civic duty is encapsulated in a program printed for his company's annual staff dinner in 1944. The program began with a toast to the King, then to the staff, the firm and, somewhat oddly, the press. On the right-hand side of the program was a manifesto titled 'My Vocation'. It was unattributed, but it seems reasonable to surmise that Moorhouse Snr penned it. It reads, in part: 'Therefore, it shall be my purpose: To consider my job worthy, affording me not merely a means of material gain and self-expression, but also a distinct opportunity to serve society.' These are clearly not the words of a man who regarded manufacturing dairy equipment simply as a means of providing for his family.

There was, however, a darker side to the family history, which Moorhouse characteristically winkled out of his father when he was researching Purth's history. Moorhouse Snr's father, Frederick Curtis Moorhouse, had suicided in 1909. Moorhouse Snr asked Moorhouse to keep this fact a secret from his brothers until his death.

'It was, I suspect, Dad's darkest secret and his shame,' he reflected. 'What Dad showed me at that time was a newspaper clipping he had kept hidden in a book. It told of the death of his father, Frederick Curtis Moorhouse, aged 43, by self-strangulation (by using his torn-up shirt) in a padded police cell in Wanganui between August 5 and 6, while "temporarily insane".'

How remarkable it was, Moorhouse said, that his father was so driven while living under what he must privately have seen as a dark shadow. 'He would have feared that it might happen to him—that is, insanity, alcoholism and suicide. Or that the secret would be discovered by someone in Nowra.'

Moorhouse arguably explored the fear that may have shadowed his otherwise stalwart and determined father in one of his seminal characters T. George McDowell—the central character in *The Electrical Experience*, and a minor but key character in his League of Nations trilogy. The relationship between fiction and life is, of course, always unclear. But it would be hard to ignore the influence Moorhouse Snr had on his son's life— including, as we will see, his own interrogations of how much we might reveal about ourselves without inviting shame.

Moorhouse's mother was an even stronger influence on him than his father. The branch president of the Nowra CWA in 1954, 1960–62 and 1964, Purth was described by her son Arthur as being well known in the district as the type of person 'who wanted to help other folk'. As a middle-class woman married to a successful man, Purth Moorhouse was expected to model civic virtue through both her organisational skills and domestic talents.

In her book *Country Women and the Colour Bar*, historian Jennifer Jones writes: 'CWA social occasions, such as a branch opening, provided a public stage for the celebration of CWA values, including the display of traditional feminine skills such as cooking and food service.' At the Nowra branch of the CWA, women were taught handicraft skills, from glove-making, pottery and cake decorating to making French flowers and fashioning winter hats.

Jones observes that the CWA was an organisation that reinforced existing class hierarchies, and that having been 'placed' according to known facts, including family background, residence and occupation, rural people were pressured to moderate their behaviour in keeping with their class position. The CWA and other associations such as Rotary were important glue that bound the Nowra community together, while nevertheless reinforcing the differing social status of their members.

In Nowra, Jones' research reveals, Purth Moorhouse was among several members of the CWA who were 'wished "bon voyage" as they embarked on overseas trips during the period 1961–1964. Travel slides and souvenirs provided entertainment for branch members on their return.' Purth Moorhouse was a middle-class woman of her time and place, but she was, equally, a bright woman whom Moorhouse often said he admired. He talked of how she had influenced his preoccupation with committees, conferences and the rules of living well, a fascination shared by the heroine of his League of Nations series, Edith Campbell Berry.

Despite his rejection of the bourgeois conformism of his upbringing, Moorhouse was profoundly shaped by both his parents. His father's influence can be seen in his disciplined work ethic when it came to writing, and his mother's in his fascination with committees, protocols and the role of aesthetics in creating the right setting and atmosphere to facilitate formal discourse and convivial conversation.

———

Moorhouse grew up in a home where he had access to books—a collection of classic literature which included Sir Walter Scott and Charles Dickens, as well as a selection of 18th- and 19th-century poets—and he was a constant reader from an early age. As a child, he was already foreshadowing his future career as a writer. He recalled of his years in primary school, 'I was good at painting . . . I wrote a novella . . . I enjoyed primary school.'

He was profoundly influenced by reading *Alice's Adventures in Wonderland* while bed-ridden for months at the age of twelve. The book was given to him by Muriel Lewis, a young university graduate, who was visiting Nowra and the Moorhouse family for the first time. Muriel would become his sister-in-law. Moorhouse credited her with furthering his fascination with becoming a writer, saying, 'After experiencing the magic of this book, I wanted to be the magician who made the magic.'

His father, however, had different ideas about his son's future when he sent him to Wollongong Technical High. 'He thought that all his sons should have a trade,' Moorhouse recalled. 'My two brothers went through Wollongong Tech and went into the factory. He thought that I would go into the factory and that I should have a technical background. Probably, I don't know, do an apprenticeship or something like that, like my two brothers had done.'

Peter Martin remembers being surprised when Moorhouse was sent to Wollongong Tech for his first three years of secondary education: 'I said to him: "Why aren't you going to boarding school?" Because they were considered wealthy. He said his father wanted him to have a technical education. It was quite interesting, I thought . . . Nowra was the headquarters of a big dairy farming area where everyone just sort of subsisted. Yet the Moorhouse brothers went to this intermediate technical high school.'

Moorhouse was billeted with a local family, the Churchins, in Wollongong and learnt metalworking, woodworking and technical drawing, along with English, maths and science. 'It was a really old, prison-style school,' he said, 'that was built around an asphalt playground that was virtually enclosed by the four sides of the high school . . . it was a very tough sort of school physically, structurally, because there was no real recreational area . . .'

A letter of reference for Moorhouse written by the deputy headmaster in 1953 read, in part: 'Frank's character and personality may be judged from the fact that this year he was School Captain; in performing the duties of this office, he displayed qualities of leadership, reliability and maturity which marks him as an outstanding boy.' The letter went on to note his sporting and academic prowess as a first-grade rugby footballer, as a cadet and as the schoolboy member of the annual school magazine's editorial committee.

It goes without saying that Moorhouse was first in his year in English. For topping the year in the subject he received a copy of The King's English by H.G. and F.G. Fowler, the then compilers of *The Concise Oxford Dictionary of Current English*. One can only imagine what the Fowlers would have made of the uses to which Moorhouse later put their beloved English language in his vivid descriptions of the era that brought sexual liberation to Australia—the 1970s.

In his third year of high school, a vocational guidance counsellor asked Moorhouse to fill in a form with his preferred vocations. 'I wrote short story writer, then I just put army officer and then expressive dancer,' he recalled. As improbable as it seems, he really did put down option three—it is in the archive.

In 1954, having been dux of Wollongong Tech, Moorhouse moved to Nowra High for his last two years of school. He wanted to study art along with other traditional subjects, but his father and the headmaster insisted he do general maths instead.

Fay Martin remembers Moorhouse's arrival in Form Four at Nowra High: 'He was an impressive newcomer—handsome, good at sport, self-assured with a hint of sophistication. Charisma, maybe—a word we didn't have in our vocab in 1954. Previously he had been at a boys' school but was very much at ease in a mixed classroom.'

In his second term Moorhouse began producing a newsletter titled *The Student Voice*. It was stencilled with the help of friends and sold for a penny a copy. In the 1954 edition of the high school's magazine, *The Platypus*, Moorhouse had a story titled 'Is This Us?', which began with a character called Johnny Australia sitting in a classroom and musing on his future.

He had often wondered what made some of his friends live. They had no fixed purpose in life, they just drifted. When asked of the future, they would, with a suck of their teeth and raised eyebrows, shrug their shoulders and say 'Don't ask me. Whatever comes along; I'm easy!' Johnny wanted to create, to make; he wanted to leave something behind him for the world to know he had been alive.

Moorhouse once again became school captain in Form Five, the final year of high school in the 1950s. In his spare time, Moorhouse often hung out with his friend Peter Martin, who says that 'our lynchpin together was push bikes . . . We used to do all sorts of marvellous things on push bikes . . . We used to travel a long way, get on the bike and ride and go down the coast for 30 miles [50 kilometres] and go to the beaches . . . Your mother wouldn't know—I'd go away all day with Frank. Sometimes we'd go over two days. We'd go out of the town, hide our bikes in the bush somewhere on the highway and start hitchhiking . . . We just used to play it by ear a bit and try and find somewhere where we could get some shelter. There was generally a beach there so you could always find shelter somewhere.' He also recalls weekend shenanigans: 'We used to go up to the creeks, jump off the big rocks and bomb the snakes in the water, all that stuff.'

In a piece titled 'They Said We Were Mad', published in the 1955 school magazine, Moorhouse recounted his adventures with Martin. It captured the strength and ebullience of their friendship and set the scene for an enduring aspect of Moorhouse's life—his appetite for challenging himself physically and emotionally with long solo bushwalks where he was separated from comfort and safety.

The piece begins: 'When we two boys planned a cycling trip to cover approximately seven hundred miles [1130 kilometres] of hot black bitumen, our friends stared, firstly with amazement and secondly with derision. Our parents laughed sympathetically and hoped that we did not have the will to attempt such a trip.'

They set out on 14 December 1954 and arrived back in Nowra on 29 January 1955. They covered over 1600 kilometres, riding their bikes and hitching lifts on trucks. They camped and occasionally found rough-and-ready accommodation through family friends or acquaintances. When they reached Leeton they picked apples and oranges for £2 and 10 shillings a day for three days, working in the morning and swimming in the afternoon. They moved on to Griffith, where they were given work on a friend's rice farm, digging burrs and thistles from the levee banks. Moorhouse wrote: 'Christmas came, a day to us which was hardly any different to the others, except for a wild duck which we had for dinner. We swam in the irrigation channels and listened to the boring repetition of Christmas tunes on the radio.'

Characteristically, Moorhouse detailed the equipment they took and the style of bikes in an amusing approximation of military language:

> HOW: On push bikes of the sports-racing type, equipped with four speed external chain type gears and generator powered head and taillight. Our gear was strapped over the back wheel on steel carriers.
>
> EQUIPMENT: Owing to our earlier experience in touring, we were able to travel lightly. Our lightweight tent and clothes folded into a groundsheet forming a waterproof pack about two feet six inches by three foot and strapped onto the carrier.

Little changed throughout the course of his life. Moorhouse loved regaling friends with tales of exciting new camping and bushwalking technologies involving tents, GPS devices, water-proof fabrics—right up until his eighties, when he no longer had the stamina for bushwalking and camping.

Despite a plan to ride 70 miles (113 kilometres) a day, the intrepid friends swiftly settled into a routine of hitching rides between towns in which they were seeking work, a mode of travel they dubbed 'hitch-biking'. They arrived in Forbes, having travelled over 1100 kilometres, and landed a job in the meatworks.

Another close childhood friend, Paul Coombes, remembers first meeting Moorhouse at Nowra High and being put off by his cadet's uniform. He soon came to realise that his friend was far more interested in being a writer than a soldier. Even so, Moorhouse's membership of the cadets and the Scouts did speak to his lifelong interest in outdoor pursuits. 'I didn't care much for the military at that time at all,' says Coombes. 'I thought, "Christ". That didn't give me a very strong impression because I didn't like wars and I didn't like violence. I didn't like kids getting in there and being brainwashed. On the other hand, of course, it was a bit of a lark. You go out and have fun and play with guns and then come home, take off your uniform, put on your bathers and run around and chase the girls.'

Coombes, like Peter and Fay Martin, has a strong memory of how early Moorhouse's identity as a writer was forged. He recalled that in 1950s Nowra:

'You were press-ganged into something you didn't want to do, and that equally you were being press-ganged to get into the family business . . . [Frank] was sufficiently strong and smart to play one game and follow the other. He only wanted to be a writer, not a soldier, and he figured that if he wanted to be a writer then that's the thing he had to do, write, and practise every day.'

Coombes's observations bear out my own as his biographer going through the voluminous Moorhouse archive at the Fryer Library. It's indeed remarkable how young Moorhouse was when he self-identified as a writer. From an early age, many key facets of his adult personality were already there, all but fully formed: his interest in the bushman's craft, his leadership abilities, his fascination with creating and facilitating democratic order, and his strong work ethic.

In an undated typewritten piece in the archive, titled 'My Reasons for Entering Journalism' Moorhouse stated that he was fourteen when he 'begot the urge to write', which he described as 'an internal urge'. He listed his reasons for his decision to enter journalism:

1. Writing gives me the fullest satisfaction. The finishing of an original story imbues me with a feeling of contentment and achievement. The desire to express my opinions and have them noticed.
2. My aversion to prejudice and bigotry which compells [sic] me to try and destroy false notions and to always give the truth . . .
3. My wish to see the world a free and just place not a world of propaganda, lies, censorship and bias.
4. My interest in other people and in current affairs because I believe that only by being fully conscious of the world about us can we live and judge fairly.
5. To learn to be a skilful and honest journalist.
6. To serve my fellow citizens.

From the somewhat stilted style and the typeface, which matched that of stories he wrote in high school, it seems likely that these notes were made when Moorhouse was fifteen or sixteen. The notes betray a certain tension for the young would-be writer. On one hand, a recognition that he needed to make a convincing case for choosing a career outside the family business, coupled with an acceptance of the values his parents championed: civic virtue and hard work.

His juvenilia are in his archive, comprising a large box full of typewritten attempts at essays on the emotional life of an adolescent, as well as on the political and social issues he detected in the world around him. In one, titled 'The World and Me' and dated 1955, he wrote:

> I am adolescent and to outline a few of those qualities which our sort are supposed to possess I will mention inexperience, half-education and a sensitivity which presents life in unreal proportion. I am prepared to accept these labels but I demand in return recognition and a hearing. I demand these because we are the people who inherit the world you are trying to manage at present. We suffer your mistakes. It seems unjust and strange that life should be nothing more than a 'passing the buck' organisation. Parents unintentionally pass on their combined character and ability to their children through hereditary [sic] the children are then compelled to live as these 'passed on' qualities demand in a 'passed on' world already twisted by attempts at organisation.

It's an indignant passage, and one that anyone who has parented an independent-minded teenager will recognise. What marked Moorhouse's copious juvenilia out from the stock standard adolescent protests and musings that populate so many teenage notebooks and diaries was the length to which he went to ask astonishingly big-picture questions. 'The World and Me' swiftly moved on from the usual complaints about parental hypocrisy to a discussion of systemic global and economic inequity and governance, the problem of censorship, and the sexual double standards that dogged heterosexual relationships.

Throughout these typewritten pieces, Moorhouse constantly returned to the problem of finding an outlet for expressing his views. In 'Rambling in the Mind of an Adolescent—Part 11', he wrote:

> I was lying on my back bemoaning the position of the world and the fact that no one would listen to me if I did try to have my essays published. I then became scared that someone else would think the same thoughts as I had just written and that I would read them tomorrow in some magazine and read of how the adolescent who wrote them was a world saviour.

What writer hasn't experienced the fear of being gazumped when they are in the middle of a writing project? Indeed, the most striking thing about Moorhouse's teenage essays was the urgency with which he was seeking a forum for his ideas. They are shot through with a growing knowledge that writing was his vocation, and that his vocation was at odds with his father's expectations that he join the family business.

———

Moorhouse's remark that he was 'always writing about Nowra' is a dry-humoured reference to his early desire to escape the parochial aspects of his upbringing, which he did in his late teens. It is certainly not meant to be taken literally. Yet, at the same time, there is some incidental truth to his observation. His life and his oeuvre, on closer inspection, are marked by a continual abstract tussle with concerns about the limits of identity and its relationship to place, family of origin, and assigned social roles. Moorhouse was interested in what props up the boundaries of our identities, how fluid they are and whether it is possible to ever 'escape' our origins.

His third book, *The Electrical Experience*, published in 1974, centred on the character of T. George McDowell, a character who recurs throughout his oeuvre. The book was a marked departure from Moorhouse's first two books, which were set firmly in a bohemian inner-city milieu. The importance of T. George McDowell in Moorhouse's oeuvre can be measured by the fact that he appears first in *The Americans, Baby* (1973) and later in *Grand Days* (1993). As a foreword to the ebook edition of *The Electrical Experience* puts it: 'T. George McDowell was a man who believed in "getting the job done". ' A manufacturer of soft drinks on the South Coast of New South Wales, McDowell prides himself on advocating for the virtues of progress. A Rotarian, he is an exponent of the wireless, refrigeration and electricity—a rationalist and a realist. It is easy to imagine him leading an early campaign to put fluoride in drinking water, or his wife promoting better hygiene education for young women embarking on homemaking.

Above all, McDowell is a man with a passion for order, which runs slightly against the grain of his enthusiasm for innovation. He believes that '[t]he South Coast produced a better sort of person. Quicker to take to new techniques, quick to understand technical matters. Independent of the city. Fishermen, farmers and business men. Not having the railway helped. Kept the coast separate. Made it what is was.' He defines himself against the city. After a confrontation with a unionist from the city who is in town to encourage a strike by local domestic workers, McDowell reflects on his opposition to unionism: 'He said to Margoulis that freedom of enterprise, freedom to organise our own lives, would be finished if we let inspectors, city Union people and all the rest push us around.'

McDowell is particularly sceptical of sophistry: 'I do not care for words in top hats,' he says in *The Electrical Experience*. 'I believe in shirt-sleeve words. I believe in getting the job done. We're like that on the coast. We believe in the right technique and the right machine.'

He goes about sex with his wife in a similarly efficient manner. They practise family planning using a diaphragm *and* a condom—better safe than sorry—and wash immediately afterwards. Darker thoughts gnaw, however, at the edges of his sexual psyche. His 'morbid feeling about Gypsies' stemmed from an encounter with a pretty gypsy girl just out of childhood who had, he believes, 'smiled at him in a certain way'.

> He rather thought, self-control slipping, that . . . maybe . . . the gypsy girl . . . would . . . he had lost his self-control for that instant, she called her mother, his hand on her arm, groin against her, she her mother, and the mother was morbidly attractive too, aroused in his trousers, he wanted to offer money to lie down in the bushes with the gypsy girl . . .

Maintaining self-control emerges as an obsession for McDowell, whose spirit 'cries out' to let go, just for one day.

> To say, drink alcohol, like some of the others. To lay down the burden. He could see nothing in gambling. But yet there must be something in it for men to pursue it so fanatically. That

was just another pleasure he could not touch. He was locked in place. He feared the rules. He was frightened the relaxation was irreversible. That, once relaxed, the rules would not return to place. A slide would begin. Into what? What did he fear?

McDowell is not only a refracted version of Frank Moorhouse Snr, he is a cipher for a series of questions Moorhouse contends with throughout his writing. How many rules are required to maintain a social order? When does the pursuit of pleasure collapse into a surrender to chaos?

These questions found their fullest expression in the character who drives the narrative in Moorhouse's League of Nations trilogy of novels, Edith Campbell Berry. Like Moorhouse, Edith hails from a provincial town on the South Coast of New South Wales. And like Moorhouse, she is interested in questions about how the regional speaks to the national, and how the national speaks to the international.

In the first volume of the trilogy, *Grand Days* (1993), Edith reflects on her journey from small-town Jasper's Brush to Geneva:

> Being in Geneva had permitted her to behave in a way she would never have dreamed back in Australia. This was not only the refashioning of self on which she knew she was embarked. She supposed that it could be seen as a coming out of self, as well as a becoming of self. That is, if she had any 'original self' left. Back home too many people watched her with their own expectations of her, and she'd had to acknowledge this and respond to them.

While Moorhouse always remained in contact with his family, he thought his parents found his writing, in both form and content, mystifying. Moorhouse Snr once suggested that his son should write 'a bestseller', something his mother, who was more literary, intuitively understood was not his aim. Moorhouse gave them copies of his first three books and wrote them 'a long letter explaining that there were headlines in the afternoon paper about obscenity and my books'. Then, when he was researching *The Electrical Experience*, he interviewed them a few times. 'But every time I turned on the tape recorder they would make a speech.'

His sense of disconnection with his parents is made explicit in an article published in *The Monthly* in 2013 titled 'Road to Nowra', in which he recalled his childhood Christmases.

> The Christmas feast of my childhood was roast chicken and stuffing. Chickens were an expensive, special-occasion food back then, before they became degraded into mass-consumption factory takeaway. Many families bought a live chicken and killed and plucked it themselves. It was accompanied by roasted vegetables, rich gravy, homemade Christmas pudding and whipped cream with coins and fortune-telling trinkets cooked inside the pudding (the coins having been hygienically boiled before being put in the pudding; you never know, they could've been 'in a Chinaman's pocket'), nuts, raisins, some beer perhaps for the guests, only one glass, or maybe two, and Schweppes soft drinks too bitter for children but we tried anyway . . .

He then recounted what happened the Christmas he announced he was going to be a writer instead of going into the family business: '[I]t was about as shocking for my family as if I'd said, "Hey, guess what? I'm gay." My father was fond of Mark Twain and considered I wasn't Mark Twain and unlikely to be Mark Twain.'

Later in the *Monthly* piece, he wrote about deciding that he could no longer face family Christmases:

> I remember vividly the day in my early 30s when I decided family Christmas was over for me. It came with the realisation that my family and I didn't like each other very much—that is, my parents, my brothers, didn't particularly like me. Well, at least, they didn't enjoy my company. I don't blame them.

———

By his late teens, Moorhouse was already planning his escape from the constraints of family and life in a country town. He had made plans to find a job as a journalist on a newspaper, and in his last year of high school successfully applied for a cadetship on *The Daily Telegraph*, a Sydney tabloid.

Before he left town, however, a young woman in the year below him at Nowra High had come to his attention—his future wife Wendy Halloway. 'I feel she and Frank were very similar in their manner,' Fay Martin remembers. 'Wendy was very intelligent—dux of her class—she was a high achiever. Quietly confident and a strong personality. Neither she nor Frank seemed to need lots of friends. Both were very self-contained, and Wendy was a very private person. She was a Fourth Form prefect and became vice-captain.' By the end of his final year, Moorhouse was pursuing a passionate relationship with Halloway and was to marry her only four years later.

In his final year at school, he wrote about a young boy falling in love for the first time which is in his archives:

> His eyes looked around the inactive classroom and tried to imagine the future appearance of some. His eyes stopped at

one of the girls. The prettiest girl. He occupied himself by accessing her talents and then in undressing her. She gazed around lazily and her eyes met his. Both stared. Both broke the visual collision—a little redness flowed to their faces. The boy returned to his pencil rolling and she returned to her dress designing.

Halloway—now Wendy James—was an intellectual match for Moorhouse, as her letters to him from Nowra, while she was finishing school and Moorhouse was working as a copyboy at *The Daily Telegraph*, show. Despite her own ambitions to be a writer, she entered nursing training at Sydney's Royal Prince Alfred Hospital, a typical pathway at the time for young women craving independence.

Halloway and Moorhouse were married in Nowra in 1959 at the All Saints Anglican Church, where they had attended Sunday school together. David Gyger, whom Moorhouse had met at *The Daily Telegraph*, was his best man and, for most of Moorhouse's life, a close friend.

Gyger came from the US state of Maine. When he graduated from Amherst College in New England in 1952, the draft for the Korean War was hanging over his head. He was sent to Korea in the final stages of the conflict, arriving in Busan in April 1953, a few weeks before the armistice. After leaving the US Army, he worked for a small weekly newspaper in a town outside of Cleveland before migrating to Australia in 1956 and landing a job as a reporter on *The Daily Telegraph*.

At the time, Gyger recalls, *The Daily Telegraph* was far less tabloid than its afternoon competitors, *The Mirror* and *The Sun*. 'Certainly, the remains of the *Telegraph* style, which was established by the editor Brian Penton, were very much in evidence then,' he comments. 'Coming from the States, where the style of journalism that I'd been used to was very much more descriptive and florid, I was presented with the Penton style. No sentence was supposed to have more than seventeen words in it . . . and the active voice was required . . . What struck me at that stage was [that] the educational standard of the journalist was not anything like what would be required in the States. At that stage, to get into journalism in the States, first of all, you almost certainly had a university degree.'

Gyger's reflections on the influence of Penton, a controversial columnist and later editor, were echoed by Moorhouse. Penton was known as an irreverent progressive who opposed censorship and had a deep interest in promoting the public interest and engaging readers in sophisticated debates about democracy. His approach influenced both Moorhouse's and Gyger's writing styles.

In 1958, Moorhouse moved south to work on *The Wagga Wagga Advertiser*, where he was made a C-grade journalist. 'I went to Wagga mainly to get enough money to marry Wendy,' he said. Gyger also moved to Wagga, and started his own newspaper using his independent wealth. That was *The Riverina Express*, and Frank began writing for it at the end of 1959.

Gyger remained a significant influence throughout Moorhouse's life. They shared a house in Wagga for a year until Wendy joined Frank, leaving her nursing training behind. When Wendy arrived after marrying Frank, Gyger bought another rural paper, *The Lockhart Review*, which Frank and Wendy ran together from Lockhart, a tiny town 63 kilometres from Wagga.

Gyger recalls how provincial Australia seemed to him in the 1950s. His friends and colleagues thought he was mad to go to Wagga. 'The bitumen ended at just beyond Narrandera, 60 miles

[100 kilometres] west of Wagga,' he said. 'From there you had, it must have been, 300 miles of dirt to get to Broken Hill . . . So it was really quite primitive in some respects . . . The better country roads were gravel but many of them, in the Riverina, during the period we were there, were dirt. Which was fine to drive on if the weather was good. But if you had ten points of rain they'd turn to mud and a very treacherous surface.'

The Riverina Express was published as a fortnightly from April 1958 to September 1963. Gyger says he published the paper under 'incredibly primitive conditions'. The paper was printed on old hand-fed presses that were large enough to accommodate four tabloid pages at a time.

The Lockhart Review was printed in Wagga. According to Gyger, Moorhouse's expectations were somewhat grand. 'When we took over the paper, he [Moorhouse] went to Lockhart and actually edited *The Lockhart Review* for some time. He tried to make it into something a bit more sophisticated than it was. I don't think it worked very well. I think he ran an editorial on the birth of Prince Charles which got the people very excited, because he said that we weren't very much concerned in Lockhart, halfway around the world . . . Mostly, it was the sort of basic thing that you get in all those country weekly reports— it's Country Women's Association activities, and the local council is big news.' (Wendy James points out that Gyger's memory of what excited the burghers of Lockhart is faulty, as Prince Charles was actually born in 1948.)

Moorhouse and Halloway returned to Sydney in 1960. Moorhouse had become friendly with John Penfold, whom Sydney University had placed in the Riverina to organise adult education classes. He became a mentor to Moorhouse, who was studying for a Bachelor of Arts as an external student at the

University of Queensland, a degree he never completed. Penfold recommended him for a job in Sydney tutoring at the Workers' Educational Association.

The couple moved into a flat in Surry Hills. Halloway had landed a job as a reporter on one of Frank Packer's free newspapers, working under the experienced journalists Robin Adair and Jubal Fleming. 'The WEA provided Frank with platforms to advance his interests in philosophy and politics and took up more than his working-day,' she says. 'One of his co-workers was in her late thirties, a tiny woman (not unlike his mother), and she introduced him to sexual satisfaction. He told me about her and how he felt, how torn he was by this discovery. So I packed a bag and left.'

Halloway moved to Bathurst, where she had secured a job as a D-grade reporter on the daily paper. Moorhouse visited her from time to time and they 'sort of reconciled'. When she contracted German measles, she had to quarantine and so returned to her parents' home in Nowra. After recovering, she drove to Shoalhaven Heads, where she and Moorhouse had recently purchased a house. She found her husband there with another woman. 'That was the end of the marriage for me,' she says. Their union had lasted four years.

Unbeknown to Halloway at the time, while she was finishing her Leaving Certificate, Moorhouse had commenced an affair with a male colleague. This was a time when sex between men was not only taboo but a crime. Moorhouse recalled the psychological strain of living a double life in a 2007 interview with the journalist Richard Guilliatt:

In the 50s I was in total confusion about my sexuality. I didn't know how to describe it, I didn't know how to handle it, I didn't know how to incorporate it. It had great pleasures and great agonies. Deceptions were involved because I couldn't see how to publicly express it. The curious thing about that time was that my sexuality was in sealed compartments that didn't acknowledge each other. After a homosexual experience it would close like a sealed document. My personality was compartmentalised and totally unresolved for years and years.

It was four decades later, when Moorhouse published his memoir *Martini*, that the pain the marriage and deceptions had caused Halloway surfaced in public. Now Wendy James, she'd had a substantial career as a journalist and editor in the United Kingdom, and she read the book and took strong exception to her portrayal in it. Moorhouse had given her a thin disguise as his young wife, Margaret. She could also see that he had used actual fragments from her letters to him.

In a chapter titled 'The Lemon and the Olive Tree', Moorhouse recounted living with his male lover in a country town and losing his anal virginity to another gay man they had befriended. He wrote:

> For months I'd resisted his advances while still frequently going to visit him, flirtatiously in his office. I lost my anal virginity to Trevor behind the back of Paul, who did not like anal sex and who in, turn, was my clandestine lover behind the back of my high-school girlfriend, Margaret, soon to be my wife.

In *Martini*, Moorhouse provided something of a key to the coded characters in the book. Of the character he referred to as the 'young wife', he wrote:

What of the young wife from the martini story and our life before we were arguing about martinis? Margaret and I had grown up in a country town, had known each other since about age five, went to the same Sunday school, went to the same infant, primary and high schools, the same church, and we married in that church to please our families, even though we were atheists. We read the *Communist Manifesto* together at high school. She went on to two marriages and had two children by her second marriage and one by her third and has remained married for years now. She became a magazine editor in London . . . We are still in touch now and then.

All of which was an accurate account of their relationship and James's path in life. And James clearly had this in mind when she read the next chapter of the book, 'Memoir of a Story: Story of a Memoir'. There Moorhouse recounted returning to Nowra High as a celebrated author and locating Room 17, 'where I'd first kissed Margaret my girlfriend and put my hand on her breasts through her school uniform, the first breasts I'd touched since I was a baby'. In the chapter, he read the assembled students a story from an earlier book, *Forty-Seventeen*, titled 'A Portrait of a Virgin Girl (Circa 1955)', which was also published in an edited volume titled *School Days*.

James had not publicly objected to the publication of the original story. But this time she saw it very differently because of the context. In *Martini* the narrator glosses the story and speculates on whether his former wife was having an affair with a charismatic high-school English teacher.

As the narrator in *Martini* re-reads the fragments of letters he incorporated into the story in *Forty-Seventeen*, one of them stands out:

The sentence about the teacher and his love poem leapt up at me from the page. The teacher actually wanted her to stay back with him so that he could read her a very personal love poem? My God, had the teacher been coming on to her, making a tentative advance? Could that be true? Back then—at the time I'd received the letter, this had not occurred to me. Nor had it occurred to me ten years ago while working from her letters as I wrote this chapter of the novel. It had never occurred to me that the teacher had begun to see her as a sexual being . . . Well, well. The teacher had been flirting with her. I had never read the letter that way.

James responded to the publication of *Martini* in 2007 in a blistering 3600-word piece written for *The Weekend Australian*. She wrote, in part:

> Frank Moorhouse, my husband a long time ago, owes me and Mr W. [the teacher] a public apology for all that he has scurrilously implied in his books. Any money he made from either book should go to charity to help those suffering great depredation—like those children around the world who may have no future because of AIDS—and might never know what a martini is. And most importantly, he should return my letters.

Asked by *The Australian* to respond, Moorhouse offered to return the twenty or thirty love letters to James. He told journalist Richard Guilliatt:

> It wasn't about Wendy, it wasn't an attempt to depict her, describe her, analyse her, to deal with her . . . Maybe it's unfortunate that this book was called a memoir, but I think most

readers would be able to identify by the tone, the language and the context—even the layout—that this was game-playing. This was a demented narrator. What I was writing about was the sadness and weirdness of a young guy who was sexually adrift, who didn't know what he was, and got tangled up in a very youthful marriage.

In an interview, Moorhouse told me that fiction was 'woven out of the life the fiction writer has led'. 'Nowhere in the book is it seriously suggested that the ex-wife—not that it's purely Wendy—ever had an affair with her teacher,' he continued. 'This idea exists only in the mind of the character—of the demented narrator author . . . I hoped that at this point in my life with her that we would be able to appreciate the strange unfolding of our lives from that small country town.'

Moorhouse was as hurt and blindsided by James's attack as she was by his use of her letters, and by his apparent suggestion that she'd had an affair with her teacher. He did not see the need to apologise because he took it as read that his approach to fiction, established from his earliest work, was often to draw on real-life experience and people and create characters and scenarios which were not meant to be taken literally. But by referring to *Martini* as 'a memoir', he had left himself open to the accusation that he had dropped the fictional veil and the privileges it usually entails.

Despite this episode, Moorhouse and James remained in touch until his death. In our interviews, he often spoke of her with great fondness. They had both been very young when they wed, he acknowledged. And while they shared a strong desire to shuck off the constraints of a country town upbringing, they were ill-equipped to make a marriage work.

The ambiguous importance of Nowra in Moorhouse's writerly and psychic imaginary is perhaps best illustrated by this passage in *Grand Days*, in which Edith Campbell Berry is visited in Geneva by George McDowell, a young man from her hometown of Jasper's Brush:

> Although he was a few years younger, she'd flirted with him at balls when she had been home on vacation. As a suitor, he had been a possibility, but she had other roads to travel. George was a man with big ideas in a small town, and she could not see herself back there, living on the coast with George . . .
>
> As much as she had affectionate memories of George and of those days, Edith didn't really want George McDowell in Geneva and around her life now. She wasn't the flirtatious girl from the town balls anymore, doing the hokey-pokey and the progressive barn dance. She was certainly not 'Edy', as George had addressed her in the letter.
>
> There was something unnerving about the idea of a visit from someone she had left behind . . . George's visit would mean facing the self she'd left behind. The discarded self, even.

As Moorhouse once was, Edith is a bright young thing on the cusp of what she hopes will be a dazzling career. To fully embrace that possibility, she believes she must release herself from the ties that bind her to Australia, and to her family and her identity as a young woman from country New South Wales.

It wasn't that Australia was not a 'real' place, full of real people doing real things, finding happiness, making families, practising the arts of friendship, practising the arts of politics, and practising, albeit in a youthful way, the arts and scholarship—doing all the things she knew mattered in life. It was that she needed now in her life to put herself in a position that made her productively nervous. Even if it was a bit uncomfortable at times. She had to be where she didn't know quite what was happening next, to live precipitously.

Despite his full immersion in the Sydney bohemian culture and politics of the 1960s and '70s, Moorhouse, like Edith, felt the tug of the past. His first wife, Wendy, was, after all, part of that history, part of his childhood and adolescence. And many key stories in his oeuvre are either set in a town like Nowra—in *The Coca-Cola Kid* (a film, which is constructed from short stories first published in *Futility and Other Animals* and *The Americans, Baby*) and *The Electrical Experience*, for example. It may be more accurate to say that, rather than leaving Nowra behind, Moorhouse lived and wrote in negotiation with his upbringing. His palpable anxiety on returning to his hometown, even in his seventies, speaks to his ambivalent relationship to its psychic hold on him.

Ambivalent he may have been, but there is no doubt that his upbringing in Nowra supplied Moorhouse with some of his most memorable characters. David Marr's favourite Moorhouse book is the one partly based on Frank Moorhouse Snr, *The Electrical Experience*. 'He's one of those writers who has been able to create their own geography, their own patch,' Marr says. 'Patrick White's Sarsaparilla, Frank's South Coast, it's a fully inhabited geography which he visits and revisits. Every time it's richer and balmier and completely real for me. I'm sure if I knew just precisely where to turn off the highway, I could find all of Frank's people still working and running their little businesses and doing their inventions.'

Moorhouse is buried in Nowra. He requested that there be no funeral to mark his death. Respecting his wishes, his brothers, Owen and Arthur, had him cremated in a flag-draped coffin— the Australian flag marking his membership of the Order of Australia. His family scattered half his ashes at the Shoalhaven Memorial Gardens and Lawn Cemetery and then drove to Sassafras, where they scattered the remainder in the Budawang Range, along a track where Moorhouse often started his hikes. His friend and old hiking companion Helen Lewis joined the family there.

What Moorhouse would make of being permanently back home in a place he spent his life leaving is a fascinating question. At the very least, he would probably enjoy the irony.

2

LIVING IN THE '70S: SEX, GENDER AND POLITICS

The first short story in Moorhouse's first book, *Futility and Other Animals*, is 'The Story of the Knife'. The narrator buys a knife while living in a cabin outside the city with his twenty-year-old lover, Anne. He fashions a leather strap for it from a strap hanging from a water bottle in the shed. One evening, Anne takes the knife and hangs it around her neck so that the handle rests between her breasts while they have sex.

> They rolled hard with the knife between them, clamped in a kiss. He felt the bucking and rearing of desire. They writhed and he felt the pleasure of the knife hurting. Swept by her deft sexuality. The knife like another penis. Her penis or did he have two? Or was it their penis? They rolled with the rearing of desire.

It's a story that shows Moorhouse began his published writing career in the way he meant to go on. All the hallmarks are there: knowing self-deprecation, irony, an uneasy yet complicit relationship with the intellectual life, and a searching approach to received ideas about gender, sexuality and human relationships, all three of which were under serious interrogation in the 1970s.

From his earliest days as a writer, Moorhouse infused his work with accounts of political and social issues that have defined the society he mined for material. As we have seen, his writing was also frequently and transparently entangled with his life. It's not that he directly translated people and events—no novelist does. Moorhouse once referred to the characters in his fiction as parts of a 'discarded self'. But, like many writers, he often openly engaged with the people and issues animating the milieu he was embedded in. He drew lovers, friends and colleagues into his fiction with thin disguise, and did so repeatedly.

Characters recur in his early work: 'Milton' and 'Anderson' are two key examples. Both are open to being interpreted as semi-fictionalised, or refracted, references to his friends of the time: Milton to the literary scholar and writer Michael Wilding, and Anderson to his long-time friend, the scholar and literary critic Don Anderson. Indeed, the discontinuous narrative style that stitches together his short stories into a larger narrative relies on the device of recurring characters and themes—threads, if you like, that Moorhouse pulls together to weave a more complex and novel-like story.

The reason that Moorhouse drew indirectly on his social and cultural milieu in his work is far more complex than the fact that his bohemian social set offered such rich material for scrutiny and sometimes satire. It's a reflection of a deeper aspect of Moorhouse's literary practice—his life was always an active extension of his work, in the sense that he deliberately chose to live a life that was as grounded in conscious aesthetic and ethical choices as his writing practice.

The backdrop to the life Moorhouse was living when he wrote his earliest fiction was Balmain, a solidly working-class, inner-city Sydney suburb, which became home in the 1970s to a burgeoning community of activists, writers, artists, filmmakers, actors and journalists. It was a circle characterised, as the decade progressed, by a growing political activism focused on women's liberation, gay liberation, Aboriginal land rights, environmentalism, opposition to the Vietnam War, and putting an end to Australia's notoriously conservative and paternalistic censorship regime. It was a long way from the conventional and conformist middle-class life Moorhouse had grown up with in Nowra.

Renting or sometimes even buying real estate in 1970s Balmain was still within reach of those toiling in the creative sector. Houses in the suburb were mainly terraces or workers' cottages situated in narrow streets. The suburb sits on a peninsula which juts into Sydney Harbour and, post–World War II, it was home to substantial industry, including a coal loader, a power station and working docks. The Forth and Clyde was a wharfies' pub, as was the early opener the Pacific, nicknamed 'the Opera House' because dock workers would gather around the piano on their way to work and sing while they downed schooners. The wharfie's hook and the Gladstone bag were still a common sight.

By the end of the decade, however, the suburb would be thoroughly gentrified. But during the transition, it was a haven for a bohemian and activist set living in share houses and conjuring up strategies to get published, exhibited, performed or screened while they changed the world.

Sandra Levy, who would go on to become a successful film and television producer, was in an intimate relationship with Moorhouse for seven years in this period. They separated in 1976 but would remain close friends for the rest of their lives. In defiance of the bohemian norms, Levy had borrowed money to buy a house in the suburb in the mid-1960s. Moorhouse moved in with her in 1970. She remembers the Balmain years as 'an exhilarating time with an extraordinary group of people. So many people came to Balmain—David Williamson, Don Anderson, Elisabeth Wynhausen, Robert Adamson, Kate Jennings, and so many more artists and academics. Drawn to the constant intellectual, social, sexual and emotional stimulation there. It was invigorating. And a bit dangerous.'

Moorhouse made Balmain his home base for the next nineteen years, excepting a year spent in Brisbane living with Michele Field and her six-year-old daughter, Ophelia. He lived in a variety of rented houses with a series of partners, including the writer and academic Fiona Giles. Their relationship provided the material for his 1988 book, *Forty-Seventeen*. Most of his writing was done in a ramshackle house at Ewenton Street, where he kept a desk, his reference material and a selection of spirits, mainly Jack Daniel's.

In *Days of Wine and Rage*, a 1980 collection of journalism, poetry and commentary edited by Moorhouse, he recalled life in Balmain:

> By the early seventies, friends had drifted into Balmain and people connected with the arts and the universities came to live there . . . Francis Kelly from the *National Times* [a progressive newspaper] wrote about Australian writing for *Le Monde* and mentioned Le Ghetto Balmain. I picked this up for my

column in the *Bulletin* and for a while wrote a 'letter from the Ghetto'. I began to feel like the Vicar of Balmain as more new arrivals and visitors from other states and overseas called . . .

He wrote about the Balmain Readings of Prose and Verse, which 'began as a gathering of young writers and friends with an open invitation to anyone to read either their own work or a work they liked'. He also recalls that much of the intellectual discourse took place at one of the pubs in Balmain, which as a traditional home to wharfies and boilermakers, numbered twenty-five at the time. (And Balmain, it should be noted, is not a large suburb.) Moorhouse comments in *Days of Wine and Rage* that when the chairperson of the Literature Board visited one of these readings, she remarked: 'What they're spending on alcohol and drugs would publish a dozen books.'

In that vein, Moorhouse describes some of the social events:

We had the Balmain Pub Crawl around the twenty-five hotels (originally) of Balmain. We had annual events such as the New Year's Eve party, the waifs' and strays' Christmas party (for those who chose not to have a family Christmas, or had no family), the Chairman Mao's Boxing Day party. The hotels were filled with live music, folk, rock, and jazz.

Moorhouse was writing his early short stories and journalistic pieces at a time when the rising sun of sexual liberation was already beaming down its seductively simple promise of free love, not only on Australia's small bohemian set, but increasingly on the broader society. For most Australians, women's liberation was still a distant rumble—an unexpected storm—on the horizon. Moorhouse was one of the very few Australian male writers to tackle the intimate domestic details of how these shifts in social mores were playing out in the home and the bedroom.

In the middle of 'The Story of the Knife', Anne and the narrator, who we learn is called Roger, go to a party in the city. Roger talks to a woman he's attracted to. She's an older woman with an 'analytical toughness' he finds intimidating. He shows her the knife.

> 'I can see that you're not interested.'
> 'I don't feel anything about knives.'
> 'I felt I needed one.' He closed it up.
> 'Probably an important male symbol. Painters always doubt their masculinity.'
> 'For God's sake!'
> 'Just an impression I have.'

The growing women's liberation movement (now known more commonly as the feminist movement) was formative for Moorhouse both politically and personally. Many of his female lovers, including Sandra Grimes and Sandra Levy, were involved in the movement as were his female friends.

Levy was very active both in the International Women's Year and in promoting gender equity at the ABC, where she worked. 'I was a passionate feminist then and the battles were many and various,' she recalls. 'One of the big issues for us at the ABC was to get women to present the many news and current affairs programs. The libertarian men weren't interested in any of our issues but there was pushback from the younger women. We just went on regardless and did what we wanted to do.'

Sydney bohemia had certainly been strongly influenced by libertarian ideas about sexuality, which championed free love rather than bourgeois conformity. In the early 1970s, Moorhouse witnessed the direct challenge that women's liberation was mounting to libertarian ideas and to men who literally left women holding the baby (or dealing with the abortion) to pursue their own personal and creative freedom. Characteristically, Moorhouse engaged with the movement in his writing which makes it important to take a closer look at how women's liberation unfolded around him and how he responded to it.

In 1970, the radical US feminist Anne Koedt published a highly influential essay, which was turned into a widely circulated pamphlet titled 'The Myth of the Vaginal Orgasm'. In it she argues that the notion that all women orgasmed as a result of vaginal penetration was a myth which ignored the fact that, for most women, orgasms were related to clitoral stimulation.

The feminist scholar and writer Megan Le Masurier recalls that Koedt's essay remained highly influential in feminist circles well into the late 1970s, when Le Masurier was a first-year student in feminist philosophy at Sydney University. She wrote:

With my limited sexual experience, the title resonated. Any orgasm at that point was mythical. The essay became a kind of talisman, carried around in my bag, dog-eared beside my bed, annotated with my young anger and curiosity. The vagina was not highly sensitive, not made for orgasm. The liberated woman and her vaginal orgasm was a myth, a male conspiracy.

It says a lot about Moorhouse's appetite for frankness, regardless of the potential for serious conflict, that only two years after Koedt's essay appeared he published a piece in *Thor* titled 'The Myth of the Male Orgasm'. Moorhouse's reply was not, as his title might suggest, a flippant dismissal of feminist interrogations of what sexual liberation might actually look like for women. Rather, it was a genuine reflection on the way male pleasure is an assumed rather than interrogated category in its own right. He observes that Koedt's argument is:

> Men created this myth to deny the sexuality of women and the personality of women, and to establish male dominance by making the penis central to the pleasure act and crucial for women's pleasure. (This is the only part of the pamphlet that I agree with. The rest seems distorted by male hostility and hysteria.)

Moorhouse's book *The Americans, Baby*, first published in 1972, begins with two stories that explicitly focus on changing sexual mores and practices. In 'Dell Goes into Politics', Dell gets off a country train with her Oroton handbag and white make-up (which 'didn't seem to help'), to be greeted by her parents and a man she knows who works on the station who gives her 'a funny smile and hullo'. It's a portrait of the young urban sophisticate returning to her roots and feeling 'instantly grimy, and very countrified'.

'Got a young man yet?' her mother asked, as they went inside.

'No—at least not one.'

'What happened to that young schoolteacher?'

'Oh him . . .' Kim and his politics and sex and always wanting to be doing something different to her in bed, always teaching her, 'he was a bit odd' . . .

'What do you mean odd?' her mother said, fearfully, knowing the word had something to do with sex or madness.

In parallel with his explorations of shifting gender roles, Moorhouse was also exploring his own bisexuality. In 'The American, Paul Jonson', the narrator has his first homosexual experience with a visiting American man. It's clear that simply being American was a loaded position in the narrator's—and, by extension, the nation's—insecurely politicised and immature social psyche. 'They had not moved from the settee. He had ejaculated. The breathless slide into the pleasure of it had stopped against revulsion. He felt flung and dazed as though in a road accident.'

What's remarkable, in hindsight, is the characteristic frankness with which Moorhouse narrates and names the uncertainty and the dissonances that attended the social change affecting sexual identities and gender roles as they were unfolding around him. If writing explicitly about sex between men and women was still liable to draw the censor's ire, then writing about homosexuality was beyond the pale. *The Americans, Baby* was published in an era when homosexual acts between men were still criminalised in all Australian states, and the gay liberation movement was in its infancy. Moorhouse has never been pegged as a 'gay' writer, but he was one of Australia's earliest fiction writers to openly tackle the subject, and to do so through characters who were sometimes bisexual.

Moorhouse's accounts of sexual relationships in his early writing were overlaid with his accounts of the anxiety attending masculinity in 1960s and '70s Australia. In an early short story, 'What Can You Say?', a young man goes to the Royal George and is approached by a guy named Jimmy. 'I knew he wasn't queer because of his beard.' The narrator has left home to rent an apartment in Kings Cross, leaving his girlfriend behind. Jimmy is a lecturer in sociology.

Jimmy changed my ideas about sex. I remember at a party, him telling me that different people needed different sex lives and that the same person needed a different sex life at different times. In his slow lecturer's voice he said: 'There are a diversity of personalities requiring a diversity of sexual relationships. This society says there is only one—marriage.'

Moorhouse's early forays into writing about homosexual encounters with sympathy for the characters involved can be seen, in this light, as a breakthrough in Australian fiction. Certainly they were a breakthrough when it came to what writers perceived as straight were prepared to conjure with.

Moorhouse was also thinking through the tensions between the intense homosociality of Australian mateship, and the need most men had to constantly assert an aggressive heterosexuality. In 'The Alter Ego Interpretation', a short story in the collection *Tales of Mystery and Romance*, the narrator meets up with his close friend Milton, with whom he has an ambiguous relationship that is grounded in mutual intellectual interests but laced with sexual undertones.

When he drinks he sometimes relaxes his frantic heterosexuality (as long as he's sure of a fuck somewhere in the night) and we sometimes touch and carry on. Sometimes it's done as a way of clowning the possibility, parodying homosexuality; sometimes to sham independence of women; sometimes to confuse girls that he's interested in, as a test? as sadism? or because he's basically not interested in women . . .

Linzi Murrie writes that Moorhouse's 'determination to write directly about male sexualities' during the 'sexual liberation'

of the 1960s was 'a significant turning point in the representation of sexuality in Australian writing'. Murrie also argues that
'Moorhouse subverts patriarchal constructions of homosexuality, but his privileging of male bonding suggests anxieties about
transgressive sexualities and the threat of feminism'.

This is a criticism which has been levelled at Moorhouse in
various guises, the essence of which is that his explorations of
male sexuality are innately hostile to feminism.

Yet, contrary to the critics who detect an ambivalence towards,
even a fear of, female power in his work, Moorhouse was always
innately sympathetic to feminist concerns. My research suggests
that, in his early work, he was trying to find a language to talk
about the male anxiety that necessarily reared its head when
women began challenging established social and sexual norms.

Moorhouse was certainly aware of the frequently stultifying
constraints under which women were living out their roles in the
1960s and '70s. The young woman in the 'The Story of the Knife'
has a child whose whereabouts are not explained. In a separate
short story in *Futility and Other Animals*, 'Anderson, How Can
There Be a Baby and No Crying?', a woman tells the story of
wanting a child with her husband, whom she learns is having
an affair with another woman. The woman he is having an affair
with has two children, and tells her husband she is leaving him.
At the last moment, Anderson says he can't be involved in raising
children. Towards the end of the story, Anderson forms a relationship with a young woman, Anne, who is already pregnant, and
says he will help her raise the child. They arrange for the child
to be adopted.

'We talked about keeping it,' he went on, 'but I'm going
overseas next year and Anne's coming with me. We agreed the

baby would be a drag. Remember it wasn't my baby—I mean it's different. Anne wanted to keep it—she's cut up about it—but sense prevailed . . .'

It's a vignette that neatly parses the casual sexism which was often dispensed to women amid the 'sexual revolution' when they fell pregnant or expressed a desire to have children and cement a relationship. Anne is an echo of the woman, if not the actual character, who, later in the timeline of the discontinuous narratives, shares a cabin with Roger in 'The Story of the Knife'.

Moorhouse's early stories are resonant with attention to the dilemmas that both genders faced in the push and pull between traditional roles, and to the seismic social shifts that were underway—at least in certain social groups. He painted, through dialogue, the ambivalence with which his generation negotiated the resetting of the social moral compass. And he gives the lie to the glib cultural histories of the times that are so often paraded in documentaries and articles recounting the golden age of sexual revolution. His stories offer a close-up of the cracks and the crack-ups that marked domestic life for couples living in 'open' relationships, and the social dissonance that shadowed anyone who chose to live outside gendered roles and moral norms.

In his later work, in particular in the League of Nations trilogy, Moorhouse made a very considered choice to tell the story of that famous experiment in designing rules for civilised global living through the eyes of a young Australian woman, Edith Campbell Berry. His friend Dr Lenore Coltheart published an essay on the significance of Berry in Australian literature, describing her as a character of 'intelligence, courage, curiosity and determined idealism'.

Writing about Moorhouse's 1972 short story 'The Girl Who Met Simone de Beauvoir in Paris', Margaret Henderson reads it as a satire of 'a residual culture of Australian middle class ockerism that has already lost the battle of the sexes but, like good ANZACS, keeps on fighting'.

To understand in more depth the way Moorhouse responded to both the women's liberation and the gay liberation campaigns in his early work, it is worth examining the fingerprints the libertarian movement left on Sydney's intellectual and political life in the 1970s. Moorhouse was part of the tail end of that movement—known colloquially as 'the Push'—and the values and ideas he imbibed there profoundly influenced his later engagement with the emergent politics of gender and sexuality.

———

In his original account of Australian bohemia since 1860, cultural historian Tony Moore writes of novelist and journalist Marcus Clarke: 'The creation of one's self as a work of art was a bohemian strategy implicit in the French texts of Murger, Balzac and Baudelaire.' In a similar observation, writing of the Sydney Push libertarians, Moore recounts the role Sydney University Professor of Philosophy John Anderson played as a mentor to many future public intellectual stars. He writes: 'While [Anderson] himself preferred a life of thinking, it fell to a group of young "Andersonians" in the early 1950s to turn their mentor's mantra of critical thinking into a whole way of life.'

The Sydney Push was a loose alliance of intellectuals, writers, artists and self-styled bohemians who drank together and debated ideas at Sydney pubs such as the Newcastle and the Royal George. The Push had its origins in the late 1940s and the Free Thought Society founded by Anderson. The Push was not a formal political movement, and its members certainly had no aspirations to establish a political party. It was, rather, a fluid group for which the only qualifications to join were a commitment to free thinking, a willingness to debate social norms and a high tolerance for alcohol and partying. The group leant towards libertarian and anarchist ideals, but also included those associated with the broader left of the time.

Those who passed through the Push, however briefly, include film producer Margaret Fink, feminist author Germaine Greer, activist and journalist Wendy Bacon, feminist academic Eva Cox, author Clive James, art critic Robert Hughes, journalist Lillian Roxon and writers Sasha Soldatow and Frank Moorhouse. The senior ranking—the more or less permanent members of the group—included Darcy Waters, Roelof Smilde and Harry Hooton.

In her book on the Push, *Sex and Anarchy*, Anne Coombs writes: 'They were not like the Bloomsbury set. They were not rich or self-consciously elegant. They were not out to change the world, but to interpret it . . . They were tough, in a laconic fashion, opposed to the Church, the State, wowsers and censorship.'

Human rights activist and intellectual André Frankovits, a younger but still key member of the Push, recalls that, despite the heavy drinking, there was a great deal of emphasis placed on intellectual debate. 'There was usually a paper at the Philosophy Room at Sydney University,' he says. 'Lots of my friends [in the Push] would give papers—I've given papers there. Then for the evening there would be a paper organised at Liberty Hall [a room rented by the Libertarian Society]. There would inevitably be a party afterwards, which would spill out on the stairs. Occasionally people sort of flaked there or squatted there overnight and some lived there for a while—much against the conditions of the lease.' After the lease was (unsurprisingly) not renewed, the Push hosted papers in a back room at the Royal George hotel.

A number of the Push men supported themselves through gambling, chiefly on horses. They espoused this as a way of breaking free of the bondage of the Protestant work ethic. But they were apparently quite happy to borrow money from others in the group who were earning it the regular way—particularly the women.

The Push was an early influence on Moorhouse, who, while very much on its fringes, being a generation younger than many of its leading figures, certainly drank, ate and debated ideas with them. Elizabeth Farrelly describes their social routine:

> It was a social dance choreographed not just without mobiles but, because most people lived in tiny rented flats, largely without landlines. So each evening, after work or lectures, there'd be this mad rush downtown, by tram, by bus or on foot. If you weren't in by 6, when the pubs closed, it meant social death for the evening or even the weekend. For the quick, though, there was guaranteed congeniality just about any night of the week. After the pub or café, they'd eat at the Greeks or the Italians in Castlereagh Street, or Vadim's in Challis Avenue, then head off to the party du soir.

In *Days of Wine and Rage*, Moorhouse recalls his time consorting with the Push:

> We met and drank most nights at the Newcastle Hotel, the Royal George, later at the Vanity Fair and the United States and

then the Criterion. On some nights we would eat together and perhaps go to someone's house for what was called 'a party'. We spent the time talking—or what Jim Baker, a libertarian philosophy lecturer, called critical drinking. Sometimes later in the night we danced rock'n'roll, although there was some opposition because the music interfered with conversation.

Moorhouse also recalled attending the annual libertarian conference at Minto, held over two days and two nights, where there were readings of short stories, papers on libertarian concerns, nude swimming and abundant casual sex.

Moorhouse recalled an early Push experience in his 1995 collection of satirical essays, *Loose Living*. He was in his early twenties and visiting Melbourne for the first time with a group of Sydney Push members. Adrian Rawlins, a libertarian and music journalist, introduced him to his first camembert.

> We were being guided by Darcy Waters, who had not himself been to Melbourne since the War. He was dismayed to find that old cafes, coffee houses and billiard salons had disappeared . . . We eventually joined up at whatever hotel in Carlton was then in favour. That night there was a party and, much to my astonishment, one wall was decorated with covers and copies of little magazines in which I had published my first short stories.

At the party, where the guests went to bed in sundry parts of the house, Moorhouse danced with a man; they 'also did other nice things with each other'. The following morning, Adrian Rawlins, 'the senior ranking bohemian present', suggested everyone go to Jimmy Watson's for lunch.

We went to this renowned Carlton restaurant and found
a table in the sunny courtyard. Adrian decreed that we should
have only a camembert fermier and a light Victorian wine,
which he ordered . . . It was perfectly ripe, just beginning to
run, with a spirited nose and at the right temperature. I had
never experienced such a perfect comingling of wan sun, of
cheerful restaurant noises, of the Victorian wine, of night
flavours . . .

It's an anecdote that illustrates the seductive pull of bohemian
company in the 1960s. In a deeply conservative society, the Push
and like-minded folk in other cities offered a sensual as well as an
intellectual education to a young man from Nowra embarking
on a writing career.

In chronological terms, the Push spanned from the 1950s
to the early 1970s, from the early Menzies era to a time when
new activist political movements came of age. At the heart of
libertarian philosophy was a disrespect for authority and core
institutions that bordered on anarchy, as well as a belief that
ideas should not simply be debated but lived. Adherents aspired
to live 'without illusions' in a state of 'permanent protest',
and regarded revolution as doomed to simply enshrine a new
ruling order.

In his book *Australian Cultural Elites*, published in 1974,
John Docker analyses the way the libertarian tradition both
influenced and gave way to new left-wing political forces:

These new movements were fundamentally different from
the Libertarians . . . in feeling confident both that political
change was possible, and that political activity did not necessarily conflict with personal freedom. Libertarians have engaged

recently in oppositional activities, such as Wendy Bacon's and Frank Moorhouse's involvement in *Thorunka* and *Thor* [small radical magazines], which have continued the anti-censorship concern of the Libertarian tradition. But such activism has been given force by the political confidence of the new movements, rather than by the social pessimism of older Libertarian ideology.

Docker's then framing of Moorhouse was innately hostile, as was his ultimate assessment of the libertarian tradition. At the time, he read Moorhouse's early work as grounded in 'older Sydney freethought and romantic idealistic stances'. He also understood Moorhouse as a writer bent on attacking the new left political movements—as an inherently ideological thinker who is determined to portray lefties as 'destructive and mechanical in their sense of personality and sexuality'. Docker devotes four pages of his book to dissecting Moorhouse's then recent collection of short stories, *The Americans, Baby*. Placing Moorhouse as an heir to artist Norman Lindsay, he argues that: 'Where Norman Lindsay bitterly disliked historical revolutionary figures like Christ and Shelley . . . Moorhouse turns his fire on modern revolutionaries.'

Docker was, of course, writing in the midst of political flux and had his own ideological fish to fry. From a contemporary point of view, Docker's dismissal of Moorhouse's ironic tone as merely a device to assert his rejection of the notion that individuals can have any impact on society simply doesn't stand up to more contemporary analysis. But his critique certainly highlights the growing rifts between libertarian-anarchist thought and the rise of new left movements that were festering at the time.

Moorhouse always remained sceptical of ideological positions that are animated by a sense of self-righteousness or by claims to have a monopoly on truth. But he was as sceptical about the Push as he was about some of the more authoritarian tendencies of the left. Coombs quotes Moorhouse in a cover blurb for her book as saying of the Push: 'Really, they were romantics.' It's a dryly pointed observation about the underlying idealism that characterised the movement's rejection of any compromise with the mores and lives of the 'bourgeoisie'. Push men prided themselves on their pragmatism and their ability to live outside the norms of society.

From a feminist perspective, though, it was the women of the Push who frequently lived the genuinely hardest realities of the anti-bourgeois lifestyle. The men might have paid for the serial abortions many of them had, but the women had to go through them. It was they who lived with the constant fear of falling pregnant to men who had no intention of being tied down by a family—or of using condoms. The sexual liberation that characterised the Push lifestyle took no account of what might be needed to underpin a genuine women's revolution. As Coombs writes: 'Libertarians did not use condoms. As a new woman on the scene, you learnt that very quickly. As a new man, you learnt very quickly that there was no need to worry about contraception because the women would look after that.'

In 1950s and '60s Australia, abortion was taboo, illegal and difficult to obtain. Many women died after backyard terminations. Coombs recounts the story of a young woman from a wealthy Sydney family who fell pregnant when she was fifteen and, after having an abortion, went home and haemorrhaged all over her mother's expensive carpet. She was thrown out of home.

A few years later she fell pregnant and overdosed on pills meant to induce a miscarriage.

The sexual mores of the Push were strongly influenced by Wilhelm Reich, an Austrian psychoanalyst who was in the second generation of analysts after Freud. Reich attempted to reconcile the theories of psychoanalysis with Marxist ideas, arguing that a sexual revolution would ultimately result in social and political revolution. His ideas appealed to the Push because of their opposition to the sanctity of the family unit and their championing of sexual freedom. As McKenzie Wark writes: 'If Anderson saw a parallel between sexual repression and servility, under the influence of Reich the Libertarians saw it as its very basis. The alternative, a free circulation of sexual energy, is of course exactly what the men of the Push had in mind.'

Despite the sexist attitudes of many of the men they consorted with, the women of the Push challenged many of the structures that held women in their domestic place. In an era when sex before marriage was taboo (even if it was common), when female sexual pleasure was rarely discussed and when women's primary role was to be homemakers and mothers, the women of the Push broke the mould. They had sex with men and lived with them out of wedlock. They drank with them in pubs. And they spoke frankly and swore. To do so, as a woman at that time, was an incredibly brave act. As Coombs writes: 'The outside world had rules to hedge you into every area of your life . . . Such was the rigidity and the number of these rules that there seemed, as one participant recalled, "no option but to reject the lot of them". But in doing so—if you were a woman—you put yourself beyond the pale.'

The extent of the straitjacket that comprised gender roles from the 1950s well into the 1970s is hard to imagine from a 21st-century perspective. But in 1972, one of Australia's largest advertising firms, George Patterson, felt comfortable releasing a report that summed up Australian women this way:

> Above all, the average woman is a mother, and her whole life revolves around this basic role . . . As a good mother, she must also be a good wife and basically, a good homemaker. Her home and family are the basis of her life; they are her domain. They are the justification of her existence . . .

Women in the Push gained their status not only from whom they were fucking but equally by appearing not to give a fuck about whom else their men were fucking. A willingness to use the language of the public bar—to say fuck when references to having sex were euphemised in daily life, if mentioned at all— was also a prerequisite. Whatever emotions were bubbling below the surface for women in the Push, remaining outwardly urbane about open infidelity was critical to fitting into the milieu.

This unwritten rule, based loosely on Reichian ideas, came to characterise broader 1970s bohemia in Sydney and Melbourne, as Levy recalls wryly: 'We all behaved badly then in different ways. Frank and I dealt with the issue of infidelity by agreeing that we would have one night a week off from our relationship. Each week we would agree which night it was. It was a private night and no questions asked. It was supposedly a safe way to maintain a close domestic and emotional life. Supposedly!'

Of course, an alternative way of seeing the countercultural sexual mores of the Push is as a more transparent version of the hyper-masculine culture that characterised mainstream Australia in the 1950s and '60s: it was centred on mateship, heavy drinking, gambling and an indifference to women and domesticity.

———

The early 1970s saw a set of new political imperatives animating the old Push culture—or, more accurately, the younger or 'Baby Push' members of the loose alliance. As Moorhouse reflected: 'The Libertarians were not pushing thinking on liberation issues. It was a blindness.'

Perhaps the largest shift in the political weather for the Push was the emergence of a collective women's liberation movement in the late 1960s. Megan Le Masurier writes about the tipping point between the Push and the emergent forces of second-wave feminism. She notes that, in Sydney at least, 'the ideas behind sexual liberation carried into the early years of women's liberation'. She pinpoints some cracks in the early women's liberation movement that would eventually become unbridgeable chasms. Anne Koedt's paper, first presented in the United States in 1968, became central to a debate among Sydney feminists about whether heterosexual intercourse was, in and of itself, a form of oppression of women. Le Masurier writes that piles of the Koedt pamphlet, which Moorhouse analysed with a characteristic mix of seriousness and irony, were stacked in Women's Liberation House in Sydney, and the article was used for many 'consciousness-raising sessions'.

A pivotal figure in these debates, and in both the libertarian and women's liberation movements, was Germaine Greer. She first encountered the Sydney Push in 1959, when she arrived from Melbourne, where she had been part of that city's bohemian equivalent, the Melbourne Drift. Anne Coombs quotes her observations on the difference between the two movements:

When I first entered the dingy back room at the Royal George I was a clever, undisciplined, pedantic show-off . . . In the flabby intellectual atmosphere of the Melbourne Drift, I had been encouraged to refrain from ungainly insistence on logic and the connection of ideas, to be instead witty, joking together heterogenous notions.

In 1970, Greer published *The Female Eunuch*, which became an international bestseller. The hallmarks of Sydney libertarianism are stamped on the book, and on Greer's brand of charismatic and provocative feminism. *The Female Eunuch* remains a classic feminist text, but many contemporary readers would be surprised, if not shocked, to learn how deeply its roots are embedded in an anarchistic and libertarian philosophy. As scholar Kate Gleeson writes:

> *The Female Eunuch* is unabashedly libertarian and owes much to Reich in its premise of the manifold possibilities of a simple sexual freedom for women, at a time when much feminist thought reflected its origins in the structuralism of the New Left. While liberals like Betty Friedan were fighting for equality, Greer championed freedom.
>
> While radicals like [Robin] Morgan and Kate Millett were focused on exposing the misogyny of male sexual licence, Greer demanded that licence for herself, and any woman who cared to join her.

A year before the bestseller's publication, Greer helped to establish a pornographic magazine titled *Suck*. In one edition she posed naked, legs behind her head with her genitalia fully exposed. She invited other women to send in similar snaps. Greer, as Le Masurier writes, 'refused to settle for the clitoral orgasms of Masters and Johnson . . . Greer insisted that the vagina was not without the capacity to provide intense pleasure.' Le Masurier argues that Greer's insistence on women's capacity to take back the sexual power in heterosexual relationships by being active, rather than seeing themselves as passive victims, meant that the figure of Greer became metonymic in the popular imagination for women's liberation and its connection to sexual freedom.

Most Push women, as Anne Coombs notes, didn't exactly rush to join the ranks of women's liberationists. 'The response in the early years was, "I'm already liberated."' The libertarian strand in Sydney feminism remained strong in some quarters— and still does, as I have argued myself.

While Greer was successfully spreading her own brand of libertarian feminism, a very different political tide was coming in—one equally informed, in Sydney at least, by the Push. Women known to or associated with the Push—such as Eva Cox, Liz Fell, Gillian Leahy and Ann Curthoys—were writing for and reading feminist publications like *Me Jane*, published by the Sydney Women's Liberation Group, formed in the 1970s in Balmain. Wendy Bacon, a high-profile Push woman and someone with whom Moorhouse teamed up on anti-censorship campaigns, was a late joiner of the movement. Coombs quotes her as saying: 'I wasn't a person who had never been able to stand up and speak. I was one of the slower ones.'

Greer returned to Sydney in 1972 and took part in a panel discussion at Sydney University that included Liz Fell and Gillian Leahy. By this stage, tensions were emerging between the libertarian instincts of many women associated with the Push and their emergent support for feminist concerns. Leahy told Anne Coombs:

Women's Lib was different in Sydney because of the strong libertarian influence. We had more liberal attitudes to men. There were things in libertarianism and Freudianism which meant you had to look at things like ideology, at your own complicity in your own oppression, and to recognise that men had hang-ups too.

In early 1973, two graduate students, Jean Curthoys and Liz Jacka, proposed teaching a feminist course in philosophy. The department voted for the course, with the exception of its four most senior members, including the influential Professor David Armstrong. While the Faculty of Arts approved the course, it was later scuttled by the highly conservative Professorial Board. This rejection prompted a strike by staff and students, and ultimately resulted in a split in the department, leading to the establishment of the Department of General Philosophy and the Department of Traditional and Modern Philosophy.

Moorhouse was not a student at Sydney University, but like many in his circles he frequently participated in talks, protests and parties held on campus. In an article for *The Bulletin* that was later abridged in *Days of Wine and Rage*, Moorhouse recalled the strike and the victory celebration party that attended its successful resolution:

We found the victory celebration party and the political gossiping more to our taste than the front-lawn rhetoric or the committee politicking . . . We were told that Professor Leonie Kramer, because of her opposition to the strike, had been declared an 'honorary male'—one of the women's movement's severest epithets of scorn.

Miss Betty Archdale, who was on the senate committee of inquiry into the dispute, is reported to have asked whether the two woman tutors involved in the dispute had strong enough voices to be heard at the back of a lecture theatre.

Moorhouse explored the growing feminist consciousness not only from the perspective of elite intellectual politics, but equally with an interest in the ambivalence that many so-called 'ordinary' women felt about their roles in life and the family. In a short story published in *The Bulletin* in 1972 titled 'If Asked in a Survey, Yes, I'd Say I Was a Liberated Lady' the author contemplates the thoughts of a middle-class woman reflecting on the frustrations of her marriage and what liberation might look like for her.

> My gosh, it's all very well for young girls on the pill to go around talking about sexual freedom, but for her generation it hadn't been that damned easy. She was glad for them and good luck. But she'd come from the Dark Ages . . .
>
> She masturbated. Now, there, that was something. Marks for that.

With characteristic compassion for the contradictions inherent in human identity, Moorhouse lays out a layered inner monologue that weaves across self-doubt, assertiveness, sexual desire, conformism and despair. The story ends with a poignant line: 'Oh, she could have been a lot worse off, when she looked at some of her friends.'

Moorhouse's reflections on the impact of the emergent women's movement at the time highlight a rare quality in his writing: a capacity to genuinely empathise with women. His ability to write in a female voice became particularly evident later in his career, through his character Edith Campbell Berry in his League of Nations trilogy, but it's interesting to note how early Moorhouse was experimenting with the female voice and inner monologue.

Moorhouse recalled—and the collection of early women's liberation material in his archive bears it out—that he was inherently sympathetic to second-wave feminism, even if he was not prepared to accept some of the ideological bluntness with which its arguments were made. Many of his female friends were active in the movement, including Sandra Grimes, Sandra Levy, Liz Fell, Wendy Bacon and Lyndall Ryan. His innate curiosity about gender and sexuality, and his sense that it was more fluid than society allowed, no doubt helped him retain an open mind about radical challenges to the gendered order.

'The whole of male conditioning was under challenge,' he said of the early 1970s, 'and the male role was under challenge and men were quite fearful. Even in the intellectual world they were fearful, let alone in the wider male world, [which was] angry at the women's movement. There was a huge amount of hostility because the men had been pushed off balance.'

The academic and writer Meaghan Morris notes Moorhouse's ability to capture the contradictions and flux that defined both feminism and the relationship between the sexes in the 1970s. 'I always thought, until the [League of Nations] trilogy came out, that the most extraordinary thing that he ever wrote was *The Everlasting Secret Family*,' she reflects. 'I loved that book. I mean, it's really deeply unsettling, and that is something you associate with the really extraordinary female writers . . . Even when [Moorhouse's writing] goes into really kind of either very sad or really, really confronting places, there's always just this humane curiosity there . . . I think that's very unusual in a male writer.'

Morris also clearly recalls the tensions animating the politics of early 1970s bohemian Sydney. 'For my generation, the huge fight was between communism or Marxism and libertarianism,' she says. 'While in my social life I was saying, "Oh, you old libertarians, please drop off the twig," I was always accused of being a libertarian. The seeds of what became feminist moralism were already there . . . The theory was that you were naturally lesbian and had been perverted by patriarchal ideology. So, if you must have a heterosexual relationship, you had to be promiscuous and pluralist. You had to be committed to the overthrow of marriage in all its forms, and a monogamous couple is as good as married.'

Morris, like Moorhouse, was at first frustrated by and then increasingly disillusioned about the ideological rigidity and self-righteousness that characterised elements of the left, including some strands of feminism. In Moorhouse's writing, she recognises a similar resistance to these tendencies and an eloquent ability to describe the messy realities of relationships in times of powerful social change.

———

At the same time he was grappling with the rise of women's liberation and what it meant politically and personally, Moorhouse was also contending with changing attitudes towards homosexuality and the early demands of the gay liberation movement. He had been having sex with men since the age of seventeen but did not openly identify as gay or bisexual.

David Marr, who edited Moorhouse's work at *The National Times* in the early 1980s, says of Moorhouse: 'He was seen as a straight writer, no doubt about that . . . it was really only with the publication of *The Everlasting Secret Family* [in 1980] that I began to think, "Oh maybe Frank's a poof, maybe he's bi, whatever."' According to Marr, there was often a lag between what men who had sex with men did in private and what they wrote about, prior to the era when 'coming out' was acceptable. 'In Patrick White's words, the lag is disgraceful, and Patrick, of course, tended to make homosexuals figures of ridicule in his works for a very long time. I said to him once: "Why didn't you write [positively about homosexuality or being homosexual] earlier?" . . . He said: "It's been impossible, my publishers told me it would be completely impossible."'

The history of gay and what is now known as queer literature in Australia has been fraught with debates over how homosexual characters and their desires are represented. When Moorhouse was writing his first collection of short stories, *Futility and Other Animals*, in the late 1960s, he was deeply immersed in his first serious homosexual relationship—and it was a time when homosexual acts were illegal and outing himself as bisexual would have put him at risk of becoming a social pariah.

In the 1970s, the nascent gay liberation movement largely focused on changing laws that criminalised homosexual acts between men, and on 'normalising' the notion of gay and lesbian relationships. The notion of 'gay pride' came later; the positive use of the term 'queer', let alone 'queer fiction', was not in existence.

A number of scholarly literary critics writing in the 1980s took issue with the way Moorhouse represented homosexual characters and acts in his early work. Chelva Kanaganayakam writes, for instance, that the narrative voice in Moorhouse's work is 'instrumental in transforming a celebration of homosexuality into a castigation of it'. Stephen Kirby argues that 'the question of self-censorship within apparently "liberated" texts has considerable application to Frank Moorhouse's work'.

With his characteristic clarity, Dennis Altman refutes this kind of hunting down of an 'appropriate' representation of homosexual desire and makes the following point about Moorhouse's portrayal of homosexuality: 'To speak of "lesbian/gay" writing is to raise problems of boundaries and definition: the boundaries of politics are not those of literature, which tends to be more concerned with the ambivalences and ambiguities of individual lives than with the sociological construction of individual identities.' Altman is alluding to the way that the shifts in political and social frameworks for understanding and advocating on behalf of LGBTQI identities are historically nuanced. Essentially he is arguing that it is a misreading to project contemporary notions of queer identities back onto earlier literary texts. He also opens up the question of whether it is ever appropriate to critique a work of literature on the basis that it somehow fails an ideological test.

Gay liberation was a movement of personal as well as political interest to Moorhouse. For all their espousal of unfettered sexual relationships, the men of the Push had little interest in opposing the oppression of homosexuals. The only openly gay man in the Push for many years was a man known as Della. Coombs writes that: 'The men of the Push delighted in his stories. He sometimes fucked straight Push men when they were drunk.' Sandra Grimes hung out with a group of younger gay men from Sydney's Northern Beaches; Coombs reports that they found the Push too straight for them.

Moorhouse said he never talked about homosexuality with the Push men. But he was writing about it in his earliest fiction and had been having sexual and romantic relationships with men since he arrived in Sydney in the late 1950s. I have chosen not to name any of the men with whom Moorhouse had multiple casual and long-term sexual relationships throughout his life, although the chronology and character of some of these relationships can be pieced together from letters in his archive. And I have steered away from using that material, because to do so would be to 'out' a number of men who have lived outwardly heterosexual lives. More importantly, the quotidian details of Moorhouse's sex life are beside the point here. The interesting thing is how he grappled with his own anxieties about his sexuality in print— an act of astonishing commitment to self-interrogation and to writing.

Moorhouse recalled that he seduced an older man, a work colleague, when he first arrived in Sydney, and that their sexual as well as personal relationship continued for many decades, crisscrossing the relationships he had with other women and men. For Moorhouse, the relationship was a hinge in his sexual life. His parallel homosexual life, which continued after he married, was something that he 'compartmentalised'. But in relation to his early writing, he reflected: 'The word "gay" came a lot later. When I was writing about—drawing on—my own homosexual experiences there was no support system, and it was illegal and it was persecuted. I mean, the police persecuted gays. So it was a very different milieu to the world of the gay movement, and so it was much more furtive and dangerous, and dangerous in terms of one's occupation.' Moorhouse drew on his homosexual experiences in his work nonetheless, observing: 'I think when I was writing fiction, I had numbed myself to the risks I was taking.'

In his history of gay and lesbian activism in Australia, Graham Willett writes that the gay community in this era 'differed most strongly from the later gay community in its nocturnal nature. It was a scene of the night and was very largely invisible to the rest of society. It was also, and most obviously, a radically apolitical scene. Its members hoped for nothing more than to be left alone.'

In an Australia where same-sex marriage is legal, as it is in most Western democracies, it is difficult to imagine the violent institutionalised prejudice that gay men and lesbians faced so recently. There was scant history of organised gay politics in Australia until the Campaign Against Moral Persecution (CAMP) was established in 1970 by John Ware and Christabel Poll. Robert Reynolds writes about the shifts that were occurring in gay identity and politics at the time:

> From 1970 to 1973, the first generation of CAMP activists participated in a remaking of Australian homosexuality. More specifically, it is possible to mark off these three years as a crucial phase in the creation of a homosexual who was, in CAMP's own words, 'open' and 'proud'.

Prior to this era, homosexual life was lived clandestinely and was, for some men and women, a source of shame and conflict. In a short story published in *The Americans, Baby*, Moorhouse writes about a series of sexual encounters between the narrator, Carl, and an American journalist named Paul. After they first have sex, Carl leaves the American's flat abruptly in disgust. But he agrees to drink with him again and returns to the same apartment.

> This time they went to Paul's bed. Afterwards, he lay there bewildered, wanting to run from the flat. The distance between himself in the bed and the clothes crumpled on the floor beside the bed, was too great. He could not make the move.
>
> 'Christ,' he said bitterly, 'you said we wouldn't.'

'We're too attracted,' said Paul hopelessly.

'I didn't want it. I didn't want to do it. I'm not like this.'

'I'm not homosexual either,' said Paul defensively, 'we have affinity—it happens to people sometimes.'

Moorhouse grew up in a world where 'passing' as straight was a basic necessity if you wanted to keep the love and approval of your family and the ability to earn a living and basic social acceptance. The fact that he openly wrote homosexual characters into his first book of short stories is a mark of his commitment to his life as a writer, in the face of the undeniable pull his middle-class and conformist upbringing exercised on him. In one story in *Futility and Other Animals* he writes about a young man who develops a sexual crush on a visiting American: 'There in the alcove of the pub our hands gripped. Mine partly the grip of a mate and partly the grip of a lover. Mark's? How did Mark's hands grip? And then a blush. And then a laugh.'

Despite the growing visibility of the gay liberation movement in the Balmain milieu, straight men, even self-professed radicals, were not always comfortable with homosexuality, according to Moorhouse. He once told me that 'there's a difference between politics and what men in an intensely homosocial society were prepared to acknowledge'. Michael Wilding remarks on Moorhouse's homosexuality in his memoir, *Growing Wild*:

Frank's homosexuality was something it took me a while to realise . . . Gillian and his other ex-girlfriends joked about our friendship, but I thought that was merely a joke and didn't detect the dark undercurrents. His proud announcement that he had opened the dancing at the Purple Onion [a gay club] meant nothing to me, night clubs were never part of my world.

As far as I knew his late night runs in Rushcutters Bay park were just part of his exercise routine.

After this slightly anxious reflection on Moorhouse's homosexual side, Wilding recounts that, 'drunk or stoned after the pub or a party', he once gave into the 'experimental times' and decided to 'experiment' with his friend.

> I climbed into his bed. He lay there inert. I reached out
> in the direction of his genitals but encountered nothing.
> Significant absence, as the literary theorists put it. Then one
> of us fell out of the bed. It was a narrow one. I don't know
> whether it was then that peering over the side to see where
> he had fallen, or lying on the floor looking under the bed,
> I saw the rifle.

It's an interesting segue from the penis to the gun, and one guaranteed to waken the Freudian in Moorhouse. Wilding goes on to say that seeing the rifle caused him to harbour oddly unspecified 'grim suspicions'.

Moorhouse was open about keeping a gun at the time of this incident. Indeed, as he recounts in the documentary *A Writer's Camp*, made by director Judy Rymer in 1987, he bought a Winchester rifle with his first publisher's advance, 'to satisfy a boyish dream'. In the film, which details the nineteen years he spent at Ewenton Street in Balmain, where he had his writer's studio, Moorhouse is interviewed by his desk and goes to the corner of his office to take the rifle out of its carrying case. He used the rifle for hunting with his friend and patron Murray Sime. Moorhouse goes on to say that it played a number of parts in his life: 'If it was under the bed, it scared away the phantoms of anxiety' and that 'in very low periods it's been the rifle I've considered using to end it all'.

It seems unlikely that Wilding, who was a close friend of Moorhouse's at the time, would have been unaware that his fellow author owned at least one gun. Wilding's anecdote about the fumbled sexual encounter and the gun under the bed is, however, illuminating on another count. Moorhouse always juggled an apparent but central contradiction in his personality and his interests. On one hand, he was a man with a strong sense of his feminine side. Moorhouse had a lifelong interest in cross-dressing in private (of which, more later in this book), and he talked openly in interviews about it. On the other, he always enjoyed traditionally masculine pursuits such as going bush and hunting. In a later chapter, I explore whether this apparent contradiction in his own personality and persona is connected to his fascination with crossing borders, including the borders of gender and sexuality.

If not publicly out as bisexual at the time, Moorhouse was certainly a witness to the emerging gay liberation movement of the early 1970s. The young Melbourne gay writer Sasha Soldatow came to Sydney and assisted Wendy Bacon and Moorhouse to sell copies of *Thor*, an underground newspaper that was an offshoot of the UNSW student paper *Tharunka*. Soldatow fell in with the Push crowd and got involved with the women's liberation and gay liberation movements. As Coombs writes, 'When Sasha Soldatow first began visiting Sydney, various strands in the liberation and libertarian movements had converged.'

It was the beginning of the rise of what became known as 'identity politics'—a less monolithic politics defined by a strong personal or ideological identification with a human rights issue. The big-picture political activism of the traditional left—the revolutionary dream—was fracturing, and a host of new, more fragmented issues-based movements were emerging.

Activists for women's liberation, Indigenous rights, racial equality, land rights, environmentalism and gay liberation were all fragmenting into different camps. These were issues that would come to define progressive politics and inflect cultural production as the 1970s progressed.

3

THE WRITING LIFE

At the beginning of the 1970s, Moorhouse made the decision to become a full-time fiction writer. He was in his early thirties. His book *Futility and Other Animals* had been published in 1969 by Gareth Powell Associates but had not been distributed to bookstores because the company had gone out of business. The books were languishing in packing cases.

Nicholas Pounder, Moorhouse's archivist, made the following catalogue note for the archive:

> *Futility* was published without a title page. In the conventions of bookselling and publishing at that time a title page sent back to a publisher was marked for a credit to the bookseller as evidence that a defective copy had been provided and that the book could not be sold. Just another handicap for a local small press production.

Moorhouse was living on accumulated holiday and sick pay from a stint at the ABC, where he had been a television and radio journalist. He had been cohabiting with Gillian Burnett, a fellow libertarian, in Kings Cross. But by 1970 he was living out of a room he had originally rented to write in. 'Separated from Gillian and from the ABC, I found myself with my books, a rented television, an electric coffee percolator, my type-writer—everything I owned—in a room, sharing a bathroom, and sleeping on a single divan,' he recalls in *Days of Wine and Rage*.

It's a domestic situation in which Moorhouse would find himself many times. He had often lived and written in comfort-able circumstances, whether because he was sharing a house with a lover or minding a house for a friend or patron. But equally he often lived and worked without complaint in far more spartan conditions.

At the time, six reviewers had read his first book and favour-ably reviewed it—despite it being unobtainable in any bookshop. He applied for a fellowship from the Commonwealth Literary Fund, the precursor to the Literature Board of Australia Council. In *Days of Wine and Rage* he recalls a hinge point in his transition to becoming a full-time writer:

> I had used the good reviews for *Futility and Other Animals* and my stories published in magazines to apply . . . Elizabeth Riddell wrote about the annual awards and noted, 'Among the unsuccessful applicants is the Sydney writer Frank Moorhouse.' From being an unemployed journalist with his first book a phantom, read only by six reviewers in Australia, I had become a Sydney writer.

Moorhouse was awarded what he called 'a consolation prize' of $1500 by the minister running the fund, Peter Howson. Using these funds, he patched together an income selling short stories, teaching adult education classes at the Workers' Educational Association and writing for *The Bulletin* under Donald Horne's editorship. His friendship with Horne was to be one of the most important of his life. It was through Moorhouse that Horne and his wife, Myfanwy, came to know and socialise with many of the Balmain writers. In a memoir, Horne recalls:

> What had really pulled the curtain up was David Williamson's *Don's Party*, written for the Melbourne Pram Factory, which replaced the idiomatic language of the Bush with a city idiom that set a new charge through Australian theatre. We reported all of this, but in the case of Frank Moorhouse, we also helped it along. I had read his *Futility and Other Animals*, which presented, in 'discontinuous narrative', a 'modern urban tribe'—part of it set in Balmain, where he lived, and it seemed so good that when the Commonwealth Literary Fund knocked him back for a fellowship I rang him, offering him a 'grant' if he wrote for us regularly.

Moorhouse wrote columns on eclectic topics including 'the laundromat society', the Chinese meal as an Australian ritual, productive use of 'the sickie', hotel décor, the new revival cinemas and resident power. He introduced Horne to Don Anderson, who became *The Bulletin*'s television critic. Horne and his wife also met Sandra Levy, whom Horne describes in his memoir as 'a talented, energetic and diverting woman'. Horne says of Moorhouse's writing: 'I took to Frank's writing as an antidote to the more portentous modes that were in favour, puzzling people by finding a small thing he did, *Conference-ville*, to be more successful, in its own way, than some of the largest works of Patrick White.'

Over the next two years, he completed his second book, *The Americans, Baby*. At the same time, Moorhouse was doing more than simply advancing his own career. He was simultaneously deeply engaged in the politics of culture and in advocating for the rights of writers and others involved in the arts.

Throughout his life, Moorhouse not only wrote consistently—fiction, non-fiction, essays, screenplays and journalistic pieces—but he also reflected on what it meant to be a writer. And particularly what it meant to be an Australian writer. In *Forty-Seventeen*, a work of fiction, the narrator observes a group of poets exchanging notes on their pens:

> They handled each other's pens, writing their favourite line from Yeats or Eliot or whoever. 'Mere anarchy is loosed upon the world,' one wrote. He had not seen poets at this before . . . Australians wrote with the greatest freedom there is—writing without the fear of being read.

Moorhouse advocated throughout his life, at a not insignificant personal cost, to end regressive censorship laws, affirm copyright protection for writers, and expose and curtail the political surveillance of writers and journalists.

In this chapter, which examines Moorhouse's writing routine and the challenges he faced in making a living as a writer, I will also trace the history and extraordinary legacy of his advocacy for other Australian writers. It's a legacy which continues to benefit anyone who seeks to make a living from writing in this country.

———

In 1969, when Moorhouse first entered the fray as an anti-censorship activist, libertarian and anarchist politics were still animating the debate. From a 21st-century perspective, in the age of the internet, it is hard to imagine just how restrictive and effective the censorship laws of the time were.

Australia has a rich, enthusiastic and occasionally hilarious history of censorship. The banning of James Joyce's novel *Ulysses* in 1929 ushered in an orgy of censorship (orgy possibly being one of the words that was banned). By 1936, the list of prohibited publications comprised 5000 books, including Aldous Huxley's *Brave New World*, George Orwell's *Down and Out in Paris and London*, Ernest Hemingway's *Farewell to Arms* and Daniel Defoe's *Moll Flanders*. In 1930, the New South Wales Collector of Customs mandated that the department's censorship test was 'whether the average householder would accept the book in question as reading matter for his family'. How many implicitly male heads of households had taken the time to vet *Ulysses* for their family remains a mystery. When the uncut version of the 1967 film of *Ulysses* was released, the censor not only gave it an R18 rating but also required the audience to be segregated by gender.

By 1969, the censorship of literary works was managed by a National Literature Board of Review. But the federal government was not the only censor in town. Locally produced books, magazines and newspapers were overseen by state police departments—with predictably absurd results.

In 1930, Max Harris published a series of modernist poems by an unknown writer named Ern Malley. The fact that the poems were written as a hoax, with the use of arbitrary phrases, did not deter the prosecution witness Detective Vogelsang from giving evidence that a poem entitled 'Night Piece' was obscene. 'I have found that people who go into parks at night go there for immoral purposes,' he told the court. 'My experience as a police officer might, under the circumstances, tinge my appreciation of poetry.'

By the late 1960s, there was a growing movement to push back against the frequent banning of cultural works. A key driver of this push was the fear that censorship laws underpinned an image of Australia as culturally regressive and unsophisticated. In their book *Australia's Censorship Crisis*, Geoffrey Dutton and Max Harris write that there was:

> an urgent public feeling that censorship procedures and current actions in all the art forms do not accord with the 'community standards' held by the young and yet mature majority of Australians who are determined that this country shall enjoy the same cultural freedom in the same kind of way as other Western democracies.

Peter Coleman, an Australian journalist, writer and Liberal politician, Dutton and Harris mounted their objections to excessive and arbitrary censorship along classic liberal humanist lines. They were essentially arguing that high culture should be kept out of the hands of ignorant customs inspectors and police officers. But a more radical anti-censorship movement was already fermenting—one which would abandon the traditional liberal view that sexually explicit material was only defensible on the grounds that it had literary or artistic merit.

In 1970, Wendy Bacon, Val Hodgson and Alan Rees were elected editors of the University of New South Wales student newspaper *Tharunka*. They immediately invited what Moorhouse referred to as 'downtown writers' to contribute. As Moorhouse describes in *Days of Wine and Rage*:

It was my first experience of illegal or 'underground' journalism and it was the first time in our lives that we had written for, or had available, an uncensored public outlet for our writing. During its forty odd issues, *Tharunka* was certainly the most creatively edited and laid-out newspaper in Australia, and the only uncensored newspaper that Australians had seen. In 1972 I went to England and the USA and met with editors of other underground newspapers; looking at their papers, I found ours to be superior in content—literary, theoretical, and reporting.

The editors of *Tharunka* were able to avoid the censors because the magazine was enabled by the invention of offset printing, which allowed the professional production of a newspaper or magazine by untrained people. Traditionally, printers, who worked with the hot-metal printing method, had often acted as de facto censors.

Moorhouse recalled that, for him, writing for these underground publications 'was to be the most significant activity of the decade' and 'involve us all in about forty prosecutions and . . . put Wendy Bacon in jail for a week'.

Following a dispute with the Student Representative Council, Bacon and her team moved their publication downtown and renamed it *Thorunka* and eventually *Thor*. Her active collaborators and supporters included Moorhouse, Sandra Levy, libertarian feminist Liz Fell, cartoonist Jenny Coopes, and fellow editors Val Hodgson and Alan Rees. While the publication's name had changed, the constant was the politically and culturally radical nature of the content that frequently attracted the censor's eye.

Thorunka reported on civil liberties, feminist issues and the debate over the Vietnam War and conscription, and also published literary work. The editors printed four-letter words (some of which remain unpublishable in mainstream 21st-century newspapers), erotica, pornographic cartoons and illustrations, and serialised banned books. They also published work from a roll call of esteemed Australian writers whose work had been censored, including Tom Keneally, Thomas Shapcott, A.D. Hope, Frank Hardy, Alex Buzo and Michael Dransfield.

Thorunka was financed by sales of between 5000 and 10,000 copies per issue, and by supporters. It was sold on university campuses, at demonstrations, at Sydney pubs and at bookshops which were prepared to take the risk of being prosecuted. The magazine was eventually closed, Moorhouse said, because of 'the exhaustion of the staff'. They had forty-one summonses to answer.

Coleman shows his conservative roots when he describes the publications as a 'student pornographic movement' that was 'inspired by a complete loathing of the society we live in'. Libertarians, he claims, sought to destroy 'all forms of our trea-sured society, which includes family, church, school and other institutions'. Given the mood of the times among radicals, he probably hit the nail on the head.

In *Days of Wine and Rage*, Moorhouse reflected:

Australia, partly in the drag-stream of other English-speaking nations and partly by its own initiative, was moving through a bad-tempered renegotiation of the relationships between men and women, adults and children, and a rethinking of the sexual and emotional relationships between people of the same sex . . . With this renegotiation there was an opening up of public communication. The freeing of what can be said through the media as well as what can be said conversationally was at the heart of the change.

Moorhouse had his own brushes with the law because of his censorship activism. He recalled that he and his then partner, Sandra Levy, were shopping in Balmain one afternoon when two detectives approached them and said they wanted to search her car.

I said that it was not legal for them to search the car—not knowing at the time whether it was or not and not having a clue what they wanted to find. They then dragged me from the car and a fight between them and Sandra and I broke out. A police van was called and we were arrested and taken to Balmain police station.

Moorhouse didn't say if there were fisticuffs involved, but I for one would pay to see two policemen try to face off against the formidable Sandra Levy. As Levy herself recalls it, she had, for once, actively tried to avoid being arrested for antagonising the authorities, because she had a full-time and senior job at the ABC. She remembers that Moorhouse was the one who had loaded the cargo into her station wagon.

It turned out that the cops had spied through the car's rear window copies of *Thor* and another publication, *The Little Red Schoolbook*, which encouraged young people to challenge social norms and included information about sexuality and drug use. Moorhouse and Levy were charged with exhibiting an obscene publication, resisting arrest, assaulting police, malicious damage and insulting words. They countersued the police for false arrest and were eventually convicted only of resisting arrest, for which they were fined $5.

Moorhouse's opposition to censorship became a lifelong concern, expressed through essays and public commentary. In a satirical essay, 'The Urge to Censor', written 30 years after the early censorship battles, he takes considered aim at the rationale underpinning pro-censorship rhetoric:

> It was as if we had been in a deep after-lunch sleep and had awoken—not sometime in the future, but back in our more tumultuous past. Back in the seventies, no less. It was not an agreeable sensation: we are not up to returning to the seventies . . . This disagreeable sense of déjà vu was caused by growing evidence of a resurgence of the dreaded Urge to Censor. The internet panic, the re-establishment of federal and state censorship, racial vilification acts—all show us that the bitch is back on heat.

Moorhouse went on to make a series of arguments against censorship amassed over years of collegial battle on the part of Australia's cultural vanguard (or cultural 'elite', or 'Balmain basket weavers', depending on your political leanings).

One of his most compelling arguments against censorship centred on the fallacy that censors can know in advance how messages are received and by whom, and can therefore know who needs protecting. The history of censorship, as he has noted on many occasions, has not been one of universally applied restrictions. Beginning with the Catholic Church and later the monarchy and the state, Western censorship has singled out groups assumed to be particularly vulnerable to corruption—the working class, women and children.

Censorship is a Trojan horse, of course, for many other political concerns and anxieties. It's a blister on the social skin that we can't seem to stop worrying. In each incarnation, the battle over censorship is fought over different terrain but mustered in the name of claiming the same rights. For Moorhouse and his kind, opposing censorship has never simply been about asserting the right of writers and artists to express themselves freely—though that is a critical part of his objection. It has equally been about the nature of the democracy in which we live, and how we protect the rights of citizens to speak freely—even when that speech is repugnant or hateful.

There are plenty of people on the left, as much as the right, who are likely to find Moorhouse's views on censorship unpalatable, particularly in the current climate of rigorously patrolled identity politics. But his views remained largely unchanged from the time of his first encounters with the censors. Rather than codifying anti-vilification laws or introducing workplace policies to mandate acceptable terms of address, he believed in countering ugly or offensive speech with more speech.

————

The fight against censorship was more than just a battle against parochial and paternalistic attitudes to sexuality and other once largely taboo subjects. It was equally a battle to allow a new generation of short-story writers freedom to write in ways that broke with what Michael Wilding called 'the single mythic line of the outback story'.

In an incisive essay published in a collection of short stories, Wilding recounts the emergence of the small magazine he founded in 1972 titled *Tabloid Story*. He acknowledges that the idea for the magazine was not his alone: it grew out of conversations with Moorhouse, critic Brian Kiernan and others about their dissatisfaction with the traditional outlets for short stories such as *Meanjin* and *Southerly*. He writes:

We knew there was good prose around that wasn't surfacing into the quarterlies or the overground publishing houses; we knew once we got *Tabloid Story* going, it would attract a lot more new prose we didn't even know about; people we had never read, heard of or encountered; we shaped the first two issues from the available materials—and shaped them to show the sort of new writing we wanted to encourage—no more formula bush tales, no more restrictions to the beginning, middle and end story, no more preconceptions about a well-rounded tale.

The sixteen issues that resulted featured Australian writers such as Peter Carey, Murray Bail, Carmel Kelly and Vicki Viidikas, along with Wilding and Moorhouse. Wilding notes that the format they chose had its precursor in an inner-city newspaper Moorhouse had experimented with titled *City Voices*, modelled on the original *New York Village Voice* concept, which lasted five issues and never reached its break-even circulation of 1500 copies.

To avoid that fate—the fate of many small magazines which failed to attract advertising and were thwarted by bookshops, newsagents and printers—a decision was taken to produce a pre-packaged magazine which was edited, typeset, designed and made camera-ready, and which could be distributed by a host publication. 'The host magazine taking *Tabloid Story* would give us a run-on of 2,000 copies of the supplement for us to distribute to subscribers, contributors, bookshops and as complementarities and exchanges with other magazines internationally,' Wilding writes.

The format was innovative—not only in the stories the editors published, but also in their approach to paying writers fairly for their work. When they successfully applied for a $2000 grant from the Commonwealth Literary Fund, their proposal stated that they required sufficient subsidisation to pay contributors at the standard minimum rate the Australian Society of Authors recommended—$50 per thousand words. They allocated two-thirds of their budget to contributors and one-third to production. This move, according to Wilding, forced other literary magazines to declare their rates of payment, because 'once *Tabloid Story* had publicised the issue there was no going back'.

Wilding records that Moorhouse noted down the following record of what else they did to ensure contributors were treated fairly:

a. We didn't require them to type.
b. We didn't make them pay for a reply—the literary magazines were the only business in the world which required that their clients pay for the courtesy of a reply . . .
c. We made personal comments on the stories (which were not always appreciated).
d. We supplied multiple copies to contributors.
e. We paid on acceptance not publication.
f. We broke that haughtiness and contempt and discourtesy still found in literary magazines by recognising contributors as the source of life for a little magazine.

This list is an important one, because it demonstrates the commitment Moorhouse and some of his writing cohort had to advancing the rights of writers not only to publish freely on formerly taboo subjects but equally to earn a living. It is, in one sense, a coded manifesto on the value of cultural work

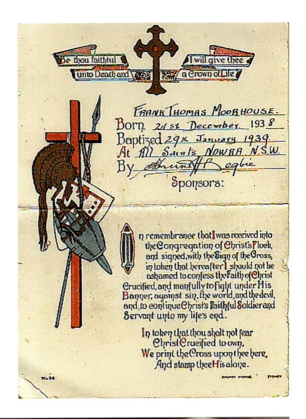

FRANK THOMAS MOORHOUSE.
Born 21st December, 1938
Baptized 29th January 1939
At All Saints NOWRA N.S.W.
By
Sponsors:

Frank (centre) with brothers Arthur and Owen, 1939.

The young 'Machinery Man'.

A family business in rural New South Wales at the centre of agricultural innovation.

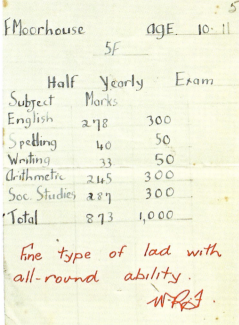

F Moorhouse   Age. 10·11

5F

Half Yearly Exam

Subject	Marks	
English	278	300
Spelling	40	50
Writing	33	50
Arithmetic	245	300
Soc. Studies	287	300
Total	873	1,000

Fine type of lad with all-round ability.

N·R·J.

Cadet and captain.

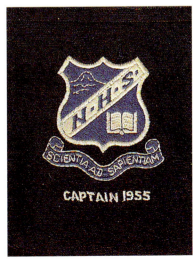

Wendy Halloway, back row centre, Frank Moorhouse, second from the right, front row. Nowra High School, Form Four class photo, 1955.

Moorhouse often hung out with his friend Peter Martin who said 'our lynchpin together was push bikes'.

'When we two boys planned a cycling trip to cover approximately seven hundred miles of hot black bitumen, our friends stared, firstly with amazement and secondly with derision. Our parents laughed sympathetically and hoped that we did not have the will to attempt such a trip.'

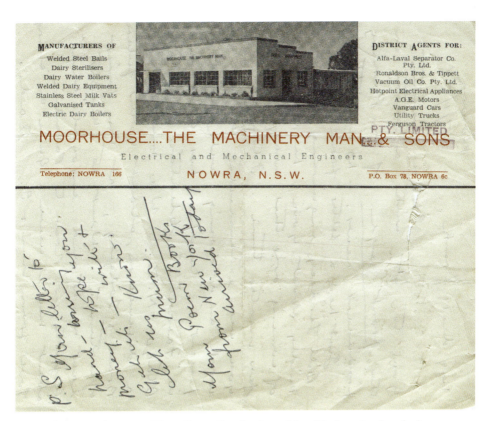

Letter from Dad, 1957. 'Your Poem Books from New York arrived today'

Frank Moorhouse and Wendy Halloway, 1957.

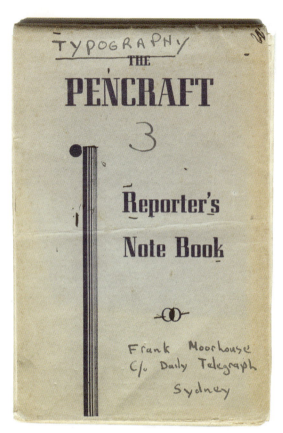

Aspirations of a seventeen-year-old cadet journalist at *The Daily Telegraph*, fresh out of Nowra High School.

Below: Editor, newspaper proprietor, and employer David Gyger. Like Moorhouse, Gyger discovered his calling as a journalist early, writing for and editing student newspapers at high school. He always regarded journalism as a craft to be practised at the highest possible level; this applied not only to the careful shaping of the prose, but also to the elegance of layout on the page.

My Dearest Wendy,

Dec 1957

My first day at work today and the only thing I wrote was an advertisement for board.

D.E.Gyger

F.T.Moorhouse

D.R.Stephenson

"POTATO PATCH"
122 Hammond Avenue
Wagga Wagga
N.S.W.

Phone 4535

Monday August 11
1958

My darling wife Wendy,

Marriage of Wendy Halloway and Frank Moorhouse, 1958.

The Daily Advertiser, Sat., May 17, 1958 3

NEW ART HAS STUDENTS "IN STITCHES"

By FRANK MOORHOUSE

Art lecturer, Lionel Gailer, is having a difficult time convincing students at the Wagga Teachers' College that some of his recent additions to the college art collection are not jokes.

The college has recently added six originals, including abstract and semi-abstract, to its £6000 collection.

The paintings are representative of modern art, and were done by Australian artists.

"I am having a hard time teaching students to appreciate the abstracts," Mr. Gailer said.

"A sound background in art is required before it is possible to appreciate some of the paintings.

Must be obtained

"I have to put up with jokes and sarcastic comments from staff members as well as students.

"But to make the college collection truly representative, painters of the modern schools must be obtained.

"The abstract paintings make students think and it gives them the opportunity to see something different from the paintings they have been used to."

The most abstract of the new paintings, titled "12 p.m." was done by Roy Fluke. The painting is an abstract of city buildings, traffic lights and tram sparks, and was painted mainly with ink rollers.

A leader

Fluke studied art after the war with the National Art Scheme, and has become a leader among Australian abstract artists.

He won the Mosman Art Prize with his controversial "Spit Bridge."

Another is a semi-abstract seascape done by Kenneth Hood and painted with a palette knife.

Hood has retained the general outlines of the original scene, but has changed colours and shapes as he felt they should be.

A less abstract painting in the collection is "Brighton Peir," by Francis Lymburner. Lymburner does not attempt to depict the world literally although "Brighton Peir" does

TO DISCUSS AGREEMENT

MELBOURNE, Friday: The chairman of the Australian Meat Board (Mr. J. I. Shute) left today for Britain to take part in the negotiation concerning the long-term meat agreement with Britain.

Mr. Shute will lead a delegation from the Board, to act in an advisory capacity to Australian Government officials.

Under the agreement, minimum prices for lamb and mutton for the three years to begin October 1, 1958, and for beef and veal for the three years to begin October 1, 1961, are to be fixed.

have some resemblance to a seaside pier.

He is one of the painters who has revolted against academic drawing and the control of the artist by his subject.

"Brighton Peir" illustrates pleasure seeking people with bright lights and fun parlours and their indifference to the turbulent storm around them. The three other paintings are more orthodox.

Some resemblance

One by George Lawrence called "South Coast Landscape" is a traditional-style painting of some farm buildings and surrounding fields. Lawrence is rated one of the best Australian landscape painters of the last 20 years.

Sydney Nolan, who became known for his paintings of the Ned Kelly legend, is represented by an unusual painting of some buildings in Sienna, Italy.

The painting is done with two colours, white and burnt sienna, and is framed with an effective wide black border.

The only woman painter represented in the group is Elaine Haxton.

Her painting, "The Dove Seller," is a brilliantly coloured portrait of an Italian with two dove cages on a yoke carrier.

The writer's first byline, 17 May 1958.

in a society which then regarded (and perhaps still regards) avant-garde cultural activity as being of dubious or marginal value.

Prior to the advent of *Tabloid Story*, writers of Moorhouse's era whose work was considered too contemporary or sexually explicit tended to publish in underground magazines (such as *Thor* and *Thorunka*) or in softcore porn magazines like *Playboy*, which published fiction along with girlie pics. (Hence that old chestnut: 'I only read it for the articles.') In the late 1960s, these magazines included *Squire*, *Casual* and *Chance International*. These magazines pre-dated and were eventually rendered obsolete by the circulation of US publications such as *Penthouse* and *Playboy* in Australia, following the liberalisation of censorship laws in the early to mid-1970s. Publishers of new fiction in these outlets included Jack de Lissa, Ron Smith and Gareth Powell. They had circulations of up to 100,000, although it is impossible to determine how many readers bought them for the fiction.

Wilding recalls of the late 1960s and early 1970s:

To us at that time the girlie magazines provided the only outlets for work that dealt with sexuality, for works that weren't committed to the old outback tale and other formulae that the established literary quarterlies ran. The girlie magazines were open to new sorts of writing—in part, for sure, because people bought the magazines to look at the tits— pre-pubic hair days, these were; it didn't matter too much about the stories since few people read them; but the editors and the publishers nonetheless did read them, did have an idea of a new writing, did have a belief in a new prose; and those editors had a wider, non-academic, non-establishment taste than the editors of the quarterlies and of the respectable publishing houses.

––––––

Moorhouse revisited the theme of censorship and surveillance in a book published in 2014 titled *Australia Under Surveillance*, in which he explored the role ASIO and allied government agencies have played in the nation's history and its people's cultural lives.

In the third book in his League of Nations trilogy, *Cold Light*, Moorhouse takes his readers to Canberra, a town in the Australian Capital Territory, which was chosen as the seat of federal parliament because it was positioned between the two main capital cities, Sydney and Melbourne. The federation of Australian states had only occurred in 1901. Australian democracy, which developed out of a penal colony built by the British, evolved slowly. Some would say it is still evolving. Australia has no bill of rights, is still governed (by the letter of the law, if not in practice) by the ruling British monarch, and has, at the time of writing, not yet formally recognised the Indigenous peoples of the land in its constitution.

In *Cold Light*, Edith Campbell Berry arrives in Canberra, in whose arid soil the symbols of Australian democracy would become rooted. For Edith, coming to Canberra is a major step down from working as a key adviser to the president of the League of Nations. Ambrose, her husband and original mentor at the League, is less than happy about being dragged to a place he describes to her over dinner as: 'a country that is ninety per cent uninhabited . . . and mostly desert'. Ambrose is, obviously, British.

Edith ignores him and continues with her vision of the new capital city—which she decides to spell as 'capitol', to acknowledge the key role that the American architects Walter Burley Griffin and Marion Mahony Griffin played in designing Canberra. She tells Ambrose:

> A capitol is not only the place of governance—a place where how we are to live our lives is decided, as if that isn't dramatic enough . . . I've realised that a capitol is also the place of communal memory. Hence the old capitols and their museums and monuments and so on, their spoils of war. Memorials. The national memory. In a capitol we are inside the living memory of the nation.

Edith's political idealism, though rocked by the fall of the League of Nations in the wake of World War II, is remarkably undimmed. She remains an advocate of participatory democracy, and a believer in the notion that everything from the design of a city to the furniture which graces someone's office can change the way people think and act. As did Moorhouse.

She is living at the best hotel in the city at the time, the Hotel Canberra, when her brother turns up. He hasn't been in contact with her for decades, and he now reveals himself to be an organiser with the Communist Party. It is 1950, and Robert Menzies is prime minister. A conservative, deeply enmeshed in Cold War politics, Menzies is preparing to ask the federal parliament to pass the Communist Party Dissolution Bill. As someone hoping for a job in the public service, Edith is not only ambivalent about her brother's politics but also concerned that, by associating with him, she will derail her chance of a senior public service job. She knows that members of the Communist Party and their associates are being watched.

Menzies' legislation passed, but the Act was declared invalid by the High Court the following year. Menzies then took his attempts to ban the Communist Party to a referendum in 1951, but it failed. Moorhouse writes:

> It may not have been illegal to be a member of the Communist Party, but this did not stop ASIO or the Liberal Prime Minister, Robert Menzies, from carrying out surveillance of these citizens and sometimes interfering with their careers. We still do not know for certain the extent of this interference, although even at the time we knew that ASIO had been ordered by Menzies to spy on writers.

Moorhouse's battles with the censoring powers on behalf of writers were staged across a long front. At the heart of the urge to censor, as he rightly detected early in the campaign, is an authoritarian impulse. It's the desire to control dressed up as the need to protect. Censorship is an essentially paternalistic, and sometimes maternalistic, approach to dealing with aspects of being human that some in power find inconvenient and confronting.

That's not to say that Moorhouse advocated freedom of expression without any limits. In *The Inspector-General of Misconception*, published in 2002, he listed the exceptions to his opposition to censorship and conceded that the community had 'legitimate cause to suppress some information':

> Protection of the young by suppressing their names in court cases; information which endangers the armed forces in times of conflict (this does not mean the suppression of debate about the rights or wrongs of a conflict, we have in mind information strategically or tactically valuable to the enemy); misleading

false product information which is physically dangerous; the spreading of information useful to those would inflict physical violence on the society (e.g. how to make postal bombs; even though attempts to censor this information may be a futile exercise). And, of course, the text-book example of shouting 'fire' at public gatherings.

On the question of child exploitation materials, he made it clear that he believed that anyone who used children to produce such images and/or coerced them into it should be prosecuted.

When it came to laws against hate speech, Moorhouse believed that, unless hate speech was offering actual instructions to people willing to commit race hate crimes, dialogue was more effective. It's worth exploring Moorhouse's views on racial hate speech because they give us an insight into his views about democracy and humanity, and his thoughts on the writer's duty to report faithfully on both.

> We all know how ugly hate speech can be, yet there is no comfortable, pragmatic, legal answer to it. If—as I do—you come from a mainstream, privileged, ethnic group, and have mixed and lived among tolerant sub-groups, you rarely experience it. But as a writer (and personally), I have had media, parliamentary and public abuse directed towards me. No matter how resilient and protected you feel, it is still disturbing. It would be almost intolerable if it were directed against someone every day in everyday situations—something that less privileged people can experience.

Moorhouse quoted Meaghan Morris, a writer he greatly admired, on the question of the limits to hate speech and why an ethics of civility is so important:

It boils down to four basic principles. Don't harp about people's differences when it isn't necessary; do try to treat everyone equally and fairly; don't use euphemisms for disabilities or make jocular remarks to people you don't know about their race, their looks, or their sexuality; do call people whatever they prefer to be called, and if you don't know, ask them.

He also quoted television personality Andrew Denton, who once said that the solution to the political correctness debate was to form 'a group of fundamentalist moderates . . . our job will be to travel the world and slaughter anyone who can't see both sides of the argument'.

On a more serious note in *Australia Under Surveillance*, Moorhouse traced a long lineage of ASIO and other government agencies spying on writers and intellectuals, and sometimes actively working to stymie their capacity to access grants. It's a history that stretches from the 1950s to the present day. Moorhouse continued to fight the censorship battle for more than 50 years. He did it because he recognised that every new generation of writers and intellectuals had to wage the war anew— and that new forms of surveillance and allied security laws were making it even easier for governments to claim immunity from the scrutiny to which they sometimes subject others.

Part of Moorhouse's case for limiting censorship was that the artistic imagination relies on challenging our boundaries. In an essay titled 'Manifesto for the Imagination', published in the *Griffith Review*, he posed two questions: why is the artistic imagination treated as a thing of angry suspicion and distaste by some people and with awe by others? And from where does the imagination claim its authority to challenge conventions and the law?

Moorhouse argued that the artistic imagination makes a particular and singular contribution to society and culture and the audience, or readership, and so is a 'crucial part of the creative equation'. There will be some who find Moorhouse's claim for a special status for artists abhorrent, and a mere excuse for flouting the standards of 'ordinary' decency. But as he has argued in a range of contexts, the kind of people who are challenged by works of the imagination are often equally challenged by the messy business of being human. In his *Griffith Review* essay, he wrote:

The artistic imagination sometimes draws its authority from the great liberal enterprise of inquiry—scientific, intellectual and artistic—which tries to lead us to be a more knowing society, a society which is in closer touch with reality and therefore safer . . . Suppression of information and freedom of expression by law, by filters and by protocols denies us a full acquaintance with reality . . . The suppressed material turns into phantoms crouching in the dark and is transformed into the forbidden; in turn, it becomes an underground commodity.

While he defended what he saw as the almost sacral role artists hold as storytellers, Moorhouse's own approach to the daily grind of writing was far removed from the romantic bohemian ideal. He was extraordinarily productive—he produced eighteen books, comprising novels, edited collections, short stories and comic essays, along with film and television scripts and a prodigious number of literary essays and journalistic pieces.

His writing routine was set up to resemble, in many ways, that of a diligent office worker. Writer Matt Condon recalls learning from Moorhouse about how to get the job of writing a novel done. 'I visited him in his little factory studio in Balmain and I remember the chaise lounge and the Persian rugs,' he says. 'And here was Frank with his white shirt on and the sleeves rolled up and he came to work every morning, read the newspaper first thing in the day and went to the office and then went home in the afternoon. It's just another example of how he taught me what was required, in terms of discipline, to get the work done. I do not know how he's survived and been a full-time writer since the 1970s.'

Condon's account of Moorhouse's writing practice was confirmed by the 1987 documentary *A Writer's Camp*, which chronicled Moorhouse's departure from his writer's studio at Ewenton Street, Balmain, where he wrote for two decades. In that studio, he produced six works of fiction, three edited volumes and the scripts for five films. What he described in the documentary as his 'office' at Ewenton Street was full of books and papers, and had a well-stocked bar. There was a filing system, reminiscent of old library catalogues, filled with cards sorted according to theme and project.

Sandra Levy recalled that Moorhouse was always taking notes, even in social situations. In an address he gave to the Fryer Library in 2015, Moorhouse described how he began to take notes as a teenage writer in an 'expensive leather, loose-leaf notebook'. He started to use index cards in 1980 after he observed his then partner Michele Field, an academic, using 3 x 5 index cards in her research. He said: 'These cards were what I needed for my writing, not a notebook. I could never find a note I wanted in a notebook.'

He went on to make an interesting link between his excitement at discovering how useful index cards were for a writer and his delight in performing magic tricks as a child. 'Perhaps I saw index cards as an infinite pack of playing cards which could be manipulated into many, many tricks—the magic of short stories, novels and all sorts of imaginative acts.' He recounted a passage in *Alice's Adventures in Wonderland* in which Alice takes charge of the King's pencil while he is writing and makes him write things he doesn't intend to write. 'Sometimes when I read the cards I feel that my own Alice—my unconscious—is manipulating my pencil,' he said, 'and that I will not know what the card fully means until it finds its way into its destined imaginative work.'

After discovering index cards, he carried them in his wallet and would jot down thoughts on them over lunch or dinner. However chaotic or quixotic his thoughts the evening before, he reviewed the cards and filed them precisely the following morning.

In the documentary, he tells the interviewer:

> I've carried these index cards for the past few years. I used to keep a notebook but I found that notebooks are a jumble of things—of shopping lists, notes about one story and notes about another project . . . With cards I can head them up [give them a title] . . . I can organise them. I keep them in my wallet and I can make notes throughout the day and through-out the night . . . I keep them beside my bed.

In the documentary, Moorhouse is filmed jogging to his writer's office, newspaper under one arm. Those with whom he had shared houses and apartments confirm that Moorhouse usually followed a strict writing routine. He was at his desk to write for four to five hours before taking a break, and he revised his work in the late afternoon or early evening over a drink. He often wrote six days a week. And when he was in the middle of a manuscript, he cut himself off from socialising and all other distractions. Yet he also insisted on taking occasional structured holidays, which helped him decompress and restored his creative energies.

In an unpublished guide to the business of becoming and being a writer, Moorhouse laid out advice to the young writer. He discussed the role of mentoring, of patrons, and the various sources of income that most successful writers use to patch together a living. Unpacking the latter, he laid bare the administrative complexity and deadline juggling that constitutes life for any writer without a full-time job that supports their practice. The sources of income he mentions include royalties, fellowships, research grants, residences, serialisation, overseas rights, films, television, radio, opinion pieces, essays, prizes and copyright payments.

Working from book to book while keeping food on the table and a roof over one's head is not the life that many readers picture when they fondly imagine their favourite author at her or his desk. It is a life without the infrastructure that those of us with salaried jobs often take for granted. Authors who choose to write full-time also have to manage their tax affairs, any legal issues, unpredictable gaps in their income, writer's block and public attacks. They have to stay on top of their invoicing schedule and maintain good relationships with the numerous editors for whom they freelance. They also need to apply for grants and fellowships. They are dependent, at times, on the friendship, patronage and advice of those who believe in their work.

Two key supporters in Moorhouse's life were the banker Murray Sime and long-time friends publisher Carol and lawyer Nick Dettmann, who represented Moorhouse in a case he brought against publisher Angus & Robertson for losing five of his manuscripts. Two and a half of them were later discovered in the State Library of New South Wales. The Dettmanns and their children were long-term and very close friends. Moorhouse frequently spent the Christmas/New Year period with them at their Jamberoo property as well as Thanksgiving Dinner in Sydney (Carol being from the US), usually accompanied by his current partner. When he was writing *Cold Light* he used their old house at Jamberoo as a retreat and often went there for a break from the city. It was a friendship that sustained Moorhouse on many levels throughout his life. When Moorhouse needed somewhere to live in his later years they purchased an apartment in Kings Cross for him to live in. He delighted in the fact that from there he could see the first flat in Sydney that he had shared with other cadet journalists—as well as the Kings Cross fire station where his maternal grandfather had been the fire chief.

Dr Rosemary Creswell was Moorhouse's lifelong friend and literary agent. Rose, as she was known, played a crucial part in Moorhouse's life and he considered her advice and care to be intrinsic to his work and career. Dr Creswell died on 19 April 2017 after a long and cruel illness. Moorhouse spoke movingly at her memorial service, paying tribute to Creswell's loyalty and the great love she had for the authors she represented. After the service Moorhouse wept, saying Rose's death had devastated him more than any other.

When the coffers are full, writers can rely on agents, accountants and lawyers to carry some of the burden. But in a life fully devoted to writing, as Moorhouse's was, there were inevitably times when they were forced to take on many of these demands alone because of a lack of funds. And it was Moorhouse's commitment to seeing writers paid properly for their work that propelled him on a mission to reform copyright law and secure the right of authors to be paid fairly for their copying and lending rights.

———

Frank Moorhouse was lying in the sun outside his writer's studio with his girlfriend. They were naked—it was the 1970s, after all. Suddenly he flung aside the book he was reading and exclaimed: 'My god, intellectual property is about the very nature of existence. Intellectual property is the key to all understanding.' It's a classic Moorhouse anecdote: there's the juxtaposition of the intimate and the abstract, an eye for sensual detail, and a delicious irony in the idea of a man lying next to his naked lover inflamed by legal prose.

The book he was reading was *Copyright in International Relations: International Protection of Literary and Scientific Works*. He unpacked his thoughts to his girlfriend this way: 'I exclaimed to her that there were three ways of seeing intellectual property and the world—the collectivist way, which argues that the state educated and made us, and what we make rightfully belongs to the state; the continental philosophy of intellectual property, which argues that a creative work is not simply "property" but also an extension of the personality of the creator, and therefore has to be treated differently to other products; and the pure market view that intellectual property was simply a product which could be traded as any other product.

'I said that in fact we held, in part and in a tangled amalgam of law, to all three positions in most English countries. That intellectual property was able to be traded, but that we honoured and rewarded the creator in special ways quite distinctive from other occupations (that is, we did see it as a creative extension of a person). Furthermore, unlike other property we also saw intellectual property as eventually returning to the community as communal property (50 years after the death of an author), which is a collectivist way of thinking.'

Apparently, he lost his girlfriend's attention some way through this monologue.

The story of how Moorhouse became so fascinated with the technical aspects of copyright law began at the Sydney Hilton's Marble Bar over a couple of martinis with two young lawyers, Peter Banki and David Catterns. They had invited him there to reveal a secret ruse they had carried out that was to change the face of copyright law in Australia, and that would have inter-national ramifications too.

Aware that Australian universities were tacitly turning a blind eye to the opportunities for breaches of copyright offered by their newly installed photocopiers, Banki and Catterns decided to act. They asked a student at the University of New South Wales, Paul Brennan, to select works from the university library and copy them in full. He did so on 28 September 1973. One of the works was Frank Moorhouse's recently published *The Americans, Baby*. They now explained to Moorhouse that they had set up the copying without his prior knowledge so there could be no suggestion that he had authorised the student to copy his work. Next, they asked Moorhouse if he would be willing to lend his name to an action against the university for implicitly licensing breaches of copyright.

Banki, who became a partner in the Sydney firm Banki Haddock Fiora, is one of Australia's foremost intellectual property lawyers. He says Moorhouse's willingness to be involved was 'a pretty courageous thing to do', and that the case they eventually won was, in terms of intellectual property law, 'the defining case of its time; not just here but worldwide'.

Moorhouse told the story of how he came to be involved in a somewhat more self-deprecating manner. He said that, 'after several martinis and witty chat', Banki and Catterns explained that they wanted a few authors to put their names to a case suing UNSW for breach of copyright by means of its photo-copying machines. They then explained that they would take on the schools, universities and libraries for illegal copying. After they won the case, they would bring the illegal use of photocopiers to a grinding halt.

> 'Hold on,' I said, 'isn't setting up an infringement an illegal act?' 'Well, yes and no,' Banki and Catterns said, 'you leave that to us, we'll handle that.' I said: 'Let me get this straight. I put my name on a case in which we prosecute school teachers, librarians, university lecturers, and school and university students?' I had enough problems in my life at that time as a young writer. I was a young writer: I had nothing else but problems in my life. I didn't need to alienate all the school teachers, university staff and library users and librarians and all university and school students in Australia, that is, just about every serious reader of books.

The case proceeded and went through three courts—eventually to the High Court. In case notes written up in a 1976 volume of the *Federal Law Review*, Pamela Nase noted, with what is now a wonderfully antique noun, that: 'The recent dramatic advance in techniques of reprography has created a problem for the legal systems of all countries which have copyright legislation: how to reconcile the rights of authors and the interests of the community.'

Nase was of the opinion that the case did not make the headway that Banki claims for the landmark nature of the judgment of the High Court. History has proved her wrong. Universities, schools and libraries now pay authors for the copying of their work through fees collected by the Australian Copyright Council (ACC). Moorhouse was at the forefront of fighting for these rights—copyright rights—which many younger writers take for granted.

The ACC was founded in 1968, the same year the *Commonwealth Copyright Act* came into existence. As Peter Meredith notes in his excellent account of the ACC and the associated body which collects fees for the reproduction of works, Copyright Agency Limited (CAL), Frank Moorhouse was actively involved from the early 1970s. In the early days of its existence, CAL signed up key authors to add weight to the negotiations it was having with educational institutions over photocopying fees. They included Moorhouse, Tom Keneally, Tom Shapcott, Peter Carey and Judith Wright.

Gus O'Donnell was a key figure in these copyright battles, along with lawyers Banki and Catterns. As Meredith recalled: 'Copyright protection and the meeting of the challenge of new technologies became [O'Donnell's] central role in life. He was dogged in pursuing what he perceived to be the [Australian Society of Authors'] and authors' interests. He had a remarkably good strategic mind in terms of what to do next. He also had a pretty good theoretical mind because copyright quite fascinated him . . .'

On 31 July 1981, Douglas Swan, the Director-General of Education in New South Wales, circulated a memo to school principals outlining strategies they could use to avoid paying for photocopying. Moorhouse, who was then the president of the Australian Society of Authors, led a deputation to Swan's office to ask him to withdraw the memo. Swan refused. As David Catterns recalls, 'We all walked out and went to Customs House and had a few schooners. And then we said. "Well, we'll sue the bastards."' They did.

When the case went on appeal to the Federal Court, authors and publishers had a significant victory. Swan was ordered to withdraw his memo and destroy it. 'This was a much more satisfactory outcome for the authors and publishers,' Meredith writes. 'It was a signal that reluctant educational institutions everywhere could not fail to miss; it told them there was no way they could artificially avoid copyright in that way.'

There ensued a conflict between the body representing publishing houses, the Australian Book Publishers Association (ABPA) and the Australian Society of Authors, over who should collect the royalties. O'Donnell was firmly of the view that authors should own the copyright and directly collect the funds. It fell to Moorhouse to head a committee, with Peter Banki and Donald Horne as members, to review and end the stalemate. Meredith writes:

> Despite his great admiration and personal fondness for Gus, Frank was prepared to make some concessions to the ABPA. He saw that having two collecting agencies was a serious mistake. 'This was very politically damaging and would weaken our position because if we appeared to be making a mess of it and making it all too hard, the federal government would take over.'

Moorhouse's early, active and passionate engagement with both the Australian Copyright Council and the Australian Society of Authors was a hallmark of his commitment to collective action to further the rights of authors and to make a contribution to their role in broader Australian culture and society. It was also a mark of his wider generosity to other authors, particularly emerging authors, who still benefit from the copyright battles he fought and won.

———

Moorhouse's other large contribution to Australian writing was, as many successful writers will attest, his commitment to mentoring younger authors. In a 2012 essay, he says the following about his advice to young writers:

> I tell new writers that the literary writer has three ever-ongoing negotiations in their life by which they gain the privilege of a literary vocation, that is, the privilege to write what one wants to write, in a way he or she wishes to write, and to spend most of one's time doing it at one's own pace.

He goes on to say that there are three negotiations any serious writer must confront. The first is with their friends and family— and, as we shall see, Moorhouse had lost the love of a handful of those he cared about because he worked them into his stories with only thin disguise. Although no character in his writing, as I have argued, is ever simply the direct translation of a living person.

The first negotiation, he argues, is not only about ethics but it is also, in part, about resources:

> In the case of shared domesticity the writer has to negotiate a space to write, the freedom to go into reclusion, the freedom to work from midnight to daybreak, the use of shared financial

resources of the relationship for research, travel (alone), and time to write, and release from some of the routine demands of domesticity.

One of the private costs of full-time writing Moorhouse discussed with me was his decision not to father children, despite opportunities to do so with partners. It was a matter of some regret to him—though not one that should be overstated. Curiosity was probably a better word for what he said he felt. He did form close relationships with the children of people who had been partners, such as Michele Field and Sarah Ducker. He was particularly close to Harry Catterns and Nick and Carol Dettmann's children, Sam, Jessica and Pete; and Donald and Myfanwy Horne's children, Nick and Julia. He spent a lot of time at the Dettmanns' property in Jamberoo, on the South Coast of New South Wales, where he often went to retreat from the city.

'He's been around all their lives,' says Carol Dettmann, 'and he's mentored each of them at various times. Sam and Jess once spent Christmas with him in Oxford . . . He was very close to Sam and very, very good with Jessie, encouraging her, I think. He was good with our youngest, Pete. Which is really lovely for us . . . I think one of the most important things for children is to have adult friends who are not family.'

Moorhouse also wrote about children and the world of childhood with insight. As Sandra Levy observes: 'Frank never talked down to anyone, including children.' Perhaps that was partly because he was someone who never lost sight of the fundamental gift of childhood—the ability to ask the questions that most adults no longer ask, and not to take the rules of the adult world as a given.

Sarah Ducker recalls that when Moorhouse moved into her Dover Heights home, she was 28 and her son, Harry, was only a child. Moorhouse formed a close bond with Harry and was very much part of the daily rituals of the household. 'It was intellectual, it was physical, it was deep emotion,' she recalls. 'We had this great sense of connection and humour and way of being in relation to the world which was sort of maverick . . . He was working down in the little garden studio and I was working at the other end of the house at my desk. So there were discussions and there was a bouncing off each other. I was writing *Difficult Pleasure*, a film about Brett Whiteley, and he was writing *Dark Palace*.'

In *Martini*, Moorhouse memorialised his relationship with Harry, whom he clearly adored, in a story about the creation of an innovation to his favoured drink. Moorhouse would turn on the SBS news and Harry would mix him a martini—although one time the ritual did not go to plan:

> During one mixing he misremembered my instructions and put the olives in the martini shaker rather than the glass. After he had finished his mixing, we fished them out of the cocktail shaker and put them in the martini glass. It was, accidentally, an acceptable innovation to the martini. From then on we called this martini a 'Harry Catterns' and now years later I sometimes make the martini this way in memory of the good times we had together. If he can still remember how to make a martini, that is a fine continuation of the pageant of learning, from Norma [an older lover] through to me to Harry—a stretch of more than fifty years.

Another negotiation with partners and close friends throughout his career was the fact that he used his relationships as source material in his work. Moorhouse was notoriously reticent about supporting the right to privacy—his own included. When I began writing this biography, he told me that it was my duty to 'dig up disgraceful things he'd done, forgotten about, and write about them'. It was, of course, a wry joke about the biographer's task, but there was a ring of truth to it.

Moorhouse always worried about the boundaries of the public and private, both in his writing and in his life. In 2012 he wrote:

> [A]s a storyteller, I coined an expression to describe my life, saying 'I was on a fiction-finding assignment.'
>
> I was quickly aware that this detached stance was not altogether attractive to others. The English novelist Graham Greene said of the writer's detachment: 'There is a splinter of ice in the heart of a writer.'
>
> It could hamper fully-felt involvement with others—but fortunately for me, some situations and involvements with others overwhelmed my 'cool' detachment and I would find myself in the thick of things, engrossed, undetached, and even unhinged. There are emotional pains which clutch us in their fingernails deeply . . .

Privacy, and the deep and complex ethical and creative negotiations that writers conjure with, was a subject Moorhouse juggled with his whole life. On one hand, there's the potential for hurting those he was (or had been) close to, but this was balanced against his need to put life as he saw it down on the page.

'While I try to live by a practice of wide personal openness,' he told me, 'I respect those people who desire to live by strict personal rules of privacy, even if they have to cower because of stigma, fear and shame. But others do not live our way and we do not have to live up to their prescription—that is, we do not have to always live our lives to the morality, desires and wishes of others.'

Moorhouse's habit of keeping letters and other documents from his earliest days as a journalist and writer also spoke to his early sense of identity as an author. He was a writer who, from his foundational work, saw life around him and even intimate relationships as material on which to explicitly draw. His archive attests to this. He has kept thousands of letters, faxes and other material, including copies of letters and faxes he sent to others. His view was always that writers have the privilege, or perhaps the duty, of writing about life as they live it. His fiction was fiction—but it was, equally, and obviously sometimes based on the people and the milieus he had encountered.

One of his former lovers told me: 'I think there was an implicit contract when I got involved with Frank that he would write me into his stories in some way. He ended up writing a whole book based on me. I entered into the relationship knowing that. But I still feel uncomfortable—even though I'm a writer myself. I'm very torn. Part of me wants to ask him to take my letters out of the archive. I know they're there because you told me. And some of them were very explicit.'

There are certainly those, and I have interviewed some for this book, who would disagree with this as a justification for a writer to draw openly, if even in a fictionalised form, on the people and experiences around them. An author who has had occasion to contemplate the issue of the relationship between fiction and life as deeply and frequently as Moorhouse is Helen Garner. She has, at times, been criticised for drawing so overtly on the stuff of life around her. And yet her honesty and clarity of vision—her extraordinary powers of observation—are precisely what give her writing such vigour and impact. She is, like Moorhouse, equally capable of turning that penetrating intellect back on herself.

In a *New Yorker* essay titled 'Helen Garner's Savage Self-Scrutiny', James Wood wrote:

> In the early nineteen-sixties, when the Australian writer Helen Garner was a student at the University of Melbourne, she had a brief relationship with a twenty-four-year-old man who was her tutor. With characteristic briskness, she tells us she learned two things from him: 'Firstly, to start an essay without bullshit preamble, and secondly, that betrayal is part of life' . . . A writing lesson and a life lesson: Garner's work as a journalist and novelist constantly insists on the connection between writing about life and comprehending it; to try to do both responsibly and honestly—without bullshit preamble, or, for that matter, bullshit amble—is what it means to be alive.

The author concluded that Garner is 'above all, a savage self-scrutineer: her honesty has less to do with what she sees in the world than with what she refuses to turn away from in herself'.

Garner and Moorhouse have more than just the tendency to mine their own lives and those around them for their fiction. Both are Australian literary icons forged in the white-hot political crucible of the late 1960s and '70s. Both have contemplated very similar subjects: the relationship between gender, sexuality and power; the formative role of the family in the making of the self; and the way in which the quotidian details of our domestic and daily lives have significance beyond the grand narratives that structure so much of the literary canon. Both writers leave us with more questions than answers—which is what has drawn me to return to their work throughout my life, and to thinking about the fundamental question of how we understand the relationship between writing and life.

The 1970s was, of course, a time when writers, filmmakers, artists and activists were worrying the boundaries between the private and the public. And many of them were doing it while living cheek-by-jowl in shared households, or at the very least in the same suburbs. A lot of collective creative energy and camaraderie was built over long lunches. But, as in all literary milieus, there was also occasional conflict and jostling for position. Australian writers had to contend with 'the tyranny of distance' from the centres of Western publishing, London and New York, and with a far smaller local readership, which raised the competitive stakes.

Moorhouse was known for his generous mentorship of many young emerging writers, including Julia Leigh, Matt Condon, Tim Herbert and Xavier Hennekinne. Writer Julia Leigh met Moorhouse in 1997, when he agreed to mentor her as part of the Australian Society of Authors mentorship program. She was working at the time on her novel *The Hunter*. She approached him, she says, because she knew he had a genuine love of the bush and she was a great fan of Edith Campbell Berry. 'I would always leave these meetings immensely heartened,' she says. 'Frank read my drafts, made comments. We'd talk. We became friends. I loved his flair. He made me laugh . . . When I did get a publishing contract at Penguin he was sincerely happy. He later wrote reference letters and sent out lifeboats when the ship was sinking.'

Although he was noted for his mentorship of emerging writers, Moorhouse lived with his own anxieties about where he sat in the literary canon, and whether, as he once told me, 'anything I've ever written makes any sense to anyone'.

Moorhouse's generosity was not always returned, as a notorious incident in 2001 showed. That October, Moorhouse's publisher, Jane Palfreyman, rang him with the wonderful news that he had been awarded the fiction prize at the Victorian Premier's Literary Awards for his book *Dark Palace*. The award was unsurprising, given the novel had just won the prestigious Miles Franklin Award. Moorhouse was elated and took congratulatory calls from friends.

In a bizarre twist, it emerged later in the day that the State Library of Victoria, which administered the awards, was retracting Moorhouse as the winner and substituting Peter Carey, who had published *The True History of the Kelly Gang* the same year. Moorhouse's agent, Rose Creswell, was told that a 'typo' had been made by a public affairs officer, who had inserted the wrong name into an embargoed press release to the media. Moorhouse found out that evening, fifteen minutes before he was due to give the Stephen Murray-Smith Memorial Lecture in Melbourne. Ironically, his speech was titled 'Civility and Urbanity: The Nature of Intellectual Dispute in Australian Life'.

Speaking to *The Age*'s Raymond Gill, Moorhouse described his reaction:

After Jane [Palfreyman] called me and told me the news, I vomited. I couldn't believe it. It felt like a nightmare I couldn't wake up from. I considered cancelling the lecture and I would have if it hadn't been the Stephen Murray-Smith Memorial Lecture, an event I was emotionally connected to.

Moorhouse's reaction was understandable. Australian writers depend on literary prizes, not only because of their prestige, but because they are part of the patchwork funding they must use to continue writing. 'I just can't believe how awful it is to do this to someone,' Palfreyman told *The Age*. 'This is an appalling way to treat a person, let alone one of our most fantastic writers. This brings shame upon the whole awards.'

The most telling reaction in the entire saga was that of the winner, Peter Carey, who responded in the least generous manner possible. He told *The Age*:

> Who won the Miles Franklin? Frank Moorhouse. Was I disappointed? I don't speak about those things. Seeing as Frank knows all this shit, who won the Booker? It does seem that literature is rarely an important subject in this country and maybe it can only become a really important subject if Frank doesn't win something. There are so many more really important things in the world. This is really trivial. We all get disappointed. Frank was disappointed in a cruel way. It's the world. It's what happens.

In other words, rub it with a brick. Moorhouse's reaction to being told he was the recipient of a prestigious award only to have it snatched back is not hard to understand. Carey's reaction perhaps says more about the lingering competitive milieu dating back to an era in which short stories were written and published in 1970s Balmain than it does about his nature. In a collection of stories edited by Brian Kiernan and published in 1977, Carey and Moorhouse appear side by side, along with Murray Bail. All three writers would go on to become internationally renowned authors. In his introduction, Kiernan writes of what animated the writers in the collection:

There was the impression of a new sensibility being expressed. These writers seemed less anxious about the historic issues of national identity that had seemed to divide Australian writers for over a century (at least in the accounts of literary historians). They were less preoccupied with establishing the social foreground, more prone to take this for granted, to assume it and write within it naturally—and critically.

Kiernan also notes:

There is no homogenous 'new' fiction, but there are many new writers exploring a variety of fictional possibilities being published at the moment, many more than in the past. The suggestion has been made on socio-demographic grounds that most of the new writers belong to a school—the Balmain school. As happened also in the late nineteenth century, in recent years the centre of literary culture has shifted from Melbourne to Sydney.

In his memoir *Home Truths*, the playwright David Williamson recounts leaving Melbourne for Sydney in 1979. He writes:

My euphoria about Sydney was soon tempered, however, when [wife] Kristin and I were summoned to Frank Moorhouse's favourite Greek restaurant, the New Hellas in Elizabeth St, to be scrutinized by the heavyweights of the Sydney literary scene, of which Frank was the king. Whether he had achieved this status by self-appointment or general acclaim I wasn't quite sure . . . I'd assumed Frank's invitation signalled a friendly intent, but I hadn't read a recent review in which he was asked whether he was glad I was coming to Sydney. He had answered that he had little in common with a playwright who merely recycled the Australian vernacular.

Kristin left the lunch early to go back to her job at *The National Times* and Williamson was left at the table with Moorhouse, Donald Horne, the publisher Sandra Forbes, the writer Robert Drewe and the literary critic Don Anderson, to contemplate the differences between the Sydney literary scene and Melbourne's. He writes:

> Sydney had different networks of cultural power and a far less earnest agenda than Melbourne. For Sydney's literati, changing society for the better wasn't part of the deal; puns, wordplay and one-upping references to obscure writers and filmmakers I hadn't heard of were all the go. I felt depressed. My ignorance had been on plain display. Was Frank right? Was I no more than a recycler of Australian vernacular?

Moorhouse's reported lack of generosity to Williamson was uncharacteristic, according to the accounts many other writers have given. But Williamson's memoir is nothing if not searingly honest, mainly about what he regards as his own shortcomings. It is very likely that Moorhouse did feel threatened by the arrival of an extremely successful and prolific playwright on his turf. What's more, Williamson's success was routinely dismissed in the 1970s as a sign that he had 'sold out'. His anecdote demonstrates that Moorhouse was not above being unfairly dismissive of another writer—which, considering Williamson's talents, was Moorhouse's loss.

When I spoke with Williamson after Moorhouse's death, he had the following to say: 'I felt he was always a very guarded personality . . . He was into personal power games—it was a real feature of his writing actually. In *Conference-ville* they're all about establishing your status and protecting it in a social situation. There was also a sense with me that Frank was protecting his persona—and it came through to me in his writing—into personal power games and being superior and having the upper hand just because he was insecure. He was not an easy person to be with and a highly competitive person.'

Williamson's perspective is valuable, given that he and Moorhouse met and moved in the same literary circles when they were both in the early stages of their careers. It prompts the question of whether Moorhouse might have found it easier to be generous to younger writers—which he was—than to some of his contemporaries, by whom he might occasionally have felt threatened.

———

Moorhouse's desire for financial independence was one of the strong motivating forces behind his interest in writing television and film screenplays, and in optioning his work. He also enjoyed the camaraderie of film crews and the experience of learning a new writing genre.

Moorhouse was friends with a number of filmmakers, including the director Mike Thornhill and the producers Richard Brennan and Errol Sullivan. Sullivan vividly remembers meeting Moorhouse in the mid-1960s at the Newcastle Hotel. Moorhouse was barefoot and wearing shorts and a singlet, he recalls, and was 'waving a reject letter from Angus & Robertson refusing to publish yet another of his submissions and being very agitated and angry about it'.

In 1974, the feature film *Between Wars*, for which Moorhouse had written the screenplay, was released. It was directed and produced by his friend Mike Thornhill. It starred Corin Redgrave and Judy Morris. The story followed a doctor, Edward Trenbow, who begins to specialise in psychiatry after treating shell-shocked soldiers at the front in World War I. He becomes increasingly interested in psychoanalysis after working with a German prisoner of war who is a Freudian. Predictably, Trenbow meets opposition from his more conservative medical colleagues. In the 1930s, he works as a doctor in a small country town. As World War II takes shape, he becomes engaged in politics around the war. The film broaches the rise of the Australia First movement, which was antisemitic, anti-war and pro-isolationism. A number of members of the movement were from the left.

The other significant screenplay Moorhouse wrote, and the most ambitious, was *The Coca-Cola Kid*, which was partly based on a character called Becker, whom he created in *The Americans, Baby*. The film, directed by Serbian director Dûsan Makavejev and produced by David Roe, was released in 1985. Makavejev had gained international renown for his 1981 black comedy feature *Montenegro*. David Roe, the producer, recalls that working with Makavejev on *The Coca-Cola Kid* meant dealing with a director who 'thrived on conflict'. He also comments that, despite their initial rapport, Moorhouse and Makavejev had very different ideas about the film, even though both men had dark and ironic senses of humour.

In his 1990 collection of essays, *Lateshows*, Moorhouse wrote about the genesis of the film. In 1975, Makavejev travelled to Australia for the Sydney Film Festival and read *The Americans, Baby*. After returning to Paris, he expressed interest in developing the book into a script. Moorhouse recounted, in characteristically faux anxious and self-deprecating detail, the twists and turns of getting Makavejev on board with the project, which included the obstacles he encountered securing an American Express card. (He obtained one only after he wrote a self-satirising piece about his difficulties in *The Bulletin* magazine.) He decides to risk all and fly to New York where Makavejev then resided.

> I cable Makavejev's agent: I INTEND ARRIVING NEW YORK OCTOBER 1 ALGONQUIN HOTEL TO MEET MAKAVEJEV PLEASE CONFIRM HIS MOVEMENTS . . .
> I receive no reply to the cable. My advisers say that in the film business you take risks. Go there and find him. This is your big chance, grasp it. I send telegrams to all Makavejev's addresses saying I will be in New York to discuss the project. No replies.
> I go anyway.

Moorhouse lost his American Express card on arrival in New York, and Makavejev turned up three weeks later.

In 1985, after eleven drafts, four potential producers and nine years from the first letter from Makavejev, the necessary $3.3 million was raised by producer David Roe. To satisfy the investors Roe had to fly to the United States to get clearance for the use of the brand name Coca-Cola in the title. Now it was time to make the film, which proved as challenging for Roe as bringing Makavejev to the pre-production table had been for Moorhouse. Roe recalls Moorhouse hiring a large Mercedes, 'which of course I had to pay for', and insisting that Makavejev, his wife and Roe accompany him on a trip to Nowra to absorb the atmosphere of the South Coast. On arrival, Moorhouse's parents insisted that the director and his wife stay at their house.

'Makavejev really had no interest in going to Nowra,' Roe says. 'But Frank saw it as crucial to him understanding the movie and the people in it. He wanted Makavejev to experience the South Coast. His parents were very generous insisting that he and his wife stay, but Makavejev really wanted to be in a motel making expensive international phone calls.'

The Moorhouse family took the director to a local Chinese restaurant, where Makavejev sat staring at the pineapple in the sweet-and-sour sauce in great confusion.

The film that resulted was a strange melange of Moorhouse's attempts to translate his affectionate but ironic depictions of small-town Australians' first encounters with corporate America and Makavejev's struggles to rein in his art-house impulses and make a mainstream movie. As David Roe notes, Makavejev's English did not extend to the nuances in the dialogue, and he had little interest in regional Australia or its inhabitants.

The director apparently did, however, have a strong interest in Greta Scacchi's fabulous breasts. They may just be the best thing in the whole movie. Eric Roberts was wooden in the lead role. And there were some incredibly clumsy and clichéd attempts to signal 'Australian identity' to an international audience. In one scene, the character Becker camps on the edge of a cliff and in the morning is woken by a man riding a camel who proceeds to swing a billy. Oh dear, as Moorhouse probably said at the time.

Makavejev and Moorhouse had a sensibility in common, but their collaboration was only successful in this sense: *The Coca-Cola Kid* was an instant top ten bestseller in video sales and rentals when first released in the US at No. 7 in 1986. To this day it remains in active global distribution through MGM and can be accessed through major streamers such as Netflix and Prime.

In 1984, Errol Sullivan also produced a Michael Thornhill–directed television docudrama titled *The Disappearance of Azaria Chamberlain*, which Moorhouse wrote and presented. It aired on Network 10. At the time, Sullivan says, Moorhouse and others involved in the film were convinced by expert witness testimony that was later discredited. 'It was very, very damning but it was wrong,' he acknowledges.

Sullivan would go on to option the rights to *Grand Days*. 'But that was really to give Frank some money,' he explains, 'because he was in Geneva and needed dough . . . Some years later Nicole Kidman read it and had fallen in love with the character of Edith. Frank let me know he had been approached . . . and they were interested in the rights. That's when she was married to Tom Cruise, so I arranged to meet the person who ran the Tom Cruise company in Los Angeles, Paula Wagner . . . Wagner asked me how come I had the rights and I said, "Well Frank's a friend and he needed the money . . . so I optioned it." It seemed to surprise her immensely and she asked me what I wanted out of all this. I said I didn't want anything I just wanted, if the thing went ahead I'd want my money back.'

Ultimately, Wagner told Sullivan that they'd develop it for no money at their cost, and there'd be nothing for Moorhouse. Sullivan remonstrated with her and told her he wasn't signing over the rights unless Moorhouse got money out of it. She demurred and he concluded they were never serious about making the film.

Moorhouse had also been working on the screenplay for a movie based on his book *The Everlasting Secret Family*, which premiered in 1988. It was directed and produced by Michael Thornhill and starred Mark Lee, Arthur Dignam, Heather Mitchell and John Meillon. The story focuses on a beautiful young man who is drawn into a web of powerful men—including a senator and a High Court judge—who secretly use him for sex. The film did woefully at the box office but did become something of a gay cult classic. It was released at a time when mainstream Australia was not yet grappling with issues like child sexual abuse and relationships grounded in coercive control. It is worth seeing, though, for the surprising sight of John Meillon in a BDSM scene.

Ultimately, Moorhouse was never involved in a film or television production that was a commercial or critical success. Sullivan believes that Moorhouse's writing style was not really suited to film. 'Film is simple,' he says. 'It's simple in the sense that it's more like a quick poem. It's got a very simple theme and one idea beautifully elaborated in some way, whereas Frank's work is not that. It's much more complex.'

Sandra Levy agrees that Moorhouse's style was not suited to screen. 'I honestly think Frank saw it [primarily] as a way of making some money,' she explains. 'He was always trying to find a cash cow to make enough money to write . . . I don't think he was a natural screenplay writer. The irony didn't translate well onto screen.' Irony rarely does.

By the late 1980s, Moorhouse had largely set aside his filmic ambitions to concentrate on the largest project of his life: the League of Nations trilogy, which consumed his life from 1989, when he began researching in the archive of the League of Nations in Geneva for *Grand Days* and *Dark Palace*, until the publication of *Cold Light* in 2011.

4

THE MOORHOUSE METHOD: RULES FOR LIVING

In his collection of humorous essays, *Loose Living*, Moorhouse recollects his first forays into gastronomy. Sent to Sydney to try out for a state schoolboy rugby league team, he was billeted with a Lebanese family. He recalled:

> I realised that our family meals lacked something.
>
> The Lebanese family had chives sprinkled on their salad and they had 'salad dressing', not mayonnaise . . .
>
> I realised that there was more and maybe infinitely more to eating and that either my family did not know about eating or did not care.

At home, he remembered they ate a salad that consisted of a sliced tomato, a lettuce leaf and Kraft cheddar cheese. Sometimes, 'on special occasions', the salad was 'saved' by factory-made mayonnaise. 'We also had salt and pepper. That was it.'

On his return to Nowra, Moorhouse took it upon himself to educate his family in the culinary arts. He announced that 'things were to be upgraded'. Having missed the fact that it was primarily oil, vinegar and garlic that had made the Lebanese family's salad special, he focused on the chives and planted some in his backyard. Eventually, when the chives ran out, he resorted to cutting grass and sprinkling that on his salad, in defiance of his older brothers' taunting.

The story is a pointed portrait of a young, curious schoolboy growing up in a conventional middle-class Nowra family, who is beginning to strain at the aesthetic parameters of his upbringing. Design, gastronomy, the rules of social engagement and conversation were all to be significant in Moorhouse's life and his work. And the character who is most like Moorhouse in this respect— the character who channels his fascination with aesthetics and rituals—is Edith Campbell Berry.

In *Grand Days*, when Edith boards the train to Geneva to work at the League of Nations, she is self-consciously aware that her knowledge of the culinary and social arts might be lacking— coming as she does from Jasper's Brush. She is, however, well defended against embarrassment. She has practised 'Her Ways', which include 'Going' and 'Dining'. She makes her way carefully down the train corridor to the dining car and has her first encounter with Ambrose—her future lover and mentor.

Wary of ordering the soup, Edith tells her dining companion:

'It is not to do so much with the soup in the plate, I am told, but more to do with the soup in the spoon on its way to the mouth. That is where the difficulty lies . . . Further, I am told that it has to do with the unexpected stopping of the train— that's the incontestable danger point. It jerks. The train jerks.'

Like Edith, Moorhouse accumulated and designed rules for living well—including rules for avoiding the bears that lurked in the woods of excess. Rituals were always important in his life. Some of his friends joke about what they call the Moorhouse Method. When asked, and often when not asked, he was always happy to advise on the correct protocols for given situations: when to order a martini, how it should be made, when to start festivities, and—importantly—when to cease them. Etiquette, or the rules of social engagement, was a subject of endless fascination to him. From his early work, he includes vignettes that centre on learning, teaching or probing aesthetic and social rules.

In *Forty-Seventeen*, he recounted time spent with a beautiful and literate eighteen-year-old lover. He teaches her how to make a martini. In the story, they are staying in a beach house in his hometown. He thinks about the fact that she is the first woman he has made love to there. He also recalls drinking martinis with his wife, Wendy, and later with a lover, an older woman, Norma Crinnion, who comes into his life after he and Wendy split up.

The young lover at the beach house observes of the olive on the toothpick:

'I could become really hooked on martinis. But what do you do with the olive, do you eat it at the beginning or the end of the drink or is it just a . . . garnish or what?'

Garnish, nice word.

'That's a personal preference. It's useful to play with during conversation. You can prick it with the toothpick and the olive oil seeps out.' He did it. 'See, the olive oil comes into the drink.'

'The olive on the toothpick gives the drink an axis.'

Yes, she was right.

She pricked her olive.

Martini used the drink as a metaphor for his life and friend-ships. There are people—and I have met them in the writing of this biography—who find it strange that Moorhouse would choose a cocktail as a lens through which to view his life. Some find it affected, others inexplicable. They are clearly not martini drinkers.

The martini appeals to Moorhouse precisely because it is a drink poised between the poetic and the pedantic. It is, on one hand, merely a glass of spirits—and a strong one at that. Yet it is also a drink that can only be appreciated in moderation when made well. It needs to be made in precise proportions, which are always in dispute, and served icy cold. It is a drink that should only be ordered in particular places and ordered with care. It is a toast to a life lived with attention to aesthetic detail and well-tempered pleasures.

Moorhouse satirised the ritualism of the drink and, by associ-ation, the rituals by which he organised his own life with a well-known joke he called 'The Martini Rescue'. He described what to do when lost in a forest:

'You do not panic. You do not walk aimlessly. You find a shady spot with a fine view, you sit down, you take out the cocktail shaker, the gin, the vermouth, and the olives from your backpack (which every sophisticated trekker carries) and mix yourself a martini. If there is a glacier nearby you chip off some ice to chill everything down.

'You will not be lost for long. Within a few minutes someone will come from nowhere and, tap your arm and say,

excuse me, you are not doing that right—that is not the way
to make a proper martini.'

As in *Forty-Seventeen*, in *Martini* he relayed the story of
teaching an eighteen-year-old lover to mix a martini. Moorhouse
also wrote about a young man from the country sitting in the
lounge of the Windsor Hotel who had ordered martinis. He was
accompanied by his young wife, who was mortified and annoyed
when he called the waiter over to announce:

'This martini is not cold enough, we asked for it very cold, and
very dry. It is neither.'

'You give me the shits,' she said. 'So much for a second
wedding anniversary.'

He said nothing.

'Fighting with waiters is not my idea of a good time.
The drink was alcohol, isn't that what you care about?'

He knew that he'd complained to the waiter as a way
of getting at her. He didn't really care about the coldness.

He wanted to be in New York drinking martinis in
Costello's bar with Thurber in the thirties.

While this exchange is going on, the narrator is privately recall-
ing a recent infidelity with a sophisticated older woman, who
had admonished him for 'doing an American bartender act' with
a cocktail shaker while mixing a martini. The contrast between
his wife, 'the country girl', forms a hinge point in the narrative.
The martini is a bridge to a cosmopolitan world where he can
shuck off the bonds of his marriage and parochial upbringing.

An interest in aesthetics is often seen as suspect—as superficial at best and corrupt at worst. On the left of politics, taking

an overt interest in beauty, fashion or gastronomy has often been denigrated as being at odds with broader struggles for human equality.

When Moorhouse wrote about aesthetics, he often did so with an ironic and even self-mocking tone. His humorous stories and essays in the books *Lateshows*, *Room Service* and *Loose Living* revolve around the anxieties and pretensions that shadow bourgeois aspirations and manners. But there was a deeper side to his fascination with the rules of refined living. Moorhouse was very conscious of the way we invent and reinvent ourselves. Aesthetics were a core part of persona for him—a pathway to trying on masks, a way of trying on new selves, of playing with alternate ways of being in the world.

In a series of brilliant essays on aesthetics, Oscar Wilde explored the role masks play in art and life. In 'The Decay of Lying', his protagonist declares: 'what is interesting about people in good society . . . is the mask that each of them wears, not the reality'. Moorhouse was a great fan of Wilde's.

———

When Moorhouse arrived in Sydney in 1957 to take up his cadetship at *The Daily Telegraph*, there were very few fine dining restaurants. Elite wine bars were for the cognoscenti. Public bars were for men. And men drank beer. The six o'clock swill— where men lined up their schooners to finish before the pub closed—remained in place until the mid 1950s. The relatively few licensed restaurants that existed could only serve drinks until 9 pm.

In his definitive history of Australian gastronomy, Michael Symons wrote that, for those eating out in Australia in the 1950s, a typical meal would have been eaten at a cafe, would cost two shillings and sixpence, and comprised steak and chips, bread and butter, tea and ice-cream for dessert. For Moorhouse and the intellectuals, activists and creatives who formed his social circle for much of his life, eating out and drinking together stimulated their conversation and their grand schemes. Where they ate and drank, indeed, is a map of how and where social connections formed that were to profoundly influence Australian political and cultural life for decades to come.

In the early 1960s, when Moorhouse began hanging out with the Sydney Push, eating out usually meant a semi-drunken collective trip to a cheap Italian or Greek establishment in the city, some of which were clubs with liquor licences. In other restaurants, wine was sometimes covertly served in teapots or cups. A favourite haunt was known as The Greeks. In a 1972 story, 'A Change of Restaurant', published originally in *The Bulletin* and republished in *Days of Wine and Rage*, Moorhouse recalled returning, after a long absence, to Diethnes in Pitt Street.

> Up the steps to old Diethnes. The old place. Nick and Mrs Nick. They ask, 'Where have you been?'
>
> Shrug, unreasonably guilty.
>
> 'Busy, maybe you too busy nowadays,' says Nick answering for me.
>
> 'Is business good?' I ask, fumbling, wishing it good, wanting the empty tables wished away, feeling that I have to say, 'Some of us are overseas now.'

In the story, Moorhouse sits down to pea soup, lamb, Greek salad and beer. He recalled the good times from the late 1950s and the early 1960s.

Up the stairs we would come, babbling, fantasies, projects, schemes. Firstly, as a cadet journalist in the fifties.

And women 'I know a rather nice little Greek place. Do you like Greek food?'

The planning of little magazines, films, books, chapters of books, conferences, reviews, attacks and counter-attacks.

The story is not just a reverie about the days when he and his friends were idealistic young writers, filmmakers and intellectuals who were permanently strapped for cash, eating spaghetti with bolognaise sauce and asking for an extra basket of bread. It's also a meditation on where those of that milieu have resettled and dispersed to. Some have married and had babies. Many of them now live in Balmain—or Le Ghetto Balmain, as it became known when the city's young creative energy collected there in the 1970s. The author reflects on a recent conversation with someone who joked that Diethnes was really a 'training restaurant', where young people learnt to eat properly.

Moorhouse goes on to a party after his meal and talks to a young woman about the old days at Diethnes. They discuss why people stop eating at restaurants they frequented for years. He tells her he told Nick that his friends were either married or 'too well off to eat at cheap cafes anymore'.

'Do you like Greek food?' she said, back along the track in her early twenties, flat-footed before my misty sense of loss, and my first experience—the first sensation I'd had—of the infuriating moving on of time.

By the early 1970s, the culturally bohemian and politically progressive set were dining at a new restaurant in Elizabeth

Street in the city: Tony's Bon Gout. It was a revolution in Sydney dining. Legendary Australian chef Tony Bilson opened the restaurant with his then wife, Gay Bilson, in 1973. The focus was on French food in the tradition of Elizabeth David—but with a modern twist. It was BYO and guests bought their wine from the pub on the corner or the Goulburn Street Cellars. Gay Bilson kept all the menus, and in her book *Plenty* she recalls what they served for lunch. The menu was fixed-price—initially $1.95 and eventually rising through a series of increases to the dizzying heights of $12.50.

> Reading at random from 1975 . . . I find first courses such as 'Stuffed Duck's Neck in Brioche with Truffles', 'Pig's Trotters in Vinaigrette Sauce', 'Galantine of Duck', and 'Hare Terrine'; simple dishes, both hot and cold, using yabbies, pipis, mussels and Balmain bugs (invariably including the last minute addition of wine, butter, garlic and parsley to make a sauce); a variety of savoury tarts with ingredients such as walnut, watercress and a *soupe au pistou*.

In the early days, Bon Gout only opened for lunch on Fridays—a lunch that frequently lasted until 6 pm. Tony Bilson remembers the eclectic crowd, which included original Push people such as Liz Fell and Margaret Fink; journalists including Vic Carroll, Max Suich, Mungo MacCallum, Robert Haupt, Brian Toohey, Lenore Nicklin, Wendy Bacon and artist Michael Fitzjames; politicians and their advisers, including Gough Whitlam and his press secretary Dick Hall, Lionel Murphy and his staffer George Negus, Labor figures Mick Young and Jim McClelland; and a slew of writers—Moorhouse, Donald Horne, Don Anderson, Peter Carey and a young Meaghan Morris among them. Art dealer Rudy Komon was a patron in both senses of the word. He lent the Bilsons key artworks, including a large Fred Williams, which hung at the entrance.

When restaurant critic Leo Schofield wrote a glowing review in *The National Times*, business exploded. Tony Bilson said he'd been down at the fish markets the day the paper hit the stands and arrived back to find a queue 50 metres long outside. 'They were lined up with paper bags of wine under their arms. I had to race back to the fish market to get more fish.'

Tony's Bon Gout opened five months after Australians elected a left-wing Labor government under the leadership of Gough Whitlam. It was more than a restaurant—it was a salon for Australia's young cultural and political elite, who were enjoying their first moment in the sun.

Michael Symons writes: 'People swapped tables bringing their bottle or coffee over . . . Donald Horne from *The Bulletin* might want to talk to Brian Johns, and they'd go off to another table. Tony and Gay themselves were interested in ideas, politics and books—a rare type of restaurateur.'

According to Gay Bilson, 'Bon Gout nourished a portion of that generation which saw the beginning of social change in Australian cities. Perhaps it was a kind of "café society" in the convivial and intellectual European sense; the people who ate and talked there were as essential to its reputation as the food.'

Moorhouse recalled his friends' first restaurant with great affection. He said it was as much a club as somewhere to eat lunch. 'You knew quite a few people at other tables,' he said. 'I remember when we had an American journalist there—I think he was the fiction editor of *Playboy*—and he was amazed that we had lunch and kept on drinking during the afternoon. There's a whole different food culture now to when they opened

Bon Gout. Our gastronomic knowledge developed as Tony went from restaurant to restaurant, and as he developed as a chef we developed as eaters. He taught us about cheese, about what wines went with what food, the intricacies of French gastronomy, and introduced us to food that we'd not eaten—snails and frogs.'

Another key lunching restaurant of the period was EJs in Macquarie Street in the city, run by Moorhouse's friend Susie Carleton and also frequented by many of the Bon Gout crowd, including Moorhouse. Carleton recalls that Whitlam's press secretary, Dick Hall, had a Friday table there: 'It was called the Round Table, Table A, at the back of the restaurant. People used to come in to watch Table A to see who would be coming today. Dick . . . he had access to whomever he wanted. It was a privilege in those days to be invited to table—God, we were wankers. But it was when there weren't that many restaurants. Sydney wasn't a big restaurant scene.'

She recalls that she only opened for lunch, 'because lunch never ended . . . Sometimes I'd let people lock up because I had to go home to my kids.' After EJs, she bought the Riverview Hotel in Balmain with Murray Sime, a good friend of Moorhouse's. Carleton says buying the pub was a 'no-brainer', given that so many of Sydney's cultural elite had collected in the suburb in the 1970s and '80s. Along with Moorhouse, they included writers David Williamson, Kristin Williamson, Peter Carey, Robert Macklin and Murray Bail, literary critics Don Anderson and Brian Kiernan, and actors Rachel Ward and Bryan Brown.

Moorhouse always had a favourite restaurant or two up his sleeve. He enjoyed knowing and chatting to the waiters and bar staff, and being welcomed when he chose to dine alone with a book. His stories and essays are full of observations about the art of dining, and he loved to recount, with faux horror, tales of Meals

Gone Wrong. I was interviewing him for *The Bulletin* in 2004 at a then fashionable Sydney bistro when he suddenly paused and told me he remembered being at the same venue when it was a different restaurant: 'I was here with Don Anderson for dinner. It was early in the evening and we'd barely begun eating when the cook lurched out of the kitchen completely drunk and collapsed on our table.'

Stories about people in allegedly civilised situations going off the rails fascinated Moorhouse. In a chapter in *Conferenceville* titled 'Café Society: Table-to-Table Fighting', Moorhouse reflected that 'so much of our life was lived out in bars and restaurants—things planned, relationships begun and ended'. The narrator goes to 'Tony's', as Bon Gout was known, to meet his friend Dick Hall. A man called Friedman joins them. Halfway through their meal, they realise that patrons at the adjoining table are talking about Friedman loudly and derisively.

> It was about now that Friedman asked Alain [the waiter] to bring him a jug of water. This was brought. Dick caught on first and covered his face with his hands. He resignedly said: 'Oh yes.' Friedman got up, took the jug of water, and in one stride walked to the other table, and emptied it over the person, without a word. He returned to our table, put down the empty jug and sat down.

Lunches in the 1970s, apparently, often provided free entertainment of this kind.

In the 1980s and '90s, Moorhouse switched his dining allegiance to the Bayswater Brasserie in Kings Cross, which friends came to describe as his 'office'. He could frequently be found holding court there over a martini or a plate of oysters and a dry

Riesling. In *Martini* he lists a selection of the Bayswater hors d'oeuvres, including:

- foie gras served with toast (foie gras is, of course, best eaten with Sauterne)
- chickpea and flat bread (Turkish bread)
- salt and pepper squid
- mixed cheese and fruit and lavosh (though cheese for me still belongs after the main course—but go ahead, have it, I won't say anything)
- hot potato chips with homemade chilli and tomato ketchup

In later years, the Bayswater even added the 'Moorhouse Martini' to its bar menu; he had certainly drunk a few there. It was just the way Moorhouse liked it—four parts Bombay Sapphire gin, one part Noilly Prat dry vermouth, served in a very cold glass with a green olive on a toothpick.

The writer Matt Condon, with whom Moorhouse stayed on his return from researching and writing *Grand Days* in Europe, recalls scores of lunches and dinners there at which Moorhouse enjoyed playing conversational games.

'We were sitting in the Bayswater one night,' he relates, 'and there was this gorgeous-looking couple sitting nearby . . . Frank and I were looking over and I said to Frank: "What do you think? . . . Let's start with the woman. Who is she? What is her background?" So this went on for an hour, and we worked out that she was probably from a wealthy North Shore family, but she spent a lot of time at her parents' property in Scone, a lot of hockey and all that sort of stuff, and he was probably a banker, but he had a bit of an edge to him so he might have been a part-time installation artist . . .'

Eventually, Moorhouse went over to the couple to test their theories. They were, he reported back, 'two Swedish backpackers who flew into Sydney this morning'.

————

Conventional bourgeois domesticity was never attractive to Moorhouse. He didn't own a house or apartment after he was 25, and he never hosted dinner or lunch parties at home.

'I once owned a house and a car,' he explained. 'I decided I had no use for a house because all houses have appalling idiosyncrasies. There's always some trick to the hot water or the front door . . . And the car disintegrated before my very eyes . . . I suppose I did once drive it into the sea. If you rent a car it's always brand new.'

Fiona Giles described Moorhouse to journalist Richard Guilliatt this way: 'He has a love of beauty and a horror of domesticity.' She recalls with wry amusement that the biggest argument she and Moorhouse ever had was the day she came back to their Balmain house carrying an ironing board. 'He totally freaked out because he took pride in sending all his clothes out to the local laundry.'

This aversion to domesticity was reflected in his lack of interest in acquiring possessions. Matt Condon told Guilliatt that when Moorhouse stayed in his apartment for a few months, he had 'a transistor radio and some books'. Condon says Moorhouse was quite happy to sleep on a stretcher bed, even after one of the legs fell off.

Writes Guilliatt:

Somehow Moorhouse has married this asceticism with a gourmand's lifestyle and a reckless generosity that can be intoxicating to be around. After winning the PEN Keneally Award in March [2007] he insisted on shouting a dozen people from the award body to a dinner that cost him a good proportion of his $2000 prize money.

When *Forty-Seventeen* was published in 1988, Moorhouse celebrated by taking his publisher and London agent to the Groucho Club, of which he was a member. Their table was eating and drinking lavishly, and other writers in the room soon came to join them, among them Howard Jacobson, Simon Schama and Clive James. The champagne inevitably continued to flow. When the cheque was brought, none of the rest of the table volunteered their wallets. Moorhouse spent an anxious hour waiting for his agent Rose Creswell to transfer money to his credit card when the Australian banks opened. As always, Creswell came through for him, however exasperated she might privately have been.

As Moorhouse recalled it: 'I rang Rose and told her she'd better move some funds off-shore. I explained what the dinner was and she was laughing hysterically. I said she could just go across to the bank and put some cash in my account, five hundred, a thousand or whatever . . . She said: "Yeah, I'll sell my car . . . or why don't we just cash in one of your gold bars."'

In the Guilliatt article, Fiona Giles explains Moorhouse's approach to living well on a writer's income: 'Smoke and mirrors, a tolerance for high financial risk and a kind of anarchistic approach to money . . . It was almost an incantation among Frank's friends, that while they were living sensible lives he was living the good life for them.'

In *Loose Living*, Moorhouse satirised his habit of eating most of his meals in restaurants with an account of the consequences of the narrator going on a fictional 1000 Great Restaurants Tour in Europe with his friend Tony Bilson. In the story, their gastronomic excesses are brought to the attention of the European Court, who sentence the narrator to serve a fortnight in an IKEA Contemporary Living Laboratory:

> . . . which the Swedes have established to create living arrange-ments, furniture and household objects for tasteful, normal, healthy living. In a sense, I was under IKEA house arrest which was very tasteful. Fortunately for me, given the dazed state I was in, nothing in the IKEA environment was breakable, there were no sharp edges, and all materials were non-toxic and non-flammable. I was placed in the living laboratory with an IKEA Model Family of a husband and wife, two children and a dog and a cat, a bird in a cage, and a fishbowl.

Regardless of his own unconventional approach to domes-ticity, the middle-class domestic lives of others were an endless source of fascination for Moorhouse as a writer. In *Lateshows*, he writes about 'the problem of the political litany' at dinner parties:

> A political litany is where the host or one of the dominant guests begins the evening with a curse against an enemy, usually a political enemy—not as an opening of discussion but as an ignition of the other dinner guests into some sort of passionate political bonding through a cursing of an assumed common enemy. It is taken as inconceivable that anyone would dissent from the litany. We are all expected to curse the enemy. As it goes around the table each guest is required

to bring to the table a curse against the enemy or to give bad news of the enemy.

In the same book, he wrote with gentle satire about middle-class parents and his mystification about their rules for raising children in a chapter titled 'The Disciplining of Other People's Children'. The narrator is asked to mind a young girl named Tom.

He consults the philosopher Jean-Jacques Rousseau's book *Emile*, which is a treatise on the nature of education and child-hood. The narrator takes a carved wooden racing car to the child and announces that it is 'gender-distinction free'. To which she replies: 'I hate gender free gifts.'

The Late Parents had been gone fifteen minutes when Tom reappeared in the room dressed in a tiger suit.

'What-ho!?' I said, having never said what-ho to anyone before in my life. 'Are we a tiger?'

'You don't talk English to tigers,' she said, 'unless you have rocks in your head.'

I did not know where she would pick up expressions like that. Tom growled and then she bit me on my leg. It caused pain.

I suggested that she go back to bed but she said that tigers didn't obey English.

I wondered if I could muster any Bengali to instruct her to go to bed.

The narrator attempts to calm Tom by reading to her from Rousseau about the futility of reasoning with young children. 'What works best with children is an appeal to greed or fear, or bribery.' Tom responds by biting him on the leg again. The saga ends with the narrator fashioning a whip out of cord and a piece of dowelling and taming the tiger into her room.

———

Moorhouse, as we have seen, grew up in a conventional middle-class home in Nowra, and the tensions that shadowed his attempts to conform to middle-class propriety are threaded through much of his writing. He always grappled with a tension, in both his life and his work, between the norms of the respectable, country-town family he grew up in and those of the wilder shores of the bohemian and creative existence to which he determinedly rowed when he left home.

In *Martini* he writes about his first impulse to design his own way of living:

> At around the age of eight or nine, I moved out of my family home and set up house in a huge box under the lemon tree. I took my books and some toys and possessions. I think my family was glad to see me go. My memory is that I stayed there at least two nights and that eventually rain forced me to take everything back into the house despite the metallic foil lining of the box which I had thought would waterproof it.

It is, of course, a familiar story. A lot of children decide to run away from home at the same age and fantasise about living free of their parents and the family rules. For Moorhouse, it was a mission he eventually made good on, after a few practice runs. He ran away from home a couple of other times, he said, 'before I ran away to the city for good at sixteen years and ten months to become a copyboy on a newspaper'.

His move to Sydney began a lifetime interest in eating and drinking well—not only in dining in restaurants, but also in understanding how food and drink should be chosen and prepared. He wrote in *Martini* about living with his lover, the poet Jennifer Rankin, in a stone hut in Bundeena surrounded by bushland on the edge of the Royal National Park.

> We were interested in first getting to know vermouth as well as drinking martinis. In our financially restricted way, we were also exploring fine dining and exotic foods using my David Jones department store credit account, a gift to me from my parents on my twenty-first birthday, on which we were living along with a small income mainly from me giving a lecture once a week at the Workers' Educational Association in the city.
>
> Each week we bought a supply of food together with French wine and imported cheeses from David Jones which would be delivered to the wharf at Cronulla and then ferried across to us at Bundeena. We would lug it up the hill to our stone hut. Our introduction to game such as grouse, pheasant and so on was as imported food.

At 28, Moorhouse was already well on the path to balancing his Protestant work ethic with his desire to live the good life. It's certainly an entertaining portrait of a young left-leaning and financially struggling writer relying on his solidly respectable middle-class parents to feed him and his poet lover on the food of the aristocracy. David Jones credit cards, one suspects, have kept body and soul together for many emerging Australian writers and intellectuals with middle-class parents in their closets.

He may have enjoyed lunching and dining out, but even in his early eighties he continued to write and read extensively each day. He had a formidable work ethic, which he always managed to balance with his healthy appetite for the pleasures of good food, wine and companionship.

———

Travelling, and the anxieties it inspires, was a recurrent theme in Moorhouse's humorous essays. *Room Service* is a meditation on the apprehensions of travellers who wish to conform to 'the rules' in strange cities, but who equally resent their own need to please others.

In a story titled 'The New York Bell Captain', he recounts the narrator's stay at the Times Square Hotel in Manhattan, where, on his way out, he places six bottles of Heineken beer on the windowsill to chill in the snow, in order to save the 50 cent ice charge, to avoid filling the sink with beer and ice, and to 'spare myself the sight of the bell captain's outstretched palm'. He returns to the room and finds the beer gone from the sill. He knows immediately what has transpired:

> I know that the bell captain has swiftly checked my room to find out if I am using the windowsill to chill my beer instead of paying him 50 cents plus tip to bring up a plastic bag full of melting ice. Quick work on his part. I open out the window to look for clues and as I do the six bottles of Heineken are swept off the sill down fifteen stories into Fifty-Fourth Street.

While the facts suggest he apparently opened the wrong window, he surmises what has really happened:

> What the bell captain has done is to come into my room to find the bottles, steal one or two, or even three, and then

switch them to where I will sweep the remaining bottles off. This way I will never know if he has been into my room to steal my beer. I will therefore be unable to bring substantiated allegations against him. Alright. This round to the bell captain.

In *Room Service*, Moorhouse argues, with tongue only slightly in cheek, that retiring to hotel rooms or visiting their bars is by far the best way to see the world. In a story titled 'Hiltonia', he writes about staying at the original Sydney Hilton, where 'my window looked out on my house in Balmain so I could watch for robbers', and where he rarely heard or saw an Australian because '[t]he Sydney Hilton is not Sydney'.

He also writes about the anxiety that travelling and staying in hotels and motels provoked in him: 'I myself have a fondness for chain motels and am something of a specialist in Ramada Inns, Travelodge, Howard Johnson's, and Holiday Inns. I know the inadequacies of the less than intrepid traveller. I know about Traveller Paranoia, imaginary bed bugs, asbestos moneybelts.'

He quips about his close friend and editor Donald Horne's book on the museums of Europe, *The Great Museum*:

> I wanted to write a sequel called *Inconsequential Europe*. I seem to spend so much of my time with the inconsequential and I find that looking at monuments worries me. I try too hard with monuments. I read too much before and after, or I worry that I haven't read enough or that I've clouded my mind with historical background and can't 'see' the monument for itself.

In another chapter in *Room Service*, the narrator writes to his fictional editor, explaining his approach to the monuments of Cairo, where he is staying:

Here in Cairo at the Rameses Hilton I hang out at the Club 36 with Gergius and Tadros, the barmen. They are forever telling me to see monuments. They insist I see the pyramids. But I say to them that to watch them construct a cocktail tells me more about Egyptian culture than the pyramids. Tadros makes the Seth. Seth was God of the Desert . . . I like the way it embodies the colours of the Nile sunset, the flamboyant variety of the market place, the eroticism of the Arabian veil dancer, and it carries the suggestion of mystic potions from ancient times—elixirs and poisons.

Tadros reveals his secret: he learnt how to make the drink at the Hilton cocktail school.

Moorhouse was writing satirically about his approach to travelling, but there was a genuine truth, on a personal level, expressed in the tensions he felt, and the pleasures he found, in making a temporary home in hotels. He frequently disappeared to a hotel on the South Coast for what he once described to me as 'a holiday from reality'. Whatever that entailed.

One pleasure it almost certainly entailed was a visit to an oyster lease to sample some freshly shucked produce. For Moorhouse, oysters had a talismanic significance akin to the martini. In an essay for *Gourmet Traveller*, he explained it this way:

I have begun to think that it is important for us as humans to know the behaviour and nature of at least one species other than our own—we should twin with another species.

A year or so back I decided to pair with the oyster. I'd eaten so many during my life and they'd given me such fine pleasure, I felt I had become something like an oyster. I hope I have. I like swimming. I like taking in the sun, and I like to close the lid on my life for a time and just have time out—as oysters do. Oh, and they change sex every so often just for fun. I like that too.

Moorhouse remembered that, as a copyboy at *The Daily Telegraph*, one of his nightly jobs was to go to a nearby restaurant and collect oyster sandwiches for Frank Packer, who owned the paper. The oysters were out of a bottle and the sandwiches were made from white bread and butter. He noted that he sometimes ate oyster sandwiches himself, but naturally the oysters were freshly shucked.

As with the martini, Moorhouse evolved rules for how oysters were to be eaten and what should accompany them. Martinis and oysters, for instance, do not go together: 'A flinty dry Riesling, a Sancerre, a Chablis, champagne or beer are the only acceptable beverages.' He had a considered approach to the eating of the oyster and conducted extensive research into its history—cultural and scientific. He told the readers of *Gourmet Traveller* that when a team of American and Italian researchers analysed bivalve molluscs, they found they were rich in amino acids, 'which trigger, ever so slightly, the levels of our sex hormones, both male and female'. He quotes Professor George Fisher of Barry University in Miami, who led the research team: 'I am amazed . . . We now know that these molluscs are very mild aphrodisiacs for men and women.'

Moorhouse also pondered the correct table implement to use when eating an oyster. Originally, he favoured the use of a small fork, but subsequently changed his mind after a visit to an oyster lease with his friend Rohan Haslam. On returning to their motel, they discovered there were no forks to eat them with and ate them with teaspoons instead.

We discovered that using a small spoon allows the oysters to be cleanly removed from the shell without being damaged by the fork. I know it sounds rather untraditional but the spoon delivers the oyster to the mouth cleanly and with some of the oyster liquid.

Subsequently, I experimented with spoons and settled on a wooden Japanese spoon a little larger than a teaspoon. Rohan, however, gave me an elegant, longer-handled, pewter spoon from Artesia Pewter in Tasmania designed in the 1980s by John Bright which he believes is perfect for oyster eating.

Moorhouse also firmly believed that we should 'say goodbye, nicely' to the oyster by arranging the shells face-down in 'a circle of tribute', so we can contemplate their intricate shells. 'I am not by inclination a spiritual person,' he writes, 'but I fancy that how we handle the shells of the creatures we have just eaten is a way of honouring those creatures and the pleasure they've given us . . .'

Eating, for Moorhouse, was not simply a matter of knowing how to eat food with the appropriate ritual or pair it with the right drink. It was also a matter of finding companions who are agreeable conversationalists, and of avoiding bores. In *The Inspector-General of Misconception*, he wrote:

Conversation is a wide spectrum of intercourse. However, ultimately, the most delicious conversation has these following characteristics: It is inquiring and sharing rather than talking to win. It is heretical in that it challenges the accepted views of the group. It is shameless, in that it does not worry about good or bad taste. It has good humour and irony.

Most of all, it is urbane. Relaxed.

In the chapter on conversation, the Inspector-General issues some edicts about what good conversationalists do not do or are not: 'galloping in, overriding', 'being doctrinaire', 'stating one's position too often or compulsive disagreeableness' and 'talking to win'.

On the question of alcohol and conversation, Moorhouse believed:

> We concede that alcohol enhances very few activities and that some people should avoid it. It doesn't help surgery, for example.
>
> But conversation, dining, and travel are the human activities that it does hugely enhance.
>
> There is an adage about drink that, 'It makes old friends seem like new friends and new friends seem like old friends.'
>
> Beyond a certain point, however, the conversation of the intoxicated person becomes 'boringly simplified, repetitious and confused'. Time to go home.

———

On his return from researching the first two books in his League of Nations trilogy in Geneva, Moorhouse moved into a room at the Royal Automobile Club of Australia (RACA) in Sydney. It was after a year as Writer in Residence at King's College, Cambridge, and time in Cannes following the publication of *Dark Palace*.

The RACA is at the bottom of Sydney's Macquarie Street, opposite the Botanical Gardens and a short walk from the Sydney Opera House. From the top-floor dining room, there is a panoramic view of the harbour and its iconic bridge. The club was founded in 1903 to 'foster motoring and assist motorists'.

Its website notes that, in 1909, 'the club issued a protest regarding the behaviour of horse drawn vehicles, responding to criticism of motor cars from horse drawn passengers'. The Club membership traditionally includes categories 'such as Town, Young Executive, Defence . . . Interstate, and Overseas'. Moorhouse was a member for at least a decade before he moved in for a year. The irony is that he hadn't owned a car for five decades.

Clubs held a considerable, if somewhat tongue-in-cheek, fascination for Moorhouse for many decades, and were strongly linked to his interest in the aesthetics of dining, drinking, conversing and living a comfortable writer's life. Prestigious clubs, usually gentlemen's clubs, have reading rooms, bars, dining rooms, rooms to stay in and patrons who understand the rules of refined conversation. You do not, for instance, get into political or religious arguments over dinner. Moorhouse said that living at a club appealed to him because 'it's sort of an institutionalised living. It quite suited my temperament.'

A member of the London Groucho Club, he liked the fact that good clubs have international affiliations. 'So if I go to New York, I stay at the Yale Club, which is affiliated with the RAC and has one of my books in the library,' he said. 'In London I would use one of three or four clubs, including the Navy and Military Club, where John Latham used to stay [Latham was a chief justice of the High Court and a character in *Cold Light*] when he was going to the League of Nations. But there are all other sorts of genteel club that the RAC is affiliated with.'

The earliest references to clubs in Moorhouse's work are not to gentlemen's clubs but to service clubs, such as Rotary clubs and the Masonic lodges, which have long been a central part of regional town life in Australia. T. George McDowell, the character we first meet in *The Electrical Experience*, is a keen Rotarian.

He is particularly proud of a visit to the United States, where he attended the St Louis Rotary Convention in 1923. McDowell is a portrait, at least outwardly, of the model Rotarian: industrious, conscious of protocol, a self-made man with a strong community spirit.

It's a long, class-based leap from parochial service clubs to the kind of gentlemen's clubs Ian Fleming described in lingeringly snobbish detail in his James Bond novels—clubs such as White's in London. When you read Fleming, the smell of aged leather, rare filet mignon and Château Mouton Rothschild practically wafts off the page.

Yet the two types are linked in some respects. Both kinds of club have historically been exclusively male, the members bound by rituals and rules. In both, membership is dictated by an unspecified ability to demonstrate you are the 'right' kind of fellow to belong.

In *Conference-ville*, the narrator is invited to a gentlemen's club by a fellow conference goer. 'The bar was panelled, red cedar, brass footrail, members' personal pewter and stainless steel beer mugs, sheep paintings—perfect,' the narrator says. He and his dining companions are interrupted by the intrusion of a young activist on a mission to out closet conservatives attending the conference. After the activist is forcibly removed, the conversation turns to the 'ideal club'.

Dim, calm, a place where you should be able to stay overnight—stay indefinitely, until you were ready to go back into the world. No speaking rooms, abundant magazines, airmail editions of the great newspapers, sandwiches 'to which much time and consideration had been given', chafing dishes for after the theatre . . . Intricate rules and customs to create the feeling of being 'initiated'. Chairs which were deep enough to surround, to enclose you partly, to still further hold off the stress of the world.

The appeal of the club for the author is related to the appeal of hotel rooms and restaurants. It's the appeal of being out in the world—away from the domestic or the workspace—yet simultaneously cocooned in a world of familiar rituals and diverted by a certain theatre.

Tim Herbert sums up the pleasure his friend Moorhouse took in dining out this way: 'He's not somebody who really likes going to houses much or dinner parties. He doesn't because he'll get trapped. So that's why he likes restaurants. He chooses a restaurant he likes because then he can leave and he doesn't have to wait for the last course. Maybe people behave a little differently in a restaurant [than they do in domestic environments].'

For all his outward urbanity, Moorhouse had a strong need to cut himself off from other people at times. It's a need that sometimes emanated from a form of depression or existential despair. He rarely alluded to this part of himself in his writing, and when he did it was always masked with humour.

Moorhouse had written on a number of occasions about the protocols of dining alone. In a humorous essay titled 'Dining Alone at Christmas', he contemplated the rules that safeguard against being pitied by others at the restaurant, including the staff. He recommended dressing in 'tails, white scarf and a homburg', not pulling the Christmas cracker on the table 'by yourself', taking reading material 'concealed within an official government binder which will imply urgent state duty', and arriving with a pre-wrapped gift with a card attached to 'create the impression that you have a friend somewhere out there'.

He also advised against looking at pornography over lunch or weeping audibly.

Moorhouse did indeed dine alone fairly frequently. In 'The Ballad of the Sade Café', a chapter in *The Inspector-General of Misconception*, he recounts dining alone on Valentine's Day when he was a Writer in Residence at King's College. Unaware of the significance of the date, he is puzzled to discover that all his favourite restaurants were fully booked. He is eventually referred to an out-of-the-way restaurant in a dark back lane, where all the diners sit alone reading thick books. As he leaves, he reflects:

> None of us were under the protection of any saint as we walked out into the dark. But no. Perhaps we were watched over by other older pagan spirits (from whom the Catholic Church had stolen St Valentine's Day). Those pagan spirits who visited such as us on other days in our lives, if not today, and who occasionally, surprisingly, bestow upon us their own strange, aberrant, pagan gifts.

It's a passage which reminds us that there were other clubs in Moorhouse's life. Darker, less conventional and more exciting clubs. Clubs which he didn't care to elaborate on in interviews, but to which he sends his audacious heroine Edith to explore in *Grand Days* and *Dark Palace*. Clubs where the boundaries of sex, gender and class were crossed. Clubs where an appetite for flouting the rules was the price of admission.

5

BORDER CROSSINGS

In 2000, Moorhouse was on the brink of publishing the second book in his League of Nations trilogy, *Dark Palace*. He had been working on the novels for twelve years. He had reached a particularly low point after *Grand Days* was rejected for consideration by the judges of the prestigious Miles Franklin Award on the bizarre grounds that it was 'insufficiently Australian'. Moorhouse also had heard on the grapevine that the Australia Council, which had awarded him a Creative Fellowship, had taken a dim view of him spending four years writing and researching in Switzerland and France. The fact that the heroine of his books is an Australian woman who goes to work at the League of Nations, the archive of which is in Geneva, was no deterrent to these objections.

Grumblings that an Australian writer had deserted our pristine shores to 'sojourn' in Europe were given full throat at a 1995 Herald/Dymocks literary lunch. Moorhouse was promoting his collection of humorous essays, *Loose Living*, which plays on the theme of an Australian adapting to living in France.

He took the opportunity to explore the decision of the Miles Franklin judges. They were, he suggested, 'struggling with a mutation of the cultural cringe'.

'Cultural cringe' is a term coined by the Australian critic and essayist A.A. Phillips, writing in the literary journal *Meanjin* in 1950. As Rollo Hesketh writes more recently in the same publication, the term has come to refer to Australians' inherent lack of faith in their own culture, often at the popular level. This, he argues, is a distortion of what Phillips originally wanted to convey. 'Phillips wished to create a national culture that conceded no inferiority to Britain, and indeed was unembarrassed to be Australian.' The term was linked explicitly to an overvaluing of European high culture at the expense of home-grown culture. Not to mention the undervaluing of the culture of First Australians, who were here long before the Invasion—which, as Moorhouse agreed, tells us a lot about Anglo Australians' fear of being invaded.

In his speech, Moorhouse related that, on his return from France, the most common question he encountered was: 'Are you going to live here or go back to France?' He continued: 'Naturally, the Miles Franklin judges had this picture of me living in a chateau and eating my way through fine dinners, enjoying the finer things of life. Not only was the book to be damned for its unAustralianness but the author was suspected of cultural treason as well.' The deeper irony, as Moorhouse pointed out, is that *Grand Days* is a book that focuses, explicitly and implicitly, on borders—on 'the crossing of borders and the meaning of borders, national and other, and identity'.

Towards the end of his address, Moorhouse was interrupted by a diner, who rose to say the following: 'Excuse me, Frank. I know this is a bit rude . . . I shared your disappointment of

Headquarters of the *Boorowa News* edited by Frank in 1966.

With Sandra Levy, c. 1969.

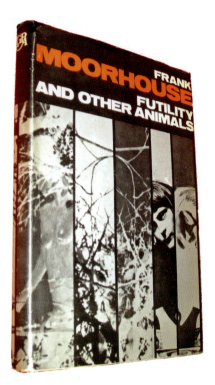

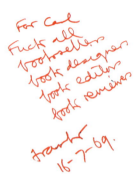

For Carl
Fuck all
booksellers
book designers
book editors
book reviewers

Frank
16-7-69.

Frank Moorhouse's first book, 1969.

With Carl Harrison-Ford and Edna Wilson. Forth and Clyde Hotel, Balmain, c. 1970.

The Moorhouse family: Frank, his mother Purthanry Moorhouse, father Frank Moorhouse Snr, brothers Arthur and Owen. Nowra, 1971.

Editing *Thor* at Ewenton Street, Balmain, 1971.

Michael Wilding, Frank and companion. Cleveland Bar & Grill, c. 1970.

On location with
filmmaker Mike
Thornhill, shooting
Frank's script
The Machine Gun,
1971.

Frank, Don Anderson, Elisabeth Wynhausen and Sandra Levy. London, 1974.

Clockwise from front right: Frank's culinary muse and great companion Tony Bilson, unknown diner, Elisabeth Wynhausen, Gay Bilson, Sandra Levy, Dick Hall, Frank Moorhouse and John Woodward. Pinocchio's Restaurant, 1976.

Michele Field and Frank Moorhouse, Fryer Library Jubilee. Brisbane, 1977.

Frank Moorhouse awarded his first Perpetual Trophy for Ballroom Dancing to Mary Lord and A.D. Hope for their performance at the 1978 inaugural Association for the Study of Australian Literature conference dinner.

Clockwise from front left: Sophia Turkiewicz, unknown diner, Tim Burstall, Richard Brennan, Barbara Gibbs, Chris Maudson and Frank Moorhouse. Sandro's Restaurant, 1979.

Launch of *Days of Wine and Rage* at the New Hellas in 1980. Penguin publisher Brian Johns, Frank Moorhouse and long-time friend Dick Hall.

Clockwise from front: Rose Creswell, Dick Hall, Suzie Malouf, Mike Thornhill and Frank. Arthur's Bar, 1981.

Train to Nowra. Don Anderson, David Williamson, Kirsty McDonald, Robert Haupt (front left), Dick Hall, Frank Moorhouse, Kristin Williamson (front right) and Susie Carleton (aloft).

the *Grand Days* [disqualification]. I came to your last luncheon, I bought your book . . . But I feel we don't want to hear what's going on, if you're not happy to be in Australia . . .' Her comment was greeted with applause from some members of the audience.

As Matt Condon reported, 'Dissent broke out like spot fires. The assembly fell into an uncomfortable rabble'.

A host of well-known writers and commentators came to Moorhouse's defence. *Sydney Morning Herald* columnist Mike Carlton wrote:

> I have never met Frank Moorhouse but I know how he feels. I have been home for nearly two years, after three years in Britain, and there are still perfect strangers who demand my assurance that Australia is God's own country. 'Betcha glad to be back,' they say. 'Greatest place in the world Straya. Dunno why y'ever left . . .' The tone is often pugnacious or querulous, challenging me to disagree, and yet betraying a nagging doubt. There is real insecurity beneath the bluster, suggesting that the Australian cultural whinge (it's a better word than cringe) is alive and thoroughly unwell.

The then leader of the New South Wales opposition Liberal Party, Peter Collins, who had been arts minister in a previous government, wrote a passionate defence of Moorhouse's 'carefully considered address':

> Far from a personal whinge, he put the case of other Australian writers who take their talent and Australian-ness into other societies and who, increasingly, win recognition for their work internationally . . . His address was humorous and witty, his horizon unlimited, his approach global but very Australian in

delivery and perspective . . . like many keen to hear Moorhouse complete his case, I was stunned by the lack of interest of a significant section of a literary audience in getting to know an accomplished Australian author better.

The literary lunching commotion predictably reignited debate about whether the cultural cringe was dead or merely resting. Prominent Australian authors commented on the question of whether *Grand Days* should have been excluded by the Miles Franklin judges. Australia's best-known art critic, Robert Hughes, opined:

> Australian writing cannot spurn the cosmopolitan and remain healthy because the writer who, from ideological pressure rather than inner need, ignores the immense menu of the world becomes a self-limiting, even a self-deforming organism. How can we value 'multiculturalism' as a healthy development within Australia and at the same time criti-cise Australian writers for immersing themselves in cultures outside their country? Cultural transmission isn't a one-way street. Do we like David Malouf for being of Lebanese descent, only to dislike him for living, part of the year, among Italians?

Tom Keneally weighed in with an observation on the anxiety animating the debate (which ironically, of course, was the theme of Moorhouse's address): the fear Australians have that they are secretly still in the grip of the cultural cringe. 'The fact that we've got to congratulate ourselves that the cultural cringe is over shows that it is still there . . . We're like 14-year-olds reassuring ourselves that last week's acne was the last we'll get,' he wrote.

Moorhouse returned to the subject in an essay in *The Inspector-General of Misconception*, published in 2002. In it he noted that, while A.A. Phillips had declared the term 'cultural cringe' dead in 1983, there was plenty of evidence that the virus had merely mutated: 'Phillips should be alive today to smell the corpse now as we stand in the graveyard of ideas, in the light rain, while gumbooted cemetery workers dig in the clay to exhume the stinking, twitching body, prematurely buried, still alive and thumping in its coffin . . .'

He goes on to identify three strains of the virus. Variant A is 'Agitated Expatriate. Or, This Little Piggy Went To Market'—the symptoms of which are recurring incertitude on the part of the expat about whether to stay away or come 'home'. Virus Variant B is 'The Unhappy Ones Who Are Stuck Here. Or, This Little Piggy Stayed Home'—the symptoms include 'a profound sense of unease on reading about fellow expatriate nationals—are they having a better life?' Virus Variant C is 'You Will Remain Seated; Do Not Attempt To Leave'. The sufferer of the latter experiences these symptoms: 'The dread that one by one anyone who is any good is leaving the country and that those who are left will be seen as second rate, poor cousins in the cultural world.'

There is no question that Moorhouse pinched a cultural nerve in his 1995 speech. What undoubtedly set him up as a target for controversy over whether he was sufficiently patriotic was that he was prepared not only to question vulgar nationalism, but also to mock it. His interjector described his speech as 'bitter'. She wished. What made the speech so inflammatory was that it was witty. Bad enough that a writer had the affront to question the maturity of Australian culture, but to do so with his tongue in his cheek was unforgivable.

———

Towards the end of *Grand Days*, Edith Campbell Berry agrees to marry Robert Dole, an English journalist. One evening they are discussing their life plans when Robert announces that, after they are wed, Edith will no longer be Australian: 'You'll be British, legally speaking.'

Edith replies: 'In the eyes of the League I will always be Australian.'

As she said this, she thought of how she'd once hoped to become an Internationalist and to shed her nationality. She'd had some notion that one day the Council would call her up and declare her International and relieve her of being Australian. Now she was assuming the burden of two nationalities.

In *Dark Palace*, Edith returns to Australia for a rest, having been embroiled in a small scandal. She struggles with the question of whether she has outgrown Australia—whether, in her heart, the border between her life abroad and her childhood home is permanently sealed. It is 1936 and she is on a train on her way home to Jasper's Brush.

As she stared out of the railway carriage at the coastal bush landscape, Edith felt a low revulsion.

Appalling, she thought, the bush is simply appalling. It appeared to her to be grasping and twisted. Grasping for water, grasping for soil—the way the roots of the eucalyptus clutched rocks and clutched the soil . . .

The disloyalty of her thinking about the bush registered. What sort of falsely superior person had she become, what dreadful snobbish disloyalty had moved through her mind, causing her to dislike the bush? . . .

There in the railway carriage she was suddenly in fear for her self, her placement in the world.

At the same time she is grappling with the borders of her national and international self, Edith is also grappling with her relationship to her sexuality and her propriety as a woman, given the mores of the era. Her friend Florence rebukes her when Edith reveals that she attended the Molly Club, a bohemian gay and cross-dressing nightclub in Geneva. Later, another acquaintance, Caroline, who is in her cups, suggests that Edith is becoming known as 'the office vamp'.

It's a classic double jeopardy that female readers will still recognise—you are damned if you're not perceived as appropriately feminine, seductive or attractive, and yet damned if you are seen as transgressing the invisible boundaries of propriety and virtue. Contemplating Caroline's remarks, Edith reflects:

> Together with this disconcerting idea, recklessly thrown at her by Caroline, there was still the earlier alarm from the unreconciled sense of herself, the sense of herself as daring, as having had a strange adventure in human passion, against the proper sense of her womanhood, about which Florence had so strongly reminded her. Somehow those had to be reconciled. Maybe her sense of womanhood was changing . . . Were we made from everything that had happened to us?

In her marriage to Robert Dole, Edith struggles with what it means to be a 'proper wife':

> She had a vocation and, as yet, she had no burning desire to have a family, she did not run the household except in

the smallest ways, she earned more than her husband, and she had private income, as well, which had survived the Depression . . .

How much of the wedding contract had she discounted?

Ultimately, she chooses to go back to her non-traditional relationship with Ambrose and forgo the conventional path of marriage and motherhood.

In Moorhouse's work, it is not only women but also men who explore the boundaries of gender identity. And it is through the character of Ambrose, Edith's lover and eventually her husband, that Moorhouse makes his personal as well as writerly interest in these border skirmishes most explicit.

In *Grand Days*, Ambrose reveals himself to Edith as a crossdresser and they incorporate it into their love-making. In the League of Nations trilogy Moorhouse explores the fluidity of sexuality and gender in a relative restrained manner. But in other work he has written in a more sexually explicit way about departures from heterosexual and gendered norms. He saw pornography—or erotica, as he preferred to call it—as having an only partially tapped literary potential.

It is particularly interesting that Moorhouse wrote his most sexually explicit work, the novella *Sonny*, at the same time he was working on *Grand Days* and *Dark Palace*. A little like his need to dress en femme when alone at home, he said working on *Sonny* was a relief and a pleasurable distraction from the task of stitching together two historically embedded novels.

There were attempts to publish *Sonny* via a private consortium of supporters, but at the time of writing it remains unpublished. Indeed it is, perhaps, unpublishable. It is nonetheless important to explore, because Moorhouse himself regarded it as a significant part of his body of work and gave copies to a number of people he regarded as significant readers of his work.

The main character is a young man named Sonny, who is sent to an elite boarding school in Switzerland, where he is trained in the arts of cross-dressing and receiving and giving sexual pleasure. Moorhouse described the work 'as an episodic, mytho-gothic, erotic gender fable which tells a continuous allegorical story from the life of a beautiful, young girl-boy'.

In an interview for this book, Moorhouse talked explicitly about his cross-dressing and the purpose it served in his life. 'Certainly, at Cambridge, when I had a flat in the College, King's College, I would dress en femme when I was working there, then I'd change if I was going out,' he said. 'But now and because I live alone, it's my preferred way of dressing. Unless I have to go out in the public, I dress en femme and sleep en femme . . . My wardrobe is two-thirds female and one-third male.'

Publisher Xavier Hennekinne, a friend who cross-dressed with Moorhouse occasionally, says that he and Moorhouse understood the practice differently. 'For me it's dressing up, it's having fun—I did that when I was a kid, cross-dress. My cousin would dress as a man and I would dress as a woman when we were twelve or thirteen and we would go down to the village in Normandy, France. I don't think it was linked to my sexuality. The aesthetic side was much stronger with Frank . . . He has this feminine aesthetic that inhabits him on a day-to-day basis.'

Moorhouse and Hennekinne went several times with their mutual friend Tim Herbert to the Seahorse Ball at Sydney's Gazebo Hotel. This was an annual party for men who like to cross-dress, where Hennekinne both annoyed and delighted his friend by winning Belle of the Ball.

Of *Sonny*, Moorhouse said:

> The book embodies a lot of my own personal preoccupations
> and pleasures—in some ways it's a spiritual autobiography . . .
> If *Grand Days* and *Dark Palace* are my attempts to write
> symphonies, *Sonny* is playing jazz on Friday nights in some
> dark bars—or perhaps dancing in drag in a chorus line is
> a more appropriate metaphor.

Moorhouse published a section of the working manuscript
in an edited collection of erotic short stories titled *Love Cries*. It
is a story that remains part of the completed work and encapsulates some of the material which is likely to be most challenging
for readers inclined to take fictional scenarios literally. And there
will be readers and reviewers of this biography who will, with
good reason, find the subject matter of *Sonny* abhorrent.

Sonny arrives at his elite boarding school in Lausanne as a
post-pubescent high-school student who has been inducted into
intercourse by his mother. Within minutes of arriving, he is
having a lesson in receiving anal sex from the school's head
counsellor. Both scenarios breach major Western taboos—and,
following revelations of the extent of child sexual abuse within
families, the church and schools in the 21st century, these are
highly charged subjects because they describe, in fictional terms,
acts which have damaged so many children.

Moorhouse was, of course, a writer who came to the territory of censorship and the dangers that can be unleashed by
exploring in fictional terms the worst of human behaviour with
his eyes wide open. He had been a politically active opponent
of censorship since his twenties and had frequently written on
the subject.

In 2009, acclaimed Australian artist Bill Henson found himself at the centre of a media firestorm for an image depicting a nude thirteen-year-old girl whose budding breasts are visible. Although he had exhibited such images for decades with little objection, including from most of the 65,000 people who attended his 2005 Art Gallery of New South Wales retrospective, Henson found himself subjected to accusations that he was a paedophile. The prime minister of the day, Kevin Rudd, weighed in on breakfast television to describe the image as 'absolutely revolting'.

In an article reflecting on the Henson controversy, Moorhouse asked: '[W]hy is the artistic imagination treated as a thing of angry suspicion and distaste by some people and with awe by others; from where does the imagination claim its authority to challenge conventions and the law?' While answering this question, he is careful not to suggest that artists and writers are automatically released from the ethical obligations that bind us as a society. He rejected the romantic view of art premised on the notion that 'the free wanderings of the imagination, especially into "dark" or irrational taboos, are not only the privilege of art but also one of its imperatives', going on to note:

> Not all taboos are nonsense: some taboos have become crimes for very good reason, but some for bad reasons. Sex with pre-pubescent children is taboo and also a crime, as it should be. In my lifetime, same-sex relationships were both taboo and criminal: an irrational taboo and an unjust crime, and ultimately one that was rejected.

In light of this statement, where should Moorhouse readers stand on subject matter that deals with incest, as well as sexual predation by a mother and a teacher?

Moorhouse's answer to these questions lies partly in the following argument:

A Shakespearean play—say, *Romeo and Juliet*—could be degraded by a classification saying that it contains mutilation, rape, suicide, incest, 'adult themes' and so on . . . Originality in an artwork at its highest, almost by definition, comes into existence outside 'standards'—and anyhow, in a pluralistic, multicultural society there is a profusion of standards, expectations and moralities. Classification robs art of its power to shock and surprise and to offend: some art is meant to be offensive and challenging.

It's a response that relies on a familiar defence: that art and the artistic imagination should be granted some licence to explore taboo themes. Certainly, there is a long literary history of works that play with themes otherwise considered profane or forbidden in mainstream or popular culture.

In a letter to his publisher in 2017, discussing his novella and the potential objections to it, Moorhouse explained that:

I feel that English literature is evolving towards, taking on, the description of sexual behaviour with the same creative detail that writers might describe a cathedral, the landscape, falling in love, a wedding, the commission of a crime, or the progress of a battle, evoking emotional responses, visceral responses, as do these depictions of human behaviours. We are accustomed to crying, laughing, and being stirred by imaginative works, so with the erotic . . . The erotic is the most under-developed and inhibited literary genre in the English language—the unfinished business of English literature.

Given that Moorhouse had explicitly defined the work as literary and erotic, it is worth pausing here to look at the history of erotic literary fiction, and how the response to it has varied according to the cultural and historical context in which it is published.

Patrick J. Kearney is widely regarded as having written one of the most authoritative works on the history of erotic literature. He reminds us that works by authors as renowned as Rabelais, Chaucer and Boccaccio were not regarded as particularly shocking in their day, but are now seen as containing themes not suitable for the young. In his memoir *Things I Didn't Know*, Robert Hughes recalls being severely chastised by a teacher for possessing a copy of James Joyce's *Ulysses*. In a book about his passion for fishing, *A Jerk on One End*, Hughes also remembers his first erotic memory: being turned on by a description of spawning salmon.

What is considered pornographic or harmful to the minds of the young or the wider public—although it is usually not considered in any way dangerous to those who seek to censor such works—varies enormously. What turns people on follows the same pattern. Some people get off on pictures of people wearing rubber kitchen gloves. Others are just reminded of the drudgery they associate with doing the washing-up.

As I argued in a 1997 book, the definitions of what is unacceptably pornographic are deeply embedded in the cultural and legal discourses of the time:

> Perhaps pornography can be most usefully understood as a blister—a tender spot on the social skin which marks a point of friction. Nothing, in these terms, is inherently, universally pornographic—the reference point for porn becomes an intersecting web of public policy, private desires and beliefs, and

culture. In concrete terms, this disjuncture is arguably what gives pornography its charge—the fear and excitement it generates flows from the transgressions of real and imagined boundaries which traverse these categories.

Erotic art and literature go back as far as art and literary historians and archaeologists have been able to discern. The sexually charged objects and frescoes uncovered at Pompeii in the 18th and 19th centuries defied the idealisation of the ancient democratic world. In *The Secret Museum*, Walter Kendrick writes of one scholar's nine-volume catalogue of these artifacts:

> Despite all appearances to the contrary, and despite his own predilection for the more 'natural' ancient world, [Pierre Sylvain] Marechal could not bring himself to believe that the Romans spent their days amid a forest of phalluses. Such things were too highly charged to be dispersed throughout the environment. They had to be set apart, and the best place for them was a brothel.

The distinction between what is seen as mere pornography and literature containing erotic material has shifted over the centuries in the Western world, but a common thread runs through objections to explicit descriptions or depictions of sex and sexuality. It's a theme that originated in a test developed in 1868 by the English chief justice Lord Cockburn known as the 'Hicklin test'. The Hicklin test set aside the intentions of the author or the publisher in writing or making a publication available. Cockburn framed it this way: 'I think the test of obscenity is this: whether the tendency of the matter charged as obscenity is to deprave and corrupt those whose minds are open to such immoral influences, and into whose hands a publication of this sort may fall.'

While courts and legislators, in the Western world at least, have significantly relaxed in their attitude to material that is classified as being of artistic or literary merit, the concerns Cockburn expressed in the mid-19th century still lie close to the surface.

What shifts is the object of concern—who is likely to be corrupted by exposure to descriptions or depictions of sex. In the 19th century, concerns about the deleterious 'effects' of novel reading were particularly focused on young, bourgeois women, who were presumed to be at risk of becoming infected with unrealistic romantic (for which, read 'sexual') ideas about their future relationships.

One of the many ironies in the long march of censorship was the attempt to suppress publication of Gustave Flaubert's *Madame Bovary* on the basis that it was liable to corrupt susceptible readers. The central character in Flaubert's novel, Emma Bovary, is a bourgeois woman who seeks escape from the chains of her married existence through reading, and eventually by escaping into the arms of lovers. Emma is a complex character and her portrayal is, in part, a meditation on the excessive vulnerability and innocence projected onto women at the time.

The potential corrupting power attributed to novels spread through the 20th century, attaching itself to postcards, erotic photographs, comic books, television and film, and finally the internet. Calls for censorship shifted largely from the tendency of erotic or violent material to corrupt women to concerns that they would corrupt the young and the uneducated.

In the 1970s, feminists shifted the locus of concern to men and reframed the need for censorship as one of civil rights for women. In her 1975 feminist classic *Against Our Will*, Susan

Brownmiller argues that pornography is both an expression of misogyny and an incitement to hate and objectify women:

> Pornography, like rape, is a male invention, designed to dehumanize women, to reduce the female to an object of sexual access . . . The staple of porn will always be the naked female body, breasts and genitals exposed, because as man devised it, her naked body is the female's 'shame', her private parts the private property of man, while his are the ancient, holy, universal patriarchal instrument of his power, his rule by force over her.

As Kendrick writes so perceptively in 1987 in *The Secret Museum*:

> The latest phase of the pornography debate seems to entail its elevation from morals to politics, the long-overdue recognition that what we have been arguing about the entire time is a matter of power, of access to the world around us, of control over our own bodies and our own minds.

Today, the most heightened political anxieties about the pernicious effects of everything from artistic and literary material to basic pornography revolve around their potential to sexualise children and/or endorse child sexual abuse. There are excellent reasons for these concerns, given what we know today about the horrific extent of child sexual abuse in institutions such as the Catholic Church and our schools—not to mention in families. I am conscious that this discussion of *Sonny* will land in an understandably heightened atmosphere of concern about child sexual abuse—and that it might be read, by some, as an endorsement of the right of adults to bend adolescents to their sexual will.

But there are other ways of reading *Sonny*. Not only is it a work of literary imagination; as Moorhouse himself said, it is 'a work that deals with pubescent sexuality with all its amoral, confused, molten, and transgressive, passion'. (This is an argument I find hard to accept, given that the novella is centred on adults intruding into the private sexual life of an adolescent and engaging in sex with him.)

Sonny is not the first time Moorhouse explored the theme of intergenerational sex. In *The Everlasting Secret Family*, Irving Bow is the proprietor of a cinema in a country town. Irving has a secret: he is sexually attracted to the children who gather in his darkened cinematic palace. When a deputation from the combined church ladies comes to see him, he is worried that a 'child has blabbed'. It turns out that their main concern is teenagers spooning each other in the dark. Moorhouse wrote in the novel:

> He had, glancing at their faces, probably pleasured children of the women present, and he looked at the pleasant faces, trying to fade back their faces, back down the years to their youth. The child, though, carried within its face, its body, the beauty of both its parents, refound there as it withered away in the parents. Children were one gender . . . How would they ever understand the shy knowing and accepting of a young person who came to him.

Irving Bow is at once portrayed as a man with a 'white popular smile behind which lay the bad, brimstone breath of a swishing dragon' and as the corruptor of youth. Yet, simultaneously, the children are portrayed as all too open to being corrupted and keen to participate in his perverse games and displays. It is ambiguous whether the perception of their eagerness lies in the mind of Irving Bow or is being posited as a reality—that adolescents actively and often seek out and initiate sexual encounters with adults.

Fiona Giles observed in a discussion we had about *The Everlasting Secret Family* how anachronistic—indeed, abhorrent—sections of it seem now. That the portrayal of the children as innately corruptible by adult sexuality is at odds with the contemporary reckoning with the imbalance of power between the perpetrator and a child. 'The difference between corruption and harm is that corruption is a moral judgment,' she notes, 'even a sign of weakness in the victim, who is considered corruptible in the first place (through lack of faith or virtue, in addition to, or as a condition of youthfulness), rather than wrongdoing in the perpetrator doing the "corrupting", whereas harm speaks of the damage caused to the victim of sexual abuse as a form of assault.'

Giles' view highlights the profound ethical differences between the libertarianism of the mid to late 20th century and mainstream thinking of the 2020s. The 1970s was a time when writers, artists and filmmakers were rebelling against what they perceived as the puritanical mores of mainstream Australia and were strongly influenced by thinkers such as the psychoanalyst Wilhelm Reich, who saw sexual repression as the root of human discontent. Since the 1990s, however, there has been widespread exposure of the endemic nature of child sexual abuse in institutions and in the family, and an increased understanding of its traumatising effects, including the lifelong suffering such abuse can cause. In this context, *The Everlasting Secret Family* rightly reads very differently.

In *Grand Days*, Moorhouse explores the themes of boundary crossing on a much grander scale: both personal, social and political. Edith and Ambrose negotiate borders both in their work at the League and in their relationship. Ambrose cross-dresses in his private life and is also bisexual. Soon after they meet on the train to Geneva, he raises the subject of homosexuality in a teasing anecdote about being acquainted with Oscar Wilde's son. Edith wonders if Ambrose is admitting something of his own sexuality. But later, when they kiss, she reflects that 'she could not tell whether there was a difference to the kiss of a man who inhabited a place at or near the border'.

Early in their love affair, Edith has occasion to dress up as an American cowgirl when she playfully takes part in an American delegation's motorcade, and she arrives at Ambrose's apartment still wearing her costume. She quickly discovers that 'dressing up' is not merely playful—it can have unexpected consequences: Ambrose takes the opportunity to dress in her undergarments.

He then came to her as a woman, as a man and a woman, for he was fully aroused in the masculine way, without any doubt. She remembered something that Nicole had said that afternoon and Edith repeated it, her voice husky, 'There is a law in Geneva against wearing masks. I think I see why.'

'Give a person a mask and they will tell you the truth,' he said softly in a new more effeminate voice.

Ambrose tells her later that his dressing up is the opposite of disguise. An English doctor who served in World War I, he dresses in conservative suits by day and often wears his regimental pyjamas to bed—when he is not clad in a silk nightdress. His character embodies border crossing of both gender and sexuality—he has sex with men on occasion while dressed as a woman.

In *Grand Days*, Edith struggles with the ambiguities that characterise his sexual persona. But later, in *Dark Palace*, following a hiatus in their relationship, Edith reconciles herself to the border crossings of gender—not only to those Ambrose embraces, but also to her own.

> As she undressed herself before him, she whispered, 'Halt. Who goes there? Man or Woman?'
>
> She removed her underpants and corset and left on only her petticoat, brassiere, garter belt, and stockings.
>
> He whispered his reply. 'Neither man nor woman' . . .
>
> Lying back under him, she whispered, 'Pass friend—all's well.'

Their love-making session comes after they have reconciled following a long rupture in their affair. In celebration of their reconciliation, Edith buys Ambrose a silk nightdress from Milan. She reflects that, in their former lives together:

> . . . she'd always told herself that Ambrose, by being something other than elementary man, had allowed her a halfway staging place, a place where she could appear to have a man in her life, a place from which she would eventually pass.
>
> Not a place towards which she had been headed.

For Edith, one of the borders she has crossed is that of conventional bourgeois mores concerning female sexuality. In accepting Ambrose's cross-dressing as part of their relationship, rather than as something adjacent to it, she finally puts aside her fears that there is something 'abnormal' about her own sexual self.

In her seminal cultural history of cross-dressing, *Vested Interests*, Marjorie Garber, analyses the way cross-dressing directs the viewer to the fact that gender is constructed rather than given. Her thesis hinges, in the first instance, on a distinction between biological sex and gender. The sex that we are told we are born with is different from what we or society more broadly make of that sex—the latter constitutes our gender. To make an obvious point, to be gendered female means something quite different in 21st-century Western society than it did in Jane Austen's England.

The distinction between biological sex and gender is now under challenge from trans and non-binary activists, who reject the idea that gender is determined by the sex an individual is assigned at birth, or even by whether they choose to alter their physical bodies to conform to standard notions of what constitutes a male or female body. The current and often fraught debate about the relationship between biological sex and gender only reinforces how emotionally, personally, culturally and politically charged that relationship can be.

Cross-dressing, which bears no necessary relationship to gender identity or sexuality, calls attention to the dress and comportment codes that frame gender in a given era or culture. (Gloria Steinem once said: 'I don't mind drag—women have been female impersonators for some time.') While dress codes for males and females seem 'natural' at any given historical moment, history shows us how mutable they are. A simple example is that, prior to World War I, it was conventional to dress boys in pink and girls in blue—pink being considered a more assertive colour and blue more feminine.

As Garber notes, cross-dressing has a long and varied history. Cross-dressing features in high and low culture: Elizabethan theatre not only relied on men dressing as women to perform female roles, but Shakespeare overtly references the practice—think of *Twelfth Night*. Billy Wilder's 1959 film *Some Like It Hot* features Jack Lemmon and Tony Curtis in drag—an interesting counterpoint to Marilyn Monroe's exaggerated, even camp, performance of femininity. And there is a rich history of men cross-dressing theatrically in hierarchical, male-dominated contexts—from the army and navy to elite male clubs like Yale University's Skull and Bones. Women, it should be noted, also cross-dress—Marlene Dietrich being a notable example.

Garber argues that the historical fascination with cross-dressing is bound up with the challenge it offers to 'easy notions of binarity, putting into question the categories of "female" and "male", whether they are considered essential or constructed, biological or cultural'. Many critics who've considered the cultural role of cross-dressing, she says, have had a tendency to 'look *through* rather than *at* the cross-dresser'. Rather than seeing the cross-dresser in terms of the male or female, Garber says, we should see him or her as a kind of third sex. As a place where both the male and the female disappear.

Garber's analysis is particularly important for understanding the way Moorhouse conjured with the significance and symbolism of cross-dressing in both his work and his personal life. He once said that he sees himself as 'bi-gendered' or 'inter-gendered'—a remark that suggests he saw gender as a fluid state of being, rather than as an either/or. Of what she terms the 'third sex', Garber has this to say: 'The "third" is a mode of articulation, a way of describing a space of possibility. Three puts in question the idea of one: of identity, self-sufficiency, self-knowledge.' It's a reflection which chimes with Moorhouse's understanding of gender and sexuality as identities which may be more permeable than we think.

————

Grand Days also deals with the consequences of more literal kinds of border crossing. The League of Nations was, of course, a grand experiment in rendering the borders of nations permeable in order to build a sustainable world order. Edith transplants herself to Geneva from Australia, an enormous leap of faith for a young woman from a provincial background. As bright, ambitious and curious young people have always done, she actively seeks out the thrill of dislocation from home and the familiar.

Edith is also a cipher for Moorhouse's reflections on the tendency on the part of would-be bohemians to glamorise life lived on the margins of conventional society. Geneva is the place where Edith discovers the cosmopolitan and the bohemian—both in nightclubs and through mixing with people with a less conventional view of social and sexual mores. Moorhouse, of course, did the same by leaving Nowra and his high-school sweetheart for Sydney. A job at *The Daily Telegraph* might not have required a passport, although a packed lunch may have been involved, but it was a significant boundary crossing in the young writer's life.

Edith's early musings on the relationship between identity and nationality or gender roles and social mores are abstract and self-focused, if occasionally self-indulgent. When her country-town friend and admirer George McDowell comes to visit her in Geneva, he notices that her accent has altered—it is less Australian and provincial. Their conversation turns to the question of whether speaking other languages unlocks new parts of the self.

'We should all have another self or part of our self perhaps which isn't tied to one nationality,' she said.

He said that he thought that learning another language might be a way of disguising oneself.

'It's perhaps a way of slipping across the border,' she said.

Like Edith, Moorhouse struggled, as his early letters and papers show, with his shifting identity. He was, at once, the country-town boy writing love letters to his intended, and equally a young man increasingly fascinated with the more bohemian side of life in the city. In *Grand Days*, Edith Campbell Berry crosses and recrosses borders which are both geographic, sexual and intellectual. In many ways, she embodies Moorhouse's fascination with the role borders or boundaries play in establishing and dissolving fixed habits of identity.

On a trip to Paris, Edith visits the Ad Lib Club, where for the first time she hears scat singing. A black musician, Jerome, explains the term and the technique to her. Later, in his dressing room, she performs oral sex on him, something she has never done to a man before.

Time and movement then became slippery, as she gracefully slid, seeing for the first time his caramel and cream shoes and without thinking too much at all about things, it seemed his warm dark hands were on her exposed and very alive breasts, which she felt she had delivered up to him; all seemed to happen in flowing fixed steps, something like a waltz, except that they were not moving from where they were adhered together in this strange way, and without any guidance at all and in no time at all, and with no impediment, with no thought at all, warmly, fleshly and flowing, it was finishing, and she took her lips, tongue, and gentle teeth away . . .

The sexual exchange mirrors the way her first encounter with scat singing affects Edith—the way it blurs the boundaries of meaning and music. The way it expresses a fluid relationship to reality and the fixed relation to it that language ordinarily suggests.

> . . . she felt that she'd had a private insight about the animal sense and the jazz sense of scats. That in every conversation there were scats, not all were rhythmical, not all of them were artful. In some conversation the scat was a glimpse of a quandary, or a befuddlement, or in some, a dropping of mystical excrement, something of their soul. True, most conversation was just drapery to make the person conversationally adorable, but the scats were always there, the noises, the rumblings of deeper unspeakable meanings of self, and definitely of quandary and befuddlement.

It's a passage which takes us to the heart of the tensions that Edith symbolically embodies for Moorhouse as an Australian writer, and by extension for all creative and idealistic Australians struggling with defining their identity and their place in a world where, they sense, their country and culture still remain largely on the fringe of Western cultural production and politics. That is, at least if they are Anglo Australians.

Journalist and author Annabel Crabb observes of Edith: 'She doesn't have that barn-door-sized, clearly discernible purpose in the novel. She is a complicated character. She's full of contradiction. She's rule-driven and yet reckless. She's foolish sometimes and very, very wise at other times. She's courageous but can also be cowardly. She's generous but she can be cruel and heedless and selfish.' And then she observes equally of Moorhouse: 'It's funny, isn't it, that one writer can be simultaneously so interested in deviance but also interested in properness.' And of the work more broadly: 'I guess it's just a bit of a study of order and disorder, isn't it?'

Literary scholar and critic Brian Kiernan, one of the most lucid analysts of Moorhouse's work, sees in Edith a character who embodies a fundamental philosophical preoccupation of the author: a fascination with unforeseen consequences. 'That, I think, was fundamental to the libertarianism that he was engaged in from the early days,' he says. 'That sort of pessimism that the Andersonians have, that no matter how you try and create a better world, something is going to go wrong . . . I think from the start that becomes very important to the trilogy because there's all of Edith's ideals. But somehow the world lets her down, doesn't it?'

———

If *Grand Days* is a meditation on a young woman from the South Coast of New South Wales crossing geographic, cultural and personal boundaries and finding a delight in toying with their limits, its sequel *Dark Palace*, as the name suggests, takes readers to a very different set of border crossings. It summons up the nightmarish world unleashed by Hitler's campaign to erase the very existence of the Jewish people, and to the tidal wave of refugees unleashed by his war on the most fundamental elements of humanity.

In the League of Nations trilogy, Moorhouse takes his fascination with border crossings and what's at stake when the established order is disrupted and trains it on the grand themes of world order, peace and the chaos unleashed on the social order by war.

6

GRAND SCHEMES

Grand Days encapsulates Moorhouse's lifelong obsession with grand schemes—or, as he would have phrased it, with Grand Schemes, the capitals a wink at the potential to give way to the ridiculous that stalks all grandiose impulses. The League of Nations was, of course, one of the most famously grand experiments of all time. It was also, tragically, a project that collapsed under the weight of its ambitions—a collapse chronicled in *Dark Palace*.

Moorhouse said, when asked why he chose the League as his subject matter:

> I am writing about the League of Nations because it is a trunk in the attic of history which has not been properly opened. It contains haunted, bitter, and embarrassing moments for the world, but it was also a human experiment of grandeur. Its stories deserve more space in our cultural imagination.

The original League of Nations covenant, adopted in 1919, sets out 'a solemn agreement between sovereign states, which consent to limit their complete freedom of action on certain points for the great good of themselves and the world at large'. Founded at the Paris Peace Conference which ended World War I, the League was the first global organisation set up to maintain world peace. Its remit, however, expanded to encompass what is, in hindsight, a breathtakingly ambitious array of projects that would literally reform the world. The League oversaw the Health Organization, the Disarmament Commission, the Permanent Court of International Justice, the International Labour Organization, the Commission for Refugees and the International Commission on Intellectual Cooperation. Through these bodies, the League campaigned to end child labour and slavery, eradicate leprosy and malaria, improve the rights of women, repatriate or resettle refugees, and promote freedom of intellectual life and speech in countries where they were under threat.

The League of Nations was headquartered in Geneva, Switzerland, and its main aim was to create a forum for resolving international disputes. Yet, despite the fact that its charter was grounded in a proposal passionately advocated by President Woodrow Wilson, the United States never joined the League—one of the many causes of its eventual demise.

Moorhouse's fascination with the League is rooted in the grand and idealistic nature of the organisation's ambitions. The League embodies many of the themes that traverse his work: the question of how many rules are necessary to maintain civility; how we might live respectfully with difference; the relationship between nationalism and internationalism; and the balance between private rights and public accountability. The

League of Nations appealed to Moorhouse because of the sheer scale of its ambition: it was, after all, an attempt to design civilised, workable rules for living for the entire planet.

Moorhouse began work on the book in Geneva at the League of Nations archive after winning a $150,000 Australia Council Creative Fellowship, also known as the Keating Fellowship after the then prime minister. He worked with the guidance of the remarkable Swedish archivist Sven Welander. Moorhouse became obsessed with the archive:

> There was something intoxicating about opening file after file, 12 kilometres of them, many unopened for 70 years. And it wasn't only files. There were gifts people had sent to the League of Nations from around the world because the idea of the League had captured the imagination of the world. They'd sent drawings of the robes for the judges of a world court, uniforms for a world police force and paintings for the walls of a whole building, the Palais des Nations. Nation states offered to furnish whole rooms; Australia offered a podium and the wood panelling to go behind that podium.

The League of Nations Museum, housed at the Palais des Nations, sits on Lac Leman, a crescent-shaped lake shared by France and Switzerland and overlooked by the Alps. Geneva, a Swiss city at its southern tip, is a cosmopolitan hub of diplomacy and high-end dining and shopping on charming cobblestoned streets. The Palais des Nations is now home to the Geneva office of the United Nations, which was established in the wake of the League's collapse.

The political historian Lenore Coltheart was teaching at the University of Adelaide in the 1990s and had formed a plan to go to the League of Nations archive in Geneva and the United Nations archive in New York to research the Australian women who had worked there. 'This was a very unusual topic,' she says. 'No one really wanted to know about the League of Nations. Nobody really cared about the Australian women involved in it and I was completely fascinated by it.' Then she read a newspaper article about the imminent publication of *Grand Days*. 'I thought, "He's stolen my idea. How could he? He couldn't really be doing this."'

It is testament to Coltheart's intellectual generosity that she got hold of a review copy of *Grand Days*, read it and reviewed it in glowing terms for the *Current Affairs Bulletin*. Moorhouse contacted her to thank her, they met for a drink and he emailed her all his contacts in Geneva. They became good friends and shared their research.

Coltheart makes an interesting connection between Moorhouse's focus on the politics of Edith's private life and how it connects to the larger political mission of the League. She sees Edith as engaged with an attempt to manage the 'federation of selves', a reference to the fact that, as she and Moorhouse both see it, 'we are not all one person'.

'You need to be able to govern your federation of selves in order to be able to be equal and have equal relationships with people around you,' she explains, 'and to deal fairly in a republican style with them . . . Only when we do that can we actually expect that we might have a national government that acts justly, [and] only when we do that can we actually think that we will have a federated world.'

Coltheart researched the remarkably significant role women played in the League of Nations more broadly, primed by the International Women's Movement of the 19th century.

'These women's organisations were actually meeting in Paris while the Versailles conference was going on, and they were feeding stuff into the Versailles conference, including a clause in the Covenant of the League of Nations that women would be employed equally. I mean, often it was breached more than it was served, but it was how some women, like Dame Rachel Crowdy from Britain, got on the secretariat and how Edith would have got onto it too. In real history there was always an Australian woman on Australia's delegations to the League.'

In conceiving of Edith, Moorhouse said, he was consciously influenced by strong women he had encountered in his life, including his mother, Purth. He was interested in early feminists such as Louisa Lawson, and, as we have seen, lived through the rise of second-wave feminism. Brian Kiernan also sees in the character of Edith the influence of a long literary tradition that has seen many male authors centre their novels on headstrong young female protagonists:

> *Grand Days* and its stand-alone sequel have grand themes and invoke some grand conventions. In its broadest outline, the narrative is akin to that which Balzac, Flaubert (who are alluded to, but so are Voltaire and Swift, Oscar Wilde and Lewis Carroll) and hundreds of other novelists worked their variations on the 19th century: the story of a young person from the provinces who aspires to make it in the metropolis against a background of tumultuous political events; the novel of a sentimental education, and of lost illusions, with the added twist of Henry James's 'international theme' of new-world innocence and a 'superstitious veneration' of Europe encountering the reality, and the decadence, of the old.

While Moorhouse was researching *Grand Days* and seeking a shape for his young protagonist Edith, the archivist at the League of Nations directed his attention to the career of a young Canadian woman, Mary McGeachy, who 'was an ambitious and productive officer who made suggestions and involved herself in in-house arguments'. Her files had remained largely unopened for 50 years. Moorhouse became fascinated by her and saw in her a model for his heroine.

While working in the archive, he lived for a time in the French town of Besançon. There he met a Canadian couple, Flora and Don Harris, and told them about his fascination with McGeachy. To his astonishment, they knew a McGeachy family from Sarina, the town where Mary McGeachy grew up. An address was procured, and a year later Moorhouse received a letter from one of her relatives, who had located Mary living in upstate New York. Moorhouse was amazed she was still alive. As soon as he could, Moorhouse got on a plane to meet her. He describes his first visit:

> Mary McGeachy was sitting in a chair in her night dress and robe, in the living room of a timber house looking out over the Adirondacks. I walked across the room, tight with almost unbearable anticipation. I knew so much about this woman, both factually and by imaginative construction. It was hard for me to accept that she did not, in turn, know me . . . By touching her hand, I was pulled back through the mirror of history.

Each day he went to see her, she'd forgotten who he was, but every day she recalled in loving detail her apartment in Geneva at 30 Place du Bourg-de-Four, from where she could walk to work at the Palais Wilson. By the time McGeachy joined the League at the beginning of 1929, its secretariat had grown from 120 to 300 people. At its largest, in the 1930s, it reached 1500.

McGeachy, like Edith, did not resile from conflict or debate when an issue mattered to her. In 1935, she helped initiate the Equal Rights Treaty, which aimed at removing all legislative restrictions on a woman's right to work. A fine gesture, but not one that translated into genuine equality for women in the workplace, not even at the League.

Despite her role at the League and her earnest commitment to social justice, McGeachy, like Edith, was not above a bit of subversive fun. She told Moorhouse that, for a time, she shared her apartment with a younger woman, an Irish painter named Gill Lyall. 'Gill was known as a naughty girl,' she said. 'Naughty girls are the best companions.' McGeachy's son-in-law David also told Moorhouse that she had once asked him to make her a drink from dry and sweet vermouth with a dash of vodka. Moorhouse recognised it as a Gin Turin, a Genevan forerunner of the martini, 'drunk by the bon viveurs in the bar of the Bavaria [a League haunt] in the 1920s'.

After his visit to McGeachy, Moorhouse learnt that Stella Zilliacus—the daughter of Konni Zilliacus, who worked with McGeachy in the information section of the League—was also writing a book on the period. They met in London, and Moorhouse informed her that he had interviewed McGeachy. She responded: 'She was my father's mistress. I believe she had a child by him.' It's an extraordinary story, but one which Moorhouse declined to explore further. 'My role as a researching fiction writer on this matter had reached a professional boundary,' he writes, 'and I had to now go off in the direction of my fictional work.'

Edith Campbell Berry is Moorhouse's most fully realised character, though interestingly one whose physical attributes remain
sketchy. It is not until halfway through *Grand Days* that we learn
she has red hair and the vestige of girlish freckles. We know she is
elegant—or at least has learnt elegance. But we know more about
her taste in clothing and lingerie than we do about her figure,
the colour of her eyes or her smile. It is a lacuna that allows the
author to play more fully and more promiscuously with her
symbolic function in narrative terms—as well as allowing each
reader the freedom to imagine their own Edith.

One of her symbolic functions, arguably, is as a cipher for the
League itself. Edith, like the League, has embarked on an idealistic journey to become a citizen of the globe, one that involves
her in uncertain reflections on the relevance of nationality in
an increasingly international world. Her careful and constant
internal testing of her comportment in meetings and social
gatherings is an echo of the League's high-minded attention to
the detail of international agreements—sometimes to the point
of absurdity, at least in hindsight.

As an example—one that clearly amused Moorhouse—the
League attempted to standardise and simplify the Gregorian
calendar. In *Grand Days*, Edith attends the meetings of the
General Transit Committee, which has been tasked with this
project.

> Frankly, she didn't care one way or another and was willing to
> accept that thirteen equal months of four complete weeks each
> might be best for the world. It was obvious that for the world
> to work together it had to have one calendar . . . Sometimes

she despaired. China had its own calendar and was totally opposed to calendar reform and the Pope didn't want to fix Easter.

Edith's idealism and deep faith in the League's mission is often challenged but never entirely shaken. Moorhouse imbues her with a sense of the absurd and a talent for self-reflection that tempers her impulse to self-righteousness. The writer and social and political commentator Annabel Crabb is the best-known member of what she calls the Edith Campbell Berry fan club. In 2012, she led a panel at the Sydney Writers' Festival titled 'What Would Edith Do?'. During the discussion, she shared her thoughts on what makes Edith so appealing to contemporary women:

> She's like a living person. Part of it is that among female readers is that joy of finding a [female] character who is complicated, who's appealing, is clever, but fallible. Of whom a point is not being made that women are reckless, or that women are wise, or that women are virtuous, or that women are stupid, because Edith is all those things at various times. She feels like a gift to me.

In his review of *Grand Days*, the literary critic Ivor Indyk argues that Moorhouse's choice of a central female character places Edith firmly in a literary tradition:

> At least since Samuel Richardson back in the 18th century, the Protestant literary imagination seems to have been fixed by the figure of the young woman poised on the verge of sexual experience, for in this way it can countenance desire while

espousing innocence, and contemplate transgression without relinquishing propriety.

For Moorhouse, one of the great joys of writing about the League of Nations and of creating a character who could channel his passions in Edith was the attention to aesthetic detail that characterised the League's grand mission. Moorhouse had an unusually high tolerance for technical detail: for the proper conduct of meetings, the protocols of governance and the role aesthetics and ceremony play in setting the stage for negotiation. Edith has a similar fascination with the proper conduct of meetings and the protocols that guide them.

> She thought of committees as parlour games where each person's contribution was their throw of the dice from which followed certain moves around the board. For her, commit-tees were the Great Basic Unit. When you understood the workings of a committee, John Latham [her mentor] said, you understood the workings of an empire.

She also believes in the subtle role that aesthetics play in social discourse. Helping to organise a conference preparing for the Disarmament Commission, she insists that the delegates are provided with custom-designed blotters and stationery stands. She explains their purpose to her colleague:

> 'And that, dear Cooper, also explains why we have the leather blotters instead of say, leatherette . . . because the objects that people handle determine how they treat themselves, how they treat each other, and treat the things they are treating. The appropriate objects can cause people to be more contemplative.'

Through the character of Edith, Moorhouse is expanding in a more considered way on habits he satirises in his earlier work, including *Conference-ville*. The narrator, who is clearly a version of the author himself, arrives at a conference on a never-revealed topic to do social and intellectual battle with an eclectic assortment of academics, writers, activists and community group representatives. He arrives on the first day of sessions early and armed with a method: Horne's Rule of Diligence—Miss nothing and take one of everything:

> Half seriously, Horne's Rule of commitment-to-the-total-experience helped overcome the temptation to skip a paper because I'd 'heard it all before' or to linger over lunch and slide into afternoon drinking. Predictions about papers were always partially wrong. Usually something unexpected in the most predictable of occasions. I used the rule too, to take me into social situations which I might have backed out of. It yielded some rewards, the undoctored experience—and also led me into a lot of wasted and tiresome times.

In *Grand Days*, Edith sets out for Geneva armed with a set of rules of comportment to ward off professional, social or personal risk. On the train:

> She moved, in what she felt was a gathered-together way, along to the dining car, having remembered not to leave anything of value back at her seat, even if it were a first-class seat, and yet not having things in her hands—something she had a phobia about, having too many things in her hands. To have free hands allowed her to ward and hold, which she considered important in the technique of travelling. It could be considered as one of her Ways of Going.

One of Moorhouse's long-term partners recognised strong echoes of the author in this description when we talked about overseas trips she'd taken with Moorhouse. He was, she said with affection, '[e]xasperating to travel with. Obsessive to the point of bloody paranoia.' This obsessiveness served him well, however, when he was working in the archive. His novels are testament to the fact that he approached his task with extra-ordinary patience and diligence. He said he wanted to make sure everything was as factual as possible, 'right down to the furniture they used in the Palais des Nations, or the food they ate and the cutlery they used'.

In his review of *Grand Days*, literary critic Ivor Indyk observes that:

> . . . the league is a grand metaphor, in Moorhouse's hands, for the way people act in their most intimate moments. Moorhouse has always been fascinated with the conference, or the committee, as a model of human life. Life makes his characters nervous: they retreat; they advance; they engage in elaborate manoeuvres; finally, they seek to negotiate.

According to David Marr, Moorhouse is 'a master of one of the things that great novelists do and are not given enough credit for, which is to vet etiquette. Tolstoy is full of etiquette. Austen is full of etiquette . . . the meanings of formal behaviour. [Moorhouse] is fantastic at that.' Marr agrees that the League of Nations trilogy is an extension of a key underlying conceptual theme in Moorhouse's work: 'Yes, etiquette for the world, this is how nations will behave. He sees the absurdity of it, he sees the value of it, he sees the way in which you can define character by failing to live up to, or living up to, those rules.'

———

In *Grand Days*, Edith's idealism about the League is challenged as she begins to encounter the unhinged and eccentric elements in society who are drawn to Grand Schemes. She meets an American man who introduces himself to her unbidden at a cafe as Captain Strongbow, 'Strongbow by name and Strongbow by nature'. With his 'associate' Mr Kennedy, he has come to Geneva, he says, on a very special mission, on which he is seeking her assistance.

> 'We have come to Geneva to aid the League. There are people out there,' he waved, gesturing Out There, 'who do not want the League of Nations to succeed, who would indeed stand to lose billions of dollars if peace came to this earth. Billions of dollars. I speak not only of the armaments manufacturers.'

As their conversation progresses, Edith becomes uncertain, in a way that is surely familiar to anyone who has worked as a serious journalist, as to whether Captain Strongbow is a passionate idealist or an utter crackpot.

> 'You think there are people who would try to harm us?' She was attentive now.
> 'I know they will. They will try to kill you. At least to assassinate those at the top, and maybe all sorts of violence will be brought to bear upon you.' Captain Strongbow said this with much emphasis.
> 'Your building may be exploded, for one thing,' Mr Kennedy put in.
> 'Hence I have plans. I have plans for an international police army. Empowered by our President Coolidge . . .'

'By President Coolidge?'

'President Coolidge. President Coolidge said that an international police force was now needed. I have designed a uniform. I have an insignia.'

Edith discovers she has serious reservations about people who design uniforms and flags unasked. 'That reservation was perhaps unreasonable, but the League had encountered a number of people who designed flags unasked and they were rarely somehow—well, on the right track.'

The reference to Calvin Coolidge, who was in office from 1923 to 1929, is an intimation of the notorious ambivalence with which US politicians regarded the League of Nations. Despite President Woodrow Wilson being the principal author of the Covenant of the League of Nations, domestic opposition undermined his efforts to bring the United States into the League as a member state. Chief among the objections was Article 10 of the covenant, which committed member states to give assistance to any member who experienced external aggression. Even Wilson himself remained conflicted, as League of Nations scholar Gary Ostrower writes:

> Wilson, along with many other internationalists, remained ambivalent about force during these years. He had not thought through the risks of collective security. Wilson at times demanded a League with 'teeth', fearing that without Article 10 the organisation would be 'hardly more than an influential debating society'. At other times, he feared substituting 'international militarism for national militarism'.

After Wilson's defeat, Coolidge kept the United States out of the League, but he engaged with foreign leaders and sponsored the Kellogg–Briand Pact of 1928, an international treaty in which the signatories resolved not to use war to resolve conflict.

Towards the end of *Grand Days*, as the League increasingly faces challenges to its idealistic vision for a world united against war, an aura of disorder and disarray shadows its mission. Edith begins to wonder if folly necessarily stalks all grand schemes. Her fears are exacerbated when Ambrose suffers a somewhat spectacular nervous breakdown after he is unmasked as a British spy. He requests an opportunity to give a presentation to the League's directors' meeting, and there he announces that he has discovered the 'key' to all humanity's predicaments in a field of hay while holidaying in Wiltshire. With great excitement, he gets to his feet and announces:

> 'While on leave, I saw an invention and was struck by the whole philosophical and organic connection to this one invention and I said to myself, "Why, here it is!" We look to conferences and assemblies and parliaments to solve the calamities of the human condition when here before our very eyes . . . here then was the answer, in a field of hay . . .
>
> 'I saw the answer to all to which we have dedicated our lives: the simple invention which will revolutionise all our lives— trust the British to come up with it, I thought—gentlemen, ladies, this invention is the New Century Hay Sweep.'

Needless to say, he is sent off to a clinic to recuperate from what was understood at the time as a 'nervous collapse'.

Moorhouse clearly invested Ambrose with some of his own tendencies, and not just his penchant for cross-dressing. Throughout his life, Moorhouse was attracted to extravagant projects. It was never entirely clear when he was being serious and when he was being playful. Once, when I was interviewing him for this book over lunch at a restaurant, I asked him about his attitude to monogamy.

'Doesn't work,' he said at first, before pausing and calling a waiter over. He asked for napkins and a pen. 'I've solved the problem,' he said with a straight face. 'We can make monogamy work. We just have to design the right sort of house.' The rest of the lunch was spent designing the Monogamy House, which, in the end, had 30 storeys and his and hers flossing rooms.

Perhaps the most audacious grand scheme Moorhouse embarked on was his plan to build a theme park called Cape Mythical National Park in the late 1990s. In typical Moorhouse fashion, the project began on a whim—almost as a joke—and then quickly evolved into a serious proposal for which he sought private funding. Cape Mythical National Park both celebrated and played in an ironic manner with the role nature plays in the Australian imaginary. Every element of the museum was designed to be incorporated into the visitor experience, including the queue for entry, a visit to the toilet and the ticket sales.

In his proposal, he wrote: 'The queue is a place to begin to engage the audience. Buskers, tv screens with introductory material including say, bacteria from the railing. "Railing Germs" sold in packages—bacteria collected from the railing. The toilet and the point of sale of tickets will be a created "activity".'

Indeed, all elements of the theme park were designed to be themselves exhibits. The signs were to be 'grouted in the way National Park signs are all over the world' and 'contain spelling and other errors, illusionism and trompe l'oeil'. There was also a 'STAFF ONLY' door designed to be left open a crack so visitors could steal a glimpse 'behind the scenes'. On entry to the park, visitors were to be greeted by attendants dressed as rangers.

'The entrance would establish the National Park tone and philosophy of "cared for" nature, nature as spectacle, the new relationship we have to nature were we to come to it as a "visitor", and the idea of public "ownership" of nature,' Moorhouse wrote in his proposal.

This play with the role nature performs in our cultural imaginaries was extended by animatronic creations described in the proposal as 'Ti-kangaroos', which are found throughout the park. Moorhouse described them this way:

They will truly embody the spirit of the Park. They will be irreverent; they will be good natured; they will infuriatingly contradict many of the ways we look at animals and at nature. They will make fun of our ways of looking at animals and nature. Ti-kangaroos also embody the human dream of being able to talk with animals, to find out their natures through speech.

The park itself was structured around a series of strange and mythical exhibits, which combined a genuine affection for the Anglo-Australian relationship to the bush and to history with ironic commentary. 'The Dog in the Back of a Ute' exhibit was described as follows:

The great Australian Dog in the Back of a Ute will also make an appearance. It will be delightful but the dog may have some things to say about being in the back of the ute. The dog and cat are the closest the human species comes to 'knowing' animals and to having intimacy with them. The Dog in the Back of a Ute is one of the most endearing Australian images of this.

There was a darker edge to the 'Shooting Gallery' exhibit, where endangered species are 'shot' in the tradition of amusement park shooting galleries. The park also incorporated a National Museum of Ideas:

This will use Donald Horne's book [*The*] *Avenue of the Fair Go* as a basis for a set of exhibits. The book has a 'tour' through the political thought of Australia with places such as The Garden of Mateship, Sights and Sounds of the British Empire, the Manning Clark Memorial Verandah, and the Chamber of Racist Horrors.

A number of the exhibits focused on the Australian experience of the bush and the way weather animates our relationship to it. 'Stormy Day at Dusk' recreated an electrical storm in the bush at dusk:

This will be a truly frightening installation with light, sound, and smells recreating an electrical storm in the bush at dusk . . . This will be the first of the 'weather' experiences in the park and will also use weather lore, the weather as art, the weather as spectacle, the weather as 'news'. It will celebrate the impact and place of climate and weather in our experience of this continent of fire or flood . . . As with nature, weather is distilled into a 'visit'.

'Hot Day in the Desert Which Becomes Cold Day in the Desert' was the second of the weather experiences and 'should be a wonderous stand-and-gape-and-feel sensory experience'. The final weather experience was 'Hot Day in the Bush Which Becomes Nice Day in the Bush'. It took place in a 'typical outback setting with intense temperatures and glare which dissolves into, and concludes with, the theme of the "nice day"'.

Finally, guests had an opportunity to visit natural mineral springs and thermal baths dubbed the 'Aphrodisiac Springs'. Visitors were issued with a caution:

> A word of warning: the Eastern Spring or 'Spring of Licentious Waters' is clinically classified as an aphrodisiac of consider-able strength and the Cape Mythical National Park Authority require the signing of a waiver of responsibility and indem-nity before permitting visitors to sample the waters. The water from this spring is not, repeat, NOT to be offered to the Ti-Kangaroos.

Cape Mythical National Park never attracted the necessary venture capital, despite Moorhouse's serious efforts to pitch the idea to potential investors. But it is interesting precisely because it illustrates the way Moorhouse always worked with large ambitions to bring the workings of the creative mind to life—to externalise it and make it breathe. In a sense, his fascination with the League of Nations was born out of his respect for the sheer implausibility of implementing such an idealistic and grand scheme—of creating rules for a civilised world.

———

By the end of *Grand Days*, a different and far darker grand scheme is brewing in Germany with the rise of Hitler and the Nazi Party. As the dark clouds of ultranationalism and fascism begin to gather on the European horizon, Edith reflects in a far less abstract manner on the circumstances of those who did not choose to become stateless. It's a revelation that casts a long shadow over her idealistic view of the League of Nations as an organisation poised to override the nation-state and bring about a global conversation.

She goes to the Molly Club with Ambrose and meets a man named Mr Huneeus, who tells her he is from Azerbaijan and is a refugee. He supposes the Molly Club is a haven for other sorts of refugees, for refugees from social and sexual norms. A rupture in this netherworld comes soon after this exchange, when ten youths with black armbands burst into the club and begin assaulting the patrons.

In *Grand Days* and *Dark Palace*, Moorhouse used the Molly Club as a device to draw an explicit link between the persecution of Jewish people and the internment of those the Nazis saw as sexually 'perverse' or 'unnatural'. Moorhouse pointedly designs the Molly Club as a haven for refugees and those escaping persecution. It stands as a symbol of honourable disorder, in contrast to the perverted fascistic obsession with order.

In his review of *Dark Palace*, Brian Kiernan argues that the Molly Club, concealed in the heart of staid Geneva, is a source of comedy until:

> Local fascist youths burst in to molest the clientele, and (in *Dark Palace*) refugees from Nazi Germany begin to arrive with stories of the persecution of homosexuals and Jews, of the sickness erupting in the depths of the seemingly rational German psyche. Bernard, the proprietor, and club members liaise secretly with the Red Cross to set up escape routes for the refugees. It is not the respectable Swiss burghers but the city's 'deviants' who act sympathetically and altruistically in this confusing situation.

Ultimately, Ambrose and the regulars of the Molly Club allowed Moorhouse to explore a theme that arguably runs through all of his work—and that animated his own life. When does a focus on rational order and the rules of civility become infected with the desire to control and subjugate anyone who doesn't comply? And what can we learn when we explore our irrational and instinctual human depths? Throughout the trilogy, Edith is torn between two impulses—she is at once the idealist who believes that the League of Nations can make rational rules to secure global peace and cooperation, and a woman who feels stifled by the conformity of conventional marriage and the constraints of her gender.

At one point Edith plans a picnic to accommodate and engage the non-diplomats who have come to Geneva with petitions and pleas for the Disarmament Conference. In typical Edith (and Moorhouse) fashion, she obsessively plans the colour scheme, the food and the drink. It is, somewhat strangely, an indoor picnic in the American library. She hopes that 'the seating arrangements might shake them out of their pious poses. Change the chairs: change the mentality. Edith's Rule.' In a metaphor for the League's attempts to fashion order out of the chaos which defined World War I, Edith's well-planned picnic rapidly descends into unexpected disorder when it is gate-crashed by mutilated veterans looking for food and booze.

This incident is echoed some years later, when Edith visits Australia to give a talk and see her family and is approached by Scraper Smith, a man from her university days, who is now hideously disfigured as a result of World War I. He manipulates Edith into masturbating him. She complies while fighting down her repugnance. She later discovers that her perfectly chosen suit, bought from a designer boutique in Europe, is now stained with semen. Moorhouse may have been fascinated by rules and well-laid plans, but he was perhaps even more fascinated by things going wrong—by 'what happens', as he once said, 'when we tip it all up'.

Kiernan comments: 'Such disruption of the codes, social and literary, already established is characteristic of Moorhouse's fiction. He is fascinated by rules, procedures, conventions of all kinds—each with its own lexicon—but equally by their limitations in the face of the unexpected, as complex interactions create confusion.'

As *Dark Palace* progresses, Edith finds herself operating as a double agent, spying on the secretary-general, Joseph Avenol, who panicked after war broke out and began issuing contradictory instructions about evacuating the League or making a stand. He even flirted openly with the idea of handing the League over to the Germans. A staff rebellion, led by the Irish deputy secretary, General Sean Lester, sidelined him. Amazingly, despite the imminent fall of Paris and declarations of war by France and England, the League had continued to operate according to its normal calendar of meetings. Moorhouse described what he found in the archive from this period as like 'watching a whole bureaucracy sleep-walk towards disaster'.

Edith comes to work one day only to discover maintenance workmen painting red arrows on the wall, which show the way to basements that can be used as shelters during air raids. There is great irony in the fact that a building designed to represent a grand scheme to secure peace for the world is now protecting itself from the very thing those it housed were dedicated to preventing.

Moorhouse asked Mary McGeachy to recollect those dark times during which she helped organise the flight of League personnel from Geneva through Portugal. 'These were sad days,' she told him. 'Grim days. We weren't the cause of it. We were not the only thing that cracked apart. The whole world cracked apart.' Moorhouse countered that the League had been set up to stop the world cracking apart. 'We were never strong enough,' she replied.

In 1946, the last Assembly of the League of Nations met in Geneva, and the League was dissolved. The Palais des Nations was handed over to the new United Nations. By the time he was finishing *Dark Palace* and searching the archive to document the ruin of the League's grand ambitions, Moorhouse said, he had come to identify so closely with Edith and her compatriots that he felt devastated as he wrote the final chapters of the book.

The ultimate ignominy comes when the members of the League delegation arrive to witness the first conference of the United Nations and discover that they have not been allocated seats on the floor. History has shut the door on the League.

It was an affront that made Moorhouse all the more determined to prise that door open. Towards the end of the writing of *Grand Days*, he said in a number of interviews that he was finished with Edith—that he had said everything he had to say about her. That is, until he started thinking about the birth of Canberra and a different design for democracy in a corner of the world far removed from Europe.

Bushwalking in the Budawang Range in the mid-1980s.

Frank with Meg Stewart at Mario Percuoco's Pulcinella Restaurant, 1982.

Clockwise from left: Brian Kiernan, Fiona Giles, Donald Horne, Helena Carr, Don Anderson, Frank Moorhouse, Monique Delamotte, Jean-Paul Delamotte, Suzanne Kiernan, Bob Carr and Myfanwy Horne. Pavilion Restaurant, Domain, 1986.

Don Anderson, Frank Moorhouse and Fiona Giles. Pavilion Restaurant, Domain, 1986.

Frank with Fiona Giles. River Cherwell, Oxford, c. 1986.

Moorhouse as toastmaster at a dinner to mark the 145th year of the Stenhouse Circle. Dick Hall, Susie Carleton, Peter Carey and Alison Summers. Riverview Hotel, Balmain, 1989.

Frank Moorhouse, Ross Steele, Monique Delamotte, Gough Whitlam, Fiona Giles, Jean-Paul Delamotte and Margaret Whitlam, 1987.

Entered into the 1985 Cannes Film Festival, Dušan Makavejev's film *Coca-Cola Kid* is based on short stories in *The Americans, Baby* and *The Electrical Experience* by Frank Moorhouse. Screenplay by Frank Moorhouse, with local acting talent including Max Gillies, Tim Finn, Chris Haywood, Bill Kerr, Kris McQuade, Greta Scacchi and Esben Storm.

ABC TV: Peter Allen, Clive James and Frank Moorhouse, 1990.

With his publisher Jane Palfreyman at the launch of *Dark Palace*, 2000.

Frank with Tim Herbert at the Seahorse Ball, Sydney, 2000.

Xavier Hennekinne, unknown diner, Frank Moorhouse, Tim Herbert and Julia Leigh at Chinatown's BBQ King in 2001.

Frank with his friend and patron Carol Dettmann.

With brothers Arthur and Owen at the Royal Automobile Club, 2021.

Statement to the French journal *Liberation*.

GA
020
INTLX 0641547 *
PUBTLX AA62614
GA
42641917+
TELELIB 641917F
064 0649 *
PUBTLX AA62614

CANBERRA PUBLIC TELEX 5/3/85

TLX 641917 PARIS ATTN DANIEL RONDEAU

MY WRITING ALLOWS ME FLIGHT FROM SOCIETY THROUGH SOLITUDE WHILE
PERMITTING ME TO REJOIN THE SOCIETY ON SOME OF MY OWN TERMS THROUGH
THE TRADING OF THE FINISHED WORK WITH THE SOCIETY.
MY IMAGINATIVE NARRATIVE GIVES ME RELIEF FROM PREVAILITY AND STRIDENT
IDEOLOGIES BY ALLOWING ME THE HERESY OF DECADENCE (AS IN EROTICA)
NAMELY, REVENGE AGAINST NORMALITY, REVERSAL OF NORMALITY AND
REGRESSION FROM NORMALITY.
MY IMAGINATIVE NARRATIVE IS RELIEF FROM PREVAILING SELF BY ALLOWING
THE POTENTIAL SELF, THE DISCARDED SELF, THE REJECTED SELF AND THE
NON - SELF TO HAVE PLAY.
MY IMAGINATIVE NARRATIVE (AS WITH NEW BIOGRAPHY AND AUTOBIOGRAPHY)
IS RELIEF FROM PRIVACY BY ALLOWING EXPOSURE OF SELF AND THE NETWORK
OF SELF.
FRANK MOORHOUSE

*
TELELIB 641917F
PUBTLX AA62614

7

DESIGNING A NATION

On a stainless spring day, I sat with Frank Moorhouse in the restaurant of the National Museum of Australia looking out onto the rolling green lawn which runs down to the lake. Two children tumbled into view, charmingly dressed in overalls and striped T-shirts, and began performing their amateur gymnastics. A small dog ran delightedly around them in circles.

Moorhouse remarked: 'What terrific acting in children so young. I'd love to meet the casting director.'

Moorhouse was always fascinated by performance, specifically the performance of self, shaped by social norms, rituals and status. Much of his writing is carved out of an ironic account of the absurdity of the self-conscious way we play our roles in various aspects of our lives. He was fascinated by how social and cultural contexts, including the language we speak, shape us, and alternatively constrain or enable us. His interest in the performance of identity is evident very early on in his short stories, specifically in his focus on how group identity on the left is (often pretentiously) acted out in social situations.

In *The Americans, Baby*, Moorhouse offers up this vignette of a party thrown in honour of a visiting radical American poet, which vibrates with status anxiety:

'What are you guys doing in the way of protest these days?' he asks . . . We try now to think about protest.

'Actually we don't hold much interest in protest these days,' says Wayne.

These days of all days, I think, these days of rapid dehumanisation and change. And we choose to relax on protest. Our lives, I observe, are spent wading against trend.

'Some of us might be what you call existential protestors,' I say, 'but not reformist protestors.' Everyone in the room looks at me except Gillian who looks at the ceiling. 'We see the protest thing more as a permanent thing—you know . . . a way of life . . . in conflict with the authoritarian nature of society,' Cooper puts in.

The rest look at him gratefully.

We walk up the historical elevator the wrong way. That's what we do. 'That's our bag,' I say, but no one admits to hearing me.

'That's our bag,' I say.

Gillian makes a nauseated face.

'Oh, you people should see what the Provos are doing,' his secretary says, with the enervating enthusiasm common to American business executives, folk singers, and tourists.

When Edith sets out for Geneva in *Grand Days*, she is an anxious young woman from Jasper's Brush who is acutely self-conscious about her lack of worldliness and whether she is comporting herself 'appropriately'. On her return to Australia in the final book of the trilogy, *Cold Light*, she encounters the opposite problem.

> She knew that if you were someone who had Lived Abroad, there were socially acceptable ways of talking about Australia—but as for Canberra, she was still uncertain of what was permitted in the way of jokes by those who lived there. There was one way of talking when speaking to another person who had travelled or lived abroad, and another if you were speaking to an Australian who hadn't travelled. There was yet another way of speaking if you were driven to flaunting your worldliness by exasperation or irritation because of arrant provincialism.

In Geneva, Edith reinvented herself, a country girl, as a cosmopolitan. As the philosopher Martha C. Nussbaum explains in her book *The Cosmopolitan Tradition*, the phrase originates with the Greek philosopher Diogenes the Cynic, who, when asked where he came from, answered with a single word— kosmopolitês—meaning 'a citizen of the world'. Nussbaum writes of this position:

> A Greek male refuses the invitation to define himself by lineage, city, social class, even free birth, even gender. He insists on defining himself in terms of a characteristic that he shares with all other human beings, male and female, Greek and non-Greek, slave and free. And by calling himself not simply a dweller in the world but a citizen of the world, Diogenes suggests, as well, the possibility of a politics, or a

moral approach to politics, that focuses on the humanity we share rather than the marks of local origin, status, class and gender that divide us.

Edith arrives back in Australia in 1950 with her British husband, Ambrose. 'Now she was back from the oldest cities in the world to live in the newest city of the world—she had moved from trying to make a world capital in Geneva to a dusty town that was trying to become a national capital.' Soon after her arrival, she meets up with her brother Frederick, who is a communist and whom she hasn't seen since his late teens. She observes that he disappeared on her. He replies: 'But didn't you do the same, Edith? . . . For God's sake, you ran to the other side of the world to find where you belonged.'

In *Cold Light*, Moorhouse unpacks and clarifies many of the themes embedded in the first two books in the trilogy: the tension between national identity and a global order, the insecurity that arguably lives in the heart of Australian nationhood, and the more personal question of how to live as an experienced and politically progressive woman in a conservative society. Edith is both a cipher for an emerging Australia and ultimately, as I'll argue in this chapter, a cipher for the author himself. Though Moorhouse often said he based Edith Campbell Berry on his mother, *Cold Light* reveals a more complex relationship between the author and his protagonist. Many of the challenges, intellectual, personal and political, which Edith confronts in this final book are echoes of challenges Moorhouse had faced himself and written and spoken about.

Early in *Cold Light*, Edith's brother lectures her about communist ideology. She changes the subject to their relationship.

'What should we do about us? Us—as brother and sister?'

'*What, then, is to be done?*' He looked at her as if assessing a painting in an art museum. 'I have thought about this. At first, I thought it was better that we not meet. But we have to face the objective reality: we are indeed brother and sister and we live in the same town. But what is the question? Can a consciousness be developed from this relationship that will benefit us?'

He continued looking at her with unblinking eyes. 'Do you follow me?'

Did he always talk like this?

Moorhouse had been, at times in his life, deeply involved with the socialist left and was indeed sympathetic, as Edith is, to many of the motivations that drive the broad, if fractured, socialist project. But like Edith, he had a strong dislike of ideological groupthink and the moral certainty and self-righteousness that sometimes characterises leftist movements (as much as it also can on the conservative side of politics). Moorhouse, as we have seen earlier in this book, was a sceptical leftist—a political progressive who eschewed black and white prescriptions for living and pompous polemic rhetoric on both the left and the right.

In *Cold Light*, Edith gives voice to this sentiment and her ambivalence about the seductions of hardcore ideology:

Over the years with Janice and Frederick, and in discussions with Ambrose and people at the League, she had come to understand the seductions of a Great Cause for those who wanted to live an all-embracing, all-knowing commitment. The right way to live.

Frederick's lover, Janice, is a cleaner at the hotel where Edith and Ambrose settle while they are looking for a house. She comes from an upper-middle-class family, attended a private school and secretly enjoys a bit of bourgeois decadence, despite her allegiance to the Communist Party. Janice tells Edith that the Party is campaigning to have US comic books banned.

'Being dumped here—putting Australian artists out of work. Children shouldn't be brought up to be Americans.'

'I don't remember Australian comics when I was a child. Only *Ginger Meggs*.'

'And you must have read *Snugglepot and Cuddlepie*?'

'Oh, yes, of course.'

How could a little girl who read *Snugglepot and Cuddlepie* become a communist?

The Australian campaign to ban US comic books was led by a far greater diversity of groups than the Communist Party. The crusade against American comics also brought together commercial interests, nationalists, local writers' and artists' unions, racists, religious groups and liberals. The campaign had its origins in duties imposed by Canadian and British customs on remaindered American comics, which resulted in cheap US comics flooding into Australia. As Peter Coleman notes in his book on the history of censorship in Australia, the lobby included the Australian Women's National League, the National Council of Women of Australia, the Housewives' Association of New South Wales, the (wonderfully named) Women's Vigilant Society, the Woman's Christian Temperance Union, the Federation of Parents and Citizens Associations of New South Wales, any number of church organisations, the

Australian Journalists' Association and the Children's Court Magistrates of Victoria.

What this alliance had in common was not only a fear that American culture would colonise a nascent and insecurely established settler Australian culture, but a clearly racially based fear of the Other. Coleman quotes a pamphlet titled 'Mental Rubbish from Overseas' in his book, which claimed that US comics were influenced by African-American culture as well as the 'illiterate and superstitious peoples of Central and Southern Europe' who had migrated to the United States. It stated: 'The negro and his African jungle form no part of our national heritage and consciousness, and we will not have him here, neither in person nor by proxy through the permeation of his culture.' That pamphlet was published by the Sydney Cultural Defence Committee, a left-wing organisation. By the late 1930s, a host of comic books had been banned; they would only begin reappearing in Australian newsagencies in the 1960s.

What the brief exchange between Edith and Janice points to is the parochial and frequently xenophobic instincts that the Australian left of the period shared with the Australian right. Moorhouse's own politics had always been informed by an instinct for the cosmopolitan and an abhorrence of racism. Edith gives voice to his formative political leanings when she tells Janice: 'I suppose I lean more towards Fabian socialism. Or rather, a dreamy Spanish anarchism. In the meantime, I'm a pragmatic kind of democrat.'

Moorhouse once joked with me, when I asked him to specify his political inclinations, that he was a 'left-leaning democratic anarchist'. He was certainly a closet romantic, and anarchism appealed to him precisely because it offered a release from the obligations of keeping order and following instructions, even instructions issued by his unconscious.

In *Forty-Seventeen*, Moorhouse included a short story titled 'Buenaventura Durruti's Funeral'. The narrator says the Antonioni movie *The Passenger* was a 'special film for him'. *The Passenger*, starring Jack Nicholson and Maria Schneider, is about a journalist 'who is approaching forty and who takes on the identity of a casual acquaintance after the acquaintance dies while they are together in a hotel in North Africa. Nicholson lives out the man's life and appointments.' The Nicholson character is in Barcelona, the city in which Durruti and the anarchists originally gained control and sought to have the government delegitimised and wrong-footed. It is there that he meets a young student played by Maria Schneider and drives with her through multiple towns before ultimately meeting his death, in accordance with his stolen identity's destiny, at the Hotel de la Gloria.

The movie resonated with Moorhouse because he was approaching 40 when he met Fiona Giles and took her on a long road trip from Perth. That trip is reprised in 'Buenaventura Durruti's Funeral', in which the narrator talks to the young woman about 'a possible journey to Spain as a homage to the Spanish anarchists and to *The Passenger*':

> She had laughingly refused to take the idea of a pilgrimage to Spain seriously. 'Why should I know anything about the Spanish Civil War—except to know who were good and who were bad?' He did not know whether it was because she thought the pilgrimage unlikely or whether she didn't want to be too much a part of his fantasies.

For Edith, returning to Australia means confronting a nation for which Europe, despite the recent war, remains a distant place, even if most of the population still see their country as tethered to Britain. This Australia is parochial. It is a long way off even beginning to acknowledge the brutal colonisation and dispossession of Indigenous peoples. It's a country in which white Australians are still anxiously attempting to define themselves and their nationhood. Edith masks her cosmopolitan past in case she triggers suspicions that she considers herself superior to those who haven't travelled, worked and lived abroad.

> She was a married woman in, well, midlife. Still with ideas. Over-experienced, too travelled, as they said back here. 'Too travelled' meant a person had been away for too long and was, as a consequence, no longer quite suited to Australia. Someone who had lost their Australianness. Who was a bit foreign.

A man she speaks to at a dinner at the prime minister's residence, the Lodge, observes to her: '"There are those who want us to be as British as can be, and there are some who think we would be better off aping the Americans with their Rotary Clubs, slang, chewing gum and jitterbug, and so on. And bow-ties."'

Much of Australia in the 1950s remained in the grip of a parochial, if not fawning, allegiance to British institutions and customs, which her English husband Ambrose denounces as a sham imitation.

> 'Here we are in this diplomatically insignificant country, playing out petty imitations of distant places—the private schools are imitations; the parliament and courts are

imitations, with their wigs and robes and maces; the HC pretends he's an ambassador, and I pretend to be on ambassadorial duties with him. The whole place has insufficient identity or heritage or skills. The PM and his ministers refer to themselves as Ministers of the Crown, for God's sake. They are role-playing imitations.'

For Edith, the planning of the Australian capital is an opportunity to be part of building a reimagined Australian identity—an identity which is no longer tethered to a colonial past. But Ambrose gives voice to the fear that dogs white Australia at the time: 'There is no history. The "city" is being built before the country has a history. This capitol has planted more trees than it has inhabitants.'

In the 1980s, Paul Taylor, the editor of an influential Australian art theory magazine, *Art & Text*, infamously made a virtue of the Australian fear that the nation was in fact defined by imitation. Generations of artists and critics had champed at the bit to run away to Europe and, in later generations, to America to learn from the avant-garde and establish themselves as culturally relevant, but Taylor made a virtue of the fact that Australians largely learnt about art history from slides—from reproductions. At the dawn of the 1980s postmodern turn in literature and art, which celebrated appropriation and pastiche, Taylor's achievement was to see Australia not as a cultural periphery, but as a country primed to take centre stage at the vanguard of this artistic vision. The superficial, the temporary, the popular and the inauthentic were, in Taylor's view, positive aspects of Australian cultural life.

From a 21st-century perspective, the glaring omission in this postmodern account of Australia is the failure to acknowledge that the country is home to the oldest continuous living culture in the world—that of our First Nations people. It is still a truth that our federal parliament is only beginning to reckon with.

———

A theme to which Moorhouse regularly returned in our later interviews for this book was his deep regret—indeed, shame— that he did not sufficiently understand the history of Indigenous Australians, and particularly their history on the South Coast and how they were treated under colonisation. Prior to European arrival, the part of the Nowra region south of Bomaderry Creek was inhabited by the Wodi-Wodi people of the Yuin Nation, while the region north of Bomaderry Creek was inhabited by the Dharawal people.

In 2000, Moorhouse shared the stage with Germaine Greer at a London literary festival. Greer, who has been an expat since the 1970s, broke down and sobbed when discussing the plight of Indigenous Australians, saying she had been adopted by a tribe of Aboriginal people living in Victoria. Moorhouse, when invited to say something, declined on the grounds that he didn't want to be a white man speaking on behalf of Indigenous Australians. He said he found the tenor of the conversation embarrassing, to which Greer theatrically told him to 'luxuriate in your embarrassment'.

Moorhouse was fascinated to learn belatedly that, in 2015, Jennifer Jones had published a book on the Country Women's Association, including a chapter on his mother and her relationship with his Indigenous carer, Belle McCleod. Given the interest he expressed in the neglect of Indigenous history, the erasure of extensive wrongs perpetrated by settler society on First Nations people and the history of the region he grew up in, it is worth setting out at some length what is currently known about the Indigenous history of the region—at least, what of that history is available to white settlers to know. The First Nations people of that region know far more, of course.

Pre-Invasion, the Shoalhaven River was home to a number of related tribes, divided into family groups of around twenty to 30 people. The 19th-century landscape painter Samuel Elyard depicted an Indigenous gunyah, or hut, in the Shoalhaven area. The first Europeans arrived in the region in the 1790s. Significant colonisation took place in the 1820s, when Alexander Berry took up a grant of 10,000 acres (4050 hectares) beside the Shoalhaven River. The profits to be made from the region, in the form of logging, farming and mining, were swiftly recognised. Australian humanities academic Hilton Penfold writes: 'These capitalist enterprises further operated to dispossess, enslave and displace Jerrinja and other Wandi Wandian tribes from Country.'

Farming and logging practices resulted in a significant loss of Country for Indigenous people, and enslavement and displacement ensued. Penfold notes that in 1879, the 'Roseby Park Aboriginal Reserve' at Orient Point, New South Wales, was declared by the state Aboriginal Protection Board. Penfold writes:

> The site has a long running historical significance for all Jerrinja people because it is nearby to their ancestral burial grounds . . . The establishment of the Aborigines' Protection Board led to the systematic removal of Aboriginal children from their families (Read, 2000). Waters & Moon (2013) identified that Aboriginal children in the Nowra region were frequently moved to the Bombaderry [sic] Children's home.

Jones writes at length about the Nowra Country Women's Association in the 1960s and Moorhouse's mother Purth's involvement in efforts to advance Indigenous people's living conditions. On 1 March 1962, she writes, nearly 30 concerned white citizens, drawn from the left and right of politics, united with Aboriginal people to support the formation of the South Coast Aborigines Advancement League. That meeting included Belle McCleod, who was a foundation member of the Worrigee–Wreck Bay branch of the CWA. McCleod, whom Jones interviewed, lived with the Moorhouse family and helped care for Owen, Arthur and Frank.

Born Isabelle Brown in 1927, Belle McCleod was raised in Aboriginal camps. One of the places she grew up was 'around the Bomaderry swamp. That was a big campsite for our people. They built their tin huts and bag humpies, and that's where we all lived. There was eight in our family.' After Belle graduated as dux of Bomaderry Primary School, the Nowra High School principal approached her father, imploring him to continue Belle's education, but after two years she had to leave school and instead support her family. She secured work with the Moorhouse family. McCleod told Jones:

'Mrs Moorhouse, she was a beautiful old lady, she was really kind. Mr Moorhouse was a nice old man, but a very reserved type of person. Arthur and Owen and Frank, they were only young then . . . Mrs Moorhouse did this bedroom out for me. I can remember that as if it was yesterday, I had this beautiful room and everything was in pink. She treated me like I was one of the family . . . She was more than a friend to me; she was like a mother to me. Even though I had my own mother, but when I used to work for her she was so kind.'

This was an era before the promotion of the 'assimilation' of First Nations people, and government policy had historically been to isolate Aboriginal communities from the white community on reserves and stations, based on the racist fiction that they would soon die out. The Wreck Bay Aboriginal Station was situated on the Bherwerre Peninsula, 37 kilometres south-east of Nowra, and, as Jones writes, the location 'made it very difficult for Aboriginal people to seek education and employment opportunities outside the fishing industry'.

As a result, Worrigee, an unofficial settlement on private land near Nowra, sprang up. The living conditions were so bad that a conference was held with the aim of forming an organisation steered by Indigenous people; Jones quotes their remit as 'not to be a charity organisation but one designed to remove all customary and legal discrimination, to improve housing, education, employment and health standards and to completely remould the way of life at present endured by many Aborigines'.

In parallel with this initiative, the Nowra CWA was beginning to include Aboriginal women in its activities. The close pre-existing tie between Purth Moorhouse and Belle McCleod was instrumental in other CWA members welcoming their Indigenous sisters. The Worrigee–Wreck Bay branch was founded in 1961. At the time, Belle McCleod lived at Worrigee in a tin shack with her husband and six children. She recalled her living circumstances to Jones:

'In our tin shack, we only had two rooms—one room where we ate and bathed the kids in front of the fire, on the dirt floor. In the other room, we had a big bed and we slept in the big bed . . . We used to fill the tin tub up in front of the fire and the kids used to get bathed in that. But even though we lived like that, we had wonderful clean lives.'

McCleod also told Jones that, 'in those days, Nowra was a very racist town'. She recounts how Indigenous people weren't allowed into shops, and that in the cinema they had to sit in the front rows in a roped-off section in seats painted with a big 'B' on the back of them. She remembers the Worrigee–Wreck Bay CWA 'as the first thing that ever happened that was good for our Aboriginal people'. Otherwise, they had 'no services, no organisations, and no nothing'. The CWA gave Indigenous women social access to the matrons of Nowra, many of whom employed Indigenous pickers on their farms. McCleod recalls that friendships formed through the CWA, which, in turn, helped Indigenous families get better access to employment, education and other services.

There were, of course, some serious ironies attendant on well-meaning white women helping their Indigenous sisters. Some of the support they were offered was either extremely patronising or redundant. Jones notes of the state president of the CWA, Thelma Bate, that her 'public statements reveal her assumptions of lowly class positioning, few skills and little life experience among Aboriginal recruits to the CWA'. She records the response of members of the South Coast Aboriginal Advancement League. Said one:

Mrs Bate said, 'Oh, we'll teach them how to make scones and we'll do this and that'—and the [Aboriginal] women were just looking at one another because they'd been making bloody dampers and scones for fifty years! And she was making them in a nice stove—they were making them in the hot ashes!

Jones also writes that the members of the Nowra CWA branch were 'particularly keen to ensure that Aboriginal women attended their handicraft classes', which were held on alternate Wednesday evenings. Members were only authorised to demonstrate handicrafts when they had passed a CWA-awarded proficiency certificate. As Jones observes:

> Aboriginal CWA members like Belle McCleod had a very genuine desire to improve conditions for their own people, but they were unlikely to achieve this by making 'French flowers', a millinery art whereby silk is shaped into flowers using a special brass tool . . . The flow of handicraft expertise remained one-way, with Worrigee-Wreck Bay members allotted the student role.

It is unsurprising that, in 1965, the Worrigee–Wreck Bay branch of the CWA was wound up due to a lack of interest from Indigenous members. Moorhouse told me that for many decades he had little interest or understanding of the history of First Nations people in the area. And although he was a supporter of the original Land Rights movement in the 1970s, he did not become curious about the Indigenous history of the South Coast until he read the Jones book in his seventies. In the last few years of his life he talked about writing about his desire to engage with the history of the original inhabitants of the region and rectify what he saw as an important omission in his fictional and non-fictional accounts of life on the South Coast of New South Wales.

———

In 1911, American architect Walter Burley Griffin won the National Capital Design Competition for his plans of Canberra.

These had been drawn up in collaboration with his wife, also an architect, Marion Mahony Griffin. Walter Griffin was influenced by then radical European and North American architects and, in particular, by the City Beautiful and Garden City movements, which dominated town planning in the late 19th and early 20th centuries. The actual building of Canberra was interrupted by controversy over the design, and by the world wars and the Great Depression. In 1950, when Edith arrives in Canberra, the population was only 22,000 and the iconic Lake Burley Griffin had not been built.

From the outset, Canberra was a very self-conscious attempt to frame a centre of government which not only represented but actively defined the newly federated nation. A 1965 book published by the National Capital Development Commission informed readers:

> A city is more than bricks and mortar; it is a reflection of society, and a National Capital is bound to reflect the needs and characteristics of the nation which has built it. It is essential that Canberra should work effectively as a legislative and administrative centre, but of even greater importance is the effect the city will have on the hearts and minds of the Australian people.

Hardly words guaranteed to stir the flames of patriotism. The characterisation is typically Australian, perhaps, in its cautious avoidance of large claims about the symbolism of Canberra and its role in galvanising citizens around a national identity.

Edith, on the other hand, fresh from the grand vision of the League of Nations and the Palais Wilson, situated in Geneva on the beautiful Lac Leman (Lake Geneva), believes that a capital can transport inhabitants and visitors 'inside the living memory of the nation'. She is offered a position not in the Department of External Affairs, as she hoped, but on the team planning a conference on the national capital. In a manner that mirrors Moorhouse's own approach to life, she takes what could be seen as a routine administrative job and imbues it with grandeur and significance. In one of her first letters to her superiors, she writes:

> Canberra could be a stunningly distinctive city, but also one that engenders civilised values in those who live there by inviting them—through its design and architecture—to participate in great civilising ventures and entertainments and study and deeds . . .
>
> In my humble opinion, Griffin is probably the only man in the world—together with his wife, Marion, herself an architect—who has had the talent to design a continent. If only we had let him.

The last two sentences speak directly to a quality which, in broad terms, animated so much of Moorhouse's literary pre-occupations, as well as his approach to life. Throughout his oeuvre, he took simple objects and practices of everyday life and imbued them with extraordinary significance. Martinis, chairs, food, conferences, conversation, hotel room service, bar culture, overseas travel, bushwalking, speech making. The topics Moorhouse has interrogated in his work are eclectic, yet bound by his capacity to illuminate the quotidian and make it vibrate with cultural or political resonance.

Edith brings the same intensity to her vision for implementing the development of the national capital. Where others see a set of plans for urban design, Edith sees a grand vision, not only for the Australian nation, but for the world.

> She mostly felt she saw it all so clearly, with the help of the Griffins. She saw the matching of sites to activities and the need for dramatic design, perhaps at times regardless of function—she had preference for whimsy, which seemed out of fashion . . . Yet she saw that there also had to be dignity to a capitol—the use of ennobled power of structures and landscape, by advanced amenity. The other thing she loved about the Griffins was that they saw all human functions as worthy of aesthetic recognition and distinctiveness, be they toilets, garbage disposal plants or sewers.
>
> She thought that there was an opportunity to use the new city as a model for the world.

There is, of course, an element of whimsy and an acknowledgement of the absurdity of his own obsessions in Moorhouse's accounts of Edith's aesthetically detailed grand schemes. But they were equally serious subjects for him. Throughout his work, he saw aesthetics not as something superficial and irrelevant to ethical and political issues, but as being deeply connected to them.

When Edith moves into her new offices in the Department of the Interior, she takes great care to order her furniture and plan her office. She orders furniture from an Australian designer, Fred Ward, whose designs were influenced by both the Arts and Crafts Movement and European modernism. He used native Australian timber and a natural waxed finish to highlight the grain and colour. Edith's selection of Ward's furniture is not merely an aesthetic choice—it is also a statement of her own political vision for the nation: at once uniquely Australian *and* progressive and cosmopolitan. She hangs two Margaret Preston lithographs in her office and gets permission to frame and hang Marion Mahony Griffin's drawings of her vision for Canberra. And, in a whimsical moment, she buys a cumquat tree.

The cumquat tree is the focus of a scene in which Moorhouse returned to another ongoing theme in his work: the role of government surveillance in Australian life and politics. In *Cold Light*, Edith opens the door of her new office to see the broken trunk of the cumquat tree 'bending towards the floor as if in shame. All the fruit had been stripped from the tree and stamped into the rug.' Attached is a note on a departmental stationery card with a handwritten message: 'rat'. She calls her colleague Mr Thomas, who observes that 'rat' has at least three meanings: 'to betray a political party; to be a cad; to be a Communist, as in a "commie rat". Oh, and I suppose there's a fourth—to be a furry rodent.'

In the same week, Edith is contacted by a man from the newly established Australian Security Intelligence Organisation, who wants to interview her. She meets him and he asks her questions about her relationship to her brother and his girlfriend, who are both communists. He asks her if she is a communist and suggests she cease contact with her brother and his partner. She demurs on both counts.

Like many of his generation who were targeted by ASIO in the 1970s because of their political activism, Moorhouse had a longstanding fascination with the organisation's role in Australian society. In his book *Australia Under Surveillance*, he unpacks his concerns at length. In 1955, ASIO opened a file on Moorhouse at the age of seventeen because he had visited the communist-dominated Labour Club at Sydney University.

'Back then ASIO had been in existence for only about five years,' he writes, 'and among the people I knew, its nature and role were still speculated about, as people wonder about the existence of a ghost in a haunted house. It had a ghost-like nature but it was no ghost.'

ASIO was established by Labor prime minister Ben Chifley in 1949, as a response to the Cold War between the Soviet Union and the West. It was modelled on MI5, Britain's domestic secret service, and British agents assisted Australia by advising on ASIO. Moorhouse recalled the young man in whom ASIO had taken an interest:

> I was a seventeen-year-old cadet journalist fresh from high school in the country town of Nowra from a conservative family. Admittedly, I saw myself as a socialist, a believer in free love, and an atheist. I was an evening student at Sydney University enrolled in English and Philosophy. I was a politically alive teenager with a high-school-textbook knowledge of politics, examining the political student world of the university.
>
> Looking back, I feel sad for my young self, standing there in the quad. No one in my family had been to university and I had never set foot in a university and, as yet, had no friends in Sydney. I was lonely and bewildered about how a university worked. I was baffled. What was a 'buttery', for god's sake?

He considered himself 'a Fabian socialist' at the time. The idea of surveilling a young writer like Moorhouse was not only ridiculous but, equally, heartless.

Australia Under Surveillance examines whether Australia, as a country, prioritises national security when it comes to laws, freedoms and behaviour. (To that one might also add politics, given the predictable recurrence of 'stopping the boats' in election campaigns.) Moorhouse notes that during the 1950s and '60s, ASIO devoted nearly all of its efforts to surveillance of the Communist Party, the unions and the left-leaning intelligentsia, even extending its coverage of the latter to the Commonwealth Literary Fund. 'In many ways, as a result, ASIO has the most comprehensive record of Australian writing of the 1950s and 1960s,' he jokes. 'They should publish it.'

The range of innocuously named organisations on which ASIO trained its beady gaze was extensive. Moorhouse recalled belonging to the Bush Music club: 'We went outback searching for songs and ballads from the Colonial days and some of these were recorded on Wattle Records—probably called a communist front.' He noted that the Housewives' Association was also on ASIO's list. More seriously, he wrote that Menzies instructed ASIO to begin surveillance of all writers who applied for Commonwealth grants, a group comprised of pretty much anyone who was a serious writer or academic working in an English department or the editor of a literary magazine. The prime minister also instructed ASIO to vet those who agreed to be referees for grant applicants. Moorhouse writes:

> Those writers thought to be connected in some way to the Communist Party (sometimes mistakenly) who were recommended for grants by the Advisory Board of the Commonwealth Literary Fund were either denied those grants or had them deliberately delayed, sometimes for years. Passports were withheld from suspect writers and academics to prevent overseas travel to what ASIO perceived to be communist-related conferences and other activities.

His account of ASIO's power is, like that of many others who were put under surveillance, laced with sardonic humour. On re-reading his file, he writes, 'I was hurt that Australian intelligence had overlooked the power and influence of the Sydney Balmain anarchists—all seven of us followers of non-violent anarchist theory'.

On top of his discovery that ASIO was essentially vetting anyone who was involved in producing or supporting Australian literature, Moorhouse also notes that the ABC, where he worked as a reporter in the late 1960s, was apparently responsive to ASIO's requests. Having been given an assignment to cover a large air, sea and land military exercise in the Coral Sea, Moorhouse was informed by the head of ABC News that he had been given clearance. The report from ASIO stated: 'Although recorded as a person interested in the Peace Movement there is no evidence at this time that MOORHOUSE would pose a personal security risk.' He comments: 'I don't know what ASIO meant back then by "personal security risk".'

In *Australia Under Surveillance*, Moorhouse also examines the role of security organisations in contemporary times. He writes:

> The current suppressions of freedom of expression are different from the Cold War and the sexual revolution. The enemy is now seen as ethnic and religious, not yet belonging in the mainstream—even when they are Australian citizens—who cannot be pacified by negotiation or treaty or assimilation. Communists and the sexual revolutionaries were from the mainstream, and their activity was often in mainstream organisations and with mainstream memberships academics, ministers of religion, intelligentsia and unionists.

Moorhouse notes that a third of Muslims living in Australia, at the time he wrote the book, were Australian-born. and nearly all were Australian citizens.

———

Part of Edith's preoccupation with being part of the design of Canberra is her desire to ensure that the city truly represents all Australians—at least, white settler Australians. She meets with Prime Minister Menzies and discusses the building of Lake Burley Griffin, which she champions in the novel.

> He added, 'It's an important city doing important things in the national interest.'
>
> She agreed, but said, 'What I like about it—for all its importance and its scheming—is that it still has a bush soul. Living here, we can all still see the bush from which we come.'

By throwing herself into advocating for Canberra, Edith rekindles the passionate idealism she experienced working at the League.

> She thought that there was an opportunity to use the new city as a model for the world. She was sure it was possible to create an environment, houses and public amenities that would encourage its citizens to live confidently and with mettle, with pride—themselves being shaped by the amenity of the new city into human exemplars of how to live. *We must become exemplars.*

As a vision for Canberra takes hold of Edith's mind, its symbolic role in the nation's identity assumes increasingly grand proportions. Edith's plans for Canberra are both grandiose and forensically detailed. She envisages a city in which even the smallest details are important:

> Paths to the front door would curve; would not be a dull straight line from street to door. The back garden would be for the privacy of the householders to do as they pleased. People would be encouraged to eat out more, instead of each family eating alone every night hunched over a quarrelsome table. In the local cafés, people would come to know each other and draw up their chairs and chat about things that mattered.

For Edith, Canberra is not merely a national capital. It is a design for living. A utopian city that is not only the heart of democracy but has democratic values threaded through all aspects of everyday life. Reading these passages in *Cold Light*, it is impossible not to see Moorhouse himself leaning over Edith's shoulder and gazing with fascinated awe at the sheer audacity of the city she is dreaming up.

> The city would be our Chartres Cathedral, only more: Chartres tells only the bible stories: this capitol would tell everyone's story. Everyone's name would be here; everyone's life experience would be here.

Moorhouse placed Edith—intentionally, he said—in a position where she was forced to choose between a cosmopolitan and internationalist career and dream of a bigger role for herself in the design of Canberra and the democracy it represented and her own personal life. For Moorhouse, the personal was always political.

8

THE BUSH

In his wonderful and complex book *The Bush*, Don Watson writes:

> The Australian bush is both real and imaginary. Real, in that it grows in various unmistakable bush-like ways, and dies, rots, burns and grows into the bush again; real, in harbouring life. Imaginary, in that among the life it harbours is the life of the Australian mind. It is, by many accounts, the source of the nation's idea of itself.

For much of his adult life, Moorhouse took off every year for eight days on foot with maps and compass, backpack and tent, sundry camping gear, food and bourbon whisky. He took bourbon, he said, because it has the best alcohol-to-weight ratio. He eschewed trails in favour of a map and compass and slept either in a tent or under overhangs. He said he walked because: 'What I do is a release from the world of words and human relationship—writing, reading, talking, listening, intimates, companions, associates—I want to go out into a raw, solitary, non-verbal world.'

Journalists writing profiles of him invariably described him as 'loving the bush'—to which he responded in an ironic tone: 'It seems to be a patriotic assumption that Australians love the bush.' Like Watson, Moorhouse was interested in what the bush represents in the settler Australian imaginary. It was important to him both as a place where he could decompress while physically challenging himself, and psychologically as a symbol of how quickly the best laid plans could unravel—of how, very quickly, you could find yourself lost.

Moorhouse's relationship with the Australian bush dates back to his childhood in Nowra. In an essay published in *Southerly*, he recalled:

At the age of eight as a cub scout, with a never before experienced delight, I cooked and ate my first lamb chop barbecued on a green forked stick at my first camp fire in the bush. I can still taste it. It was one of the most sensual gastronomic experiences I have had—and I have eaten many remarkable meals in many five-hat restaurants around the world. Since then I've been going into the bush, or the wilderness—mostly alone. In total, adding up the occasional nights and the eight-day stretches—my usual length of a trek—I have now spent nearly three years of my life out in the bush.

In a 1974 interview recorded by Hazel de Berg, Moorhouse spoke about his fascination with the Australian bush:

A crucially important experience was the feeling we lived on the edge of the wilderness and that the wilderness began at the end of Nowra and went thousands of miles, which—looking at the map—it did go virtually across the mountains . . . I spent many years as a very young child, exploring and rock climbing and swimming, exploring caves and setting up secret places, playing on the river with boats, or playing in the bush with friends.

Moorhouse was both a Cub Scout and a Boy Scout, his older brothers were Senior Scouts, his mother was a commissioner of the Girl Guides and his father a commissioner of the Boy Scouts. His family was steeped in the scouting ethic, and this was where Moorhouse learnt the fundamentals of his bushcraft. Despite greatly enjoying his time in the Baden-Powell army, he managed to get himself expelled for a very Moorhouse reason. He recounted the story in the 1974 interview:

I was expelled from the Scouts, much to the humiliation of my family, for organising a petition against the Scout Master for what I considered to be bad practices. I wanted to democratise the Boy Scout movement, I wanted elected troop leaders and a number of other things, and I organised a round robin. I probably only organised this petition because I'd read about the round robin, which seemed to me a fantastically good idea, with no one to take the blame; you simply draw a circle and people fill their names in on spokes of the circle so there is no name at the top of the list, so they don't know who signed it first.

The scout master swiftly figured out who had organised the petition, however, and Moorhouse was asked to pack his kitbag.

There is another, far more complex personal story that Moorhouse associates with his time in the Scouts. It's one that would have a profound effect on his psyche, and which he wrote about in his *Southerly* essay. Moorhouse was at a ceremony where Cub Scouts were to be inducted into the Boy Scouts. In the essay, he notes:

> Although it was never stated explicitly, this is a puberty ceremony or an initiation ritual found in tribal and trad-itional societies and in disguised forms in our own. Lord Baden-Powell, the founder of the scout movement, drew on his knowledge of African tribal initiation ceremonies for those rituals used in scouting.

The ceremony was held in an abandoned quarry, around the base of which were bush lairs constructed of gum tree branches. The Cubs to be initiated were waiting in these lairs. Moorhouse had been initiated the year before and was looking down on the ceremony from above. The Scout troop stood in a horseshoe formation in the quarry, with the leaders standing on a platform. Moorhouse was on the upper edge of the quarry with a Scout leader and a couple of patrol leaders. Their job was to send a bolt of fire down to the unlit fire in the quarry using a burning ball of material soaked in kerosene on a wire attached to a pulley.

Moorhouse had decided to perch up a tree to watch the ceremony. As it began, however, he slipped, and he slid a couple of metres down the trunk of the tree with his legs wrapped around it. He came to rest on a jagged branch, his crotch caught in the fork. (At this point in the story, it is permissible for all male readers to wince.) He extricated himself from the tree and found that his trousers were torn and his crotch was bleeding.

I called to one of the scout leaders who came over and shone a torch on me and said something like 'Christ, you've hurt yourself. Sit down.' He called to others.

Meanwhile I could hear the words coming up from the ceremony which was continuing 'Do you know what your honour is?' Another scout leader examined me and said that I had to be taken to the hospital—quickly, 'It's his cock.'

He was taken to the hospital, where a doctor sewed up his testicular sac and administered penicillin. After Moorhouse spent a month at home recuperating in bed, the GP concluded that no permanent damage had been done.

For Moorhouse, however, the injury was not only physical. It was deeply symbolic in light of what he has referred to as his 'gender fluidity' or 'androgyny'. In his retelling of the initiation, he questions whether his falling from the tree was really accidental or whether it was the expression of an unconscious desire to emasculate himself—to avoid becoming a man on the cusp of puberty. He remembers seeing the hairy chests and legs of men in swimming pool change rooms and 'recoiling'. He wrote:

On the night of my fall, at a ceremony so fraught with symbolism about maleness which was meant to define the male world into which I was to be propelled, my unconscious took a dramatic decision, a brutal decision, a decision which could not be ignored—it wounded me in my manhood. It said, your penis, the source of manhood and symbol of my gender, was now symbolically transfigured.

Moorhouse often speculated about whether the event was, in Freudian terms, the fulfilment of an unconscious wish or whether it was an incident which he later chose to reinterpret as a touchstone for his own ambivalence about gender. Certainly, it became bound up with his relationship to the bush and his need to return to the Budawangs, the country he first explored as a child. He said of this connection:

> Whatever we make of it, I have experienced an extraordinary incident with primeval overlays with great import for me, and it is this primeval narrative which I have been ritualistically enacting through my life in the Budawangs and which I am now trying to tell. It is about a landscape bonding—what we use landscape for—and about the amazing intricacies and workings of the mind as it makes a 'self'.

————

Moorhouse, like Henry Lawson in an earlier era, was alert to the darker side of the bush—of how it could undo you, physically and psychologically. In the short story 'From a Bush Log Book 1', published in *Forty-Seventeen*, the narrator writes about a trip taken into the Budawang Range with a lover, Belle. The Budawangs, a rugged mountain range in the Budawang National Park and the Morton National Park, were a favourite spot for Moorhouse in his real-life bush adventures. They are part of a spur of the Great Dividing Range located in the South Coast region of New South Wales, about 50 kilometres from Nowra.

'As they walked deeper into the bush,' the narrator says, 'he kept glancing at Belle to see if she was being affected by the dull warm day and the bush. He knew the creeping hysteria and dread which the Australian bush could bring on.'

When they arrive at a lookout, he remarks, 'I don't go into the bush for views.' When she asks what he does go into the bush for, he says, 'I go into the bush to be swallowed whole. I don't go into the bush to look at curious natural formations—I don't marvel at God's handiwork.'

Belle cooks Christmas dinner on the campfire—rabbit baked in mustard, corn, candied carrots and green beans with a Christmas pudding to follow. They begin the meal with a lobster bisque and drink a bottle of 1968 Coonawarra Cabernet Shiraz. Moorhouse was the kind of bushman who was not averse to making the occasional martini.

During the night, the narrator rises from their tent, 'because he liked to leave the tent in the dead of night and prowl about naked. He said to himself that although he did not always feel easy in the bush, in fact, he sometimes felt discordant in it, he'd rather be out in it feeling discordant than not be there.'

Despite the memorable meal and satisfying sex, they leave the bush with the narrator feeling uneasy:

> The disquiet came because Belle had been moved out of place in his life. The Budawang bush was the place of his childhood testing, his family's bush experience, touching base, touching primitive base. He had learned his masculinity here.
>
> She did not belong in that album.

Moorhouse's story is part of a long tradition in Australian culture of exploring the uncanniness of the bush. Following European settlement, colonial artists were prone to superimposing European light and landscape traditions onto paintings of their new home. It wasn't until the Heidelberg school of the late 19th century that there was a sustained attempt to capture the unique Australian light, including the blue haze of the bush on a hot day.

Frederick McCubbin's 1886 painting *Lost*, which depicts a young girl standing forlornly in a tangle of tall grass and eucalypts, is a famous example of this. It is equally a painting which speaks to the underlying sense of dread that the bush triggered in settler communities who were pushing deeper into Australia's interior. Stories of children lost in the bush were commonplace.

But as the Australian literature scholar Peter Pierce points out, they were not just accounts of misfortune, they were equally symbolic tales of the capacity of the bush to 'devour' those who ventured into it. In his book *The Country of Lost Children*, Pierce draws a parallel between the fascination that children lost in the bush held for writers such as Lawson, Marcus Clarke, Joseph Furphy and Henry Kingsley and the role the motif of the lost child plays in Moorhouse's work:

> Moorhouse is the lachrymosely joking chronicler of loss in contemporary Australian society, and he also represents the difficulty of belonging, of finding lodgement here. Cosmopolitan Moorhouse has yet made a central item of his work the revision of one of the oldest and most tenacious of Australian cultural (and originally rural) motifs—that of the lost child.

Analysing a number of Moorhouse's key works and characters, Pierce concludes that 'Moorhouse's lost children are not rural waifs . . . boys and girls who perish—on a simple reading—because of the harshness of the Australian bush or the delinquency of their parents . . . Moorhouse's lost children are the urban children who might have been.'

In 'From a Bush Log Book 2', also published in *Forty-Seventeen*, Moorhouse offers a less melancholy portrait of the perils of the bush—one that satirises 'the rules of bushwalking' and his attempts to break free of his family's rigid rituals. In it, the narrator returns to the Budawangs to 'apologise to the bush for taking Belle there'. On his way, he calls in at his parents' home, where he is lectured on the total fire ban and told not to go into the bush.

What he didn't say to his mother and father was that he intended to have camp fires regardless of the fire ban. He was now forty and could damn well light a fire, legal or illegal, if he damn well wanted to . . . Why else as a little boy had he crouched shivering and sodden at damp, smoking camp fires blowing his very soul into the fire to get it to flame. Or suffered fly-pestered pink eye and heat headaches in the dust of summer scout camps, his ears ringing with the madness of cicadas in the hot eucalyptus air, doggedly going about his camp routines. He'd paid.

His mother 'recreates' the Christmas lunch the narrator missed, despite his explicit wishes to the contrary, and his family grills him on his camping plans.

'What are you going to eat out there?' his nephew asked at the meal.

All questions from nephews and nieces were trick questions.

'Mainly tinned food,' he said, knowing this would lose him marks.

'You're not walking far then,' his nephew said with the smile of the experienced.

'No, I'm not walking far,' he said, an apology to the whole family for having included any tinned food for a camp. 'It's a lazy camp.'

They didn't know of such a thing.

They discuss the route he is planning to take.

He told them he was going to the upper reaches of the Clyde River which he hadn't done yet in his walking. He wanted to look at Webb's Crown, a remaining block of plateau around which the river had cut itself on both sides, leaving Webb's Crown like a giant cake in the middle of the river.

'It's nothing to look at,' his nephew said.

He couldn't very well say he was going into the bush to apologise to the bush for having taken the wrong person to that part of his metaphorical self.

He reflects on the fact that, as a boy, he'd just 'gone into the bush' and wandered, with one thing—caves, creeks, high points and clearings—suggesting another. Tired of his family's interrogation, he drops a bombshell.

'I'd like to go into the bush without a plan,' he said, to see how they'd jump, 'to go into the bush idly.' The word 'idly' was strange to the dining room.

'Plan the work: work the plan,' his father said.

'If you didn't have a plan how would you know where to go next?' asked his nephew.

An existential question.

Walking into the bush later, he finds his family's voices following him and critiquing his thoughts and actions. After striking camp and preparing to light a fire in an almost dry river bed, he discovers his lighter is missing.

> From the moment you left the car behind you things began to go against you in the bush—something always got broken, something spilled, something was lost, something forgotten. Well, rarely forgotten with his drill. Everything began to degenerate—batteries, food. From the moment you left civilisation you only had so long to live.

In his head, his family comments, 'He forgot his lighter.'

Fiona Giles says of Moorhouse that despite the anxiety that camping alone in the bush sometimes provoked in him, it also provided a space of belonging. 'He found domesticity quite stressful in all its guises . . . A kitchen represented a form of oppression,' she says. 'He didn't associate it with pleasure and fun and hospitality . . . So he avoided that at all costs, which is why he'd rather go out to lunch or dinner or stay in a hotel. Or then it would be camping. The camping provided a safe space of domesticity, in a way.'

———

Moorhouse's close friend Rohan Haslam has a delightful story about Moorhouse's impulse to create 'rules' to civilise the bush experience. They were planning a trip to the Budawangs when heavy rain set in. Moorhouse's response was to suggest a trip to Western Australia, where they could eat Albany oysters, fish and catch marron. The plan was to 'find the freshest fish in unpolluted waters, eat the oysters at the source, eat the marron where they exist'.

They took an eight-day road trip, driving from Perth down to Albany and on to Esperance. They arrived at Lake Grace, a town of only a few hundred people, and stayed overnight at a 'strange, small hotel'. The next day they drove towards Esperance with a full pack of live yabbies crawling around the back of the four-wheel drive. After a couple of hours they decided to stop for a bite to eat. At Moorhouse's instigation, they followed a dirt road into a national park.

'So we just sort of bushwhacked in a four-wheel drive in the middle of nowhere, drove until we found some shade, pulled up, cooked the yabbies on the little gas burner he uses in the bush, drank a bottle of wine, ate yabbies with fresh bread and butter from the Lake Grace bakery, and it was one of the most extraordinary meals I've had in my life.'

After lunch, they drove on to find a place to camp and slept out under the stars. Later in the trip, they drove east of Esperance and into national park, winding up at Tagon Beach for the cocktail hour. Moorhouse had in his mind that he wanted to camp on a deserted and pristine beach. 'So he spent the next half hour wandering around the dunes finding any bit of litter to remove any trace of human existence, so that it was a perfectly pristine beach.' They spent the next two days camping and fishing. 'The point was to pull the freshest fish out of the Southern Ocean so we could say we'd eaten the freshest fish.'

Haslam says that the trip was 'a couple of the best weeks of my life', and comments of Moorhouse: 'He's one of the warmest, most generous, loving and affectionate human beings I've ever met.'

Moorhouse was careful about whom he took into the bush. He mostly went alone, but one of the few people he loved bushwalking with was his friend Helen Lewis. They met in 1979 when Moorhouse was Writer in Residence at Canberra

University, where she was studying writing. Moorhouse gave some classes and mentoring advice, and Lewis and her fellow students made him an honorary member of their club—The Professional Drinkers' Writing Club. In return, Moorhouse gave them a sheepskin cloak held together with a medal inscribed: The Lawson, Drysdale, Moorhouse Drover's Wife Award for Imaginative Audacity in Writing, Marketing or Spoken English.

Lewis, who is now one of Moorhouse's literary trustees, says of her friend: 'There were many rooms in Frank Moorhouse. But there was one place that I went with Frank which became very special over the years. And that was the bush.' He went, he told her, to find 'release' and 're-creation', and to sleep in a 'raw, solitary, non-verbal world. He went to play out some of the masculinity dramas that troubled him throughout his life.'

Preparations for their treks were governed by three lists. List One, the Camp Checklist, contained 94 items. 'He was quite proud of this detail,' Lewis says. The second was the Meals Plan list. 'Not for Frank, the lightweight freeze-dried foods, they were emergency rations. Steaks, chops, potatoes, cucumbers, onions, pepperoni, garlic—all were on the plan. And of course alcohol, always bourbon, more alcohol, less weight.'

The Third List was the Count Down list: 'when surrounded by the chaos of back packs, tents and provisions, we would recheck everything, get the latest weather reports, study the topographical maps and consult Frank's note cards from his previous trips, laying them out like a divination'. When all the auguries were satisfactory, they were ready to head out.

'For me this was a moment of stripping down, as the weight of our packs bit into our shoulders and the intense physical demands of the walk began,' Lewis says. 'Through swamps and cut grass and rotting vegetation and tea-tree thickets. Through flies and snakes, heat and cold and scrambles over rock faces, through the strange effects that the bush can provoke, the layers of ego and artifice were peeled away, leaving us hyper aware of each other.'

At the end of the day's walk, they would make camp, 'having won through the pain of the day to a spectacular location, often by the water'. Moorhouse would set up the bar and serve rounds of bourbon and bar snacks, and they would sit by the campfire and watch the sun set.

Lewis makes an important observation about Moorhouse's particular love for the Budawangs, which he called his Heartlands. 'Frank wrote that "Freud talked about the topography of the psyche", and how Freud had come to see the landscape as a physical allegory for the unconscious. In that sense, then, the Budawangs is a fitting allegory for Frank. His Heartlands, fractured and fissured, confused and tangled but magnificent too, shining with brilliance, inspiring awe and wonder and love.'

———

Moorhouse not only enjoyed retreating to the bush, he enjoyed playing with its fetishised role in the psyche of what has been, for more than a century, a highly urbanised culture, and by extension the way Australia is still understood overseas.

In an essay first published in *The Bulletin* in January 1980 and later republished in his collection *The Drover's Wife*, Moorhouse wrote in the persona of an Italian student, Franco Casamaggiore, who is presenting a paper at a conference on 'New Writings in English' in Milan. The paper purports to analyse Lawson's 'The Drover's Wife', which the student interprets as 'an elaborate example of a national culture joke, a joke which has forced its way into high art'. Referring to the Lawson story, the Drysdale painting and Murray Bail's story of the same name, Casamaggiore concludes:

> Each of these works has the status of an Australian classic and each of these works, I will show, contains a joking wink in the direction of the Australian people which they curiously, I suspect, only dimly understand. Or if they do understand, they are not prepared to tell outsiders of it, to share it with a scholar such as myself.

The voice Moorhouse uses in this essay is parodying the earnest investigations of a young scholarly outsider, but it is interlaced with a genuine authorial commentary on the national subconscious revealed by the iconic cultural work:

> All cultures have a need for artworks which speak on their behalf. The cultures do not always understand what is being said on their behalf, at least what is being said on all levels. This is not a problem which concerns me today, it characterises all cultures, the artworks being made serve the role of revelation, the role of ornamentation, and the role of concealment. Art also buries shame until scholarship disinters it.

Casamaggiore speculates about the nature of Australian mateship in the absence of women, and extends these musings to the role that sheep may have played in the life of the drover: 'What historians have not been able to incorporate in their description is the special relationship which naturally grew between the drover or driver and his charges, who became an object for emotional and physical drives . . . I talk of interspecies reciprocity.'

This is, of course, a very old joke, and one which has apparently been perpetrated on an unsuspecting and earnest young Italian researcher. It contains, at the same time, some grains of truth. Jokes always do. Which is precisely Moorhouse's point.

Casamaggiore goes on to speculate about the symbolic connection between the 'sheep-wife' and the 'drover's wife':

> In the story, in the absence of her drover husband, she is looked after by a dog, as is a sheep. The climax of the Lawson story is the 'killing of the snake'—interpretation of which needs no Dr Freud—being the expression of a castration-rage by the wife/sheep at her husband's absence. In Australia, many lethal snakes roam the countryside as protected animals, and the male genitalia is referred to in Australian folklore poetically as the 'one-eyed' trouser snake.

In the essay, Moorhouse deployed literary devices which drive the ambiguity of much of his work, and which both render his writing satirical and at the same time gesture towards an underlying truth. In a section in *The Drover's Wife* following the essay, Moorhouse unpacks the tone that animated much of his writing in the form of an exchange of letters between a fictional Chinese student and a real Australian academic working in the Department of Italian Studies at the University of Sydney, Dr Suzanne Kiernan. In her reply to the student, who purports to have read the Casamaggiore essay, Kiernan writes:

> I think I should tell you what I believe you already suspect— that this is a joke on the part of the writer Frank Moorhouse, whose name has been 'Italianised' (with a little semantic liberty) to become 'Franco Casamaggiore'. This was the full

extent of what was described as my 'inspired assistance' in the introductory remarks, which are the author's own, and are part of the fiction. (In Italian, 'casa'='house', and 'maggiore'= 'more'—homophonous with 'moor', while not, of course, having the same meaning.) The use of the words 'excitedly' and 'inspired' which you single out in the original story by Frank Moorhouse has the function of signalling to the reader that the writer's intention is ironic and satiric, and that what follows is not necessarily to be taken at face value.

Throughout much of his work, Moorhouse adopted an ironic tone to write about matters he takes seriously: human relationships, gender, sexuality and national identity. In a review of Murray Bail's edited 1988 collection, *The Faber Book of Contemporary Australian Short Stories*, Moorhouse is described as part of the early 1970s movement 'that transformed Australian fiction from dreary local realism to hip metafiction and brief, understated vignettes of contemporary urban life'. Bail goes on to remark: 'The writers of the 1970s such as Moorhouse "Americanise" the archness by stripping down the prose and lightening the irony and by taking more democratic, post-1960s attitudes and voices, while bringing self-conscious complexity to classic Australian texts and themes.'

The short story and the 'discontinuous narrative' were the forms that anchored Moorhouse's writing and allowed him to play so successfully with the borders of reality and fiction. In an article for *Southerly* magazine, Adrienne Sallay discusses innovations with the short story in the 1970s: both Michael Wilding and Frank Moorhouse, she says, wrote with 'ironic, masculine voices, parodying themselves, writing and the world at large in loosely connected pieces that Moorhouse termed discontinuous narratives', and used 'experimental techniques including fracture, slippage and discontinuity . . . sometimes even inserting each other into their work'.

As we have seen in an earlier chapter Moorhouse and his contemporaries were determined to move away from stories set in the Australian bush and outback. In an afterword to *The Tabloid Story Pocket Book*, a collection of short stories that had been published in the magazine *Tabloid Story*, Wilding expands on the desire he and his contemporaries had to get away from 'formula bush tales'. What he terms 'the new nationalist critics of the 1930s, 40s and 50s had produced a particular and pre-dominant version of Australian literary tradition'. This version devalued writers not born in Australia, even if their creative life was spent there, and placed stress on 'national' traditions rather than international literary connections. There was an assumption that anything written before the 1890s was derivative writing which drew on English modes. It's not surprising that the same critical concerns also animated critical debates about art at the time, in the wake of the Heidelberg school of painting. According to Wilding:

> So there is the nationalist cult of the short story, with Henry Lawson as the particular native genius and the fount and the source. The Australian story began with Lawson, the myth read: so anthology after anthology of Australian short stories was produced beginning with Lawson. It was forgotten that anyone even wrote stories before Lawson—Marcus Clarke, for instance, and the host of forgotten magazine writers of the 1850s and 60s onwards. And this lapse of memory produced a distorted picture of the literary history of Australia . . . the late reduction of this early variety of short story to the single

mythic line of the outback story, a reduction fostered by the new nationalist critics, immensely damaged Australian writing.

The deliberate turning away from this mode of writing by Wilding, Moorhouse and their contemporaries, and towards a more experimental, modernist style which often actively engaged with the milieu they were part of, makes it all the more intriguing that, in his mid-seventies, Moorhouse turned back to Lawson and began researching his work and life.

———

In 2017, Moorhouse published a collection of stories based on Henry Lawson's short story 'The Drover's Wife'. In his own essay in the collection, Moorhouse explores what he argues was Lawson's bisexuality and his ambivalent relationship to his gender. Lawson is, at first glance, a counter-intuitive subject for an exploration of gender ambivalence and marginalised sexuality, being so strongly associated with masculine tales of the bush, but Moorhouse had come across some surprising information in his research.

In 1945, Russell Drysdale painted one of his most famous works, *The Drover's Wife*, which now hangs in the National Gallery of Australia. Drysdale denied that his work was inspired by the Lawson story, but Moorhouse doubted this claim. In 1975, Murray Bail wrote a short story inspired by both the Lawson story and the Drysdale painting. Moorhouse commented:

[I]t could be said that both the Lawson story and the Drysdale painting have become Australia's own version of the *Mona Lisa*. Leonardo da Vinci's enigmatic painting has been described by the critic John Lichfield as 'the best known, the most visited, the most written about, the most sung about, the most parodied work of art in the world'. Some of the drover's wife stories published since have taken their lead from Bail, intertwining the story and the painting. There are thirteen contemporary short stories with the title . . . It is a phenomenon unique in the Australian artistic imagination.

To that list of works we can now add Leah Purcell's wonderful 2021 novel *The Drover's Wife*, and her play and film of the same name. There are also other novels, a novella and a song cycle.

A volume of Henry Lawson's short stories and poems has long been a go-to gift for the hard-to-buy-for male relative. Lawson, like A.B. 'Banjo' Paterson, is a reassuring symbol of patriotic Australian masculinity. The prime minister at the time of Lawson's death in 1922, Billy Hughes, eulogised him at a state funeral thus: 'Lawson knew intimately the real Australia and was its greatest minstrel. He sang of its wide spaces, its dense bush, its droughts, its floods. He loved Australia . . . None was his master. He was the poet of Australia, the minstrel of the people.'

Given this reputation as the macho minstrel of the bush, it may come as a surprise to some that Moorhouse believed that Lawson was probably gay or bisexual, and that he was, at the very least, 'sexually confused'. His theory is supported by letters, by the descriptions of contemporaries and by Lawson's own diary. Moorhouse writes:

Contemporary descriptions of the personality and manner of Henry Lawson, and his own description of himself, reveal him as having a precarious sense of his sexual nature, now described academically as gender, as distinct from a person's anatomical sex. Lawson uses the word 'effeminate' to describe himself, as did others. But given the rigid and coarsened Australian masculine culture in which he mostly moved, Lawson's consciousness of his femininity, which was considerable, meant that he would have tried to suppress or modify it so that he could find acceptance in conventional male company, hence his adoption of the big moustache.

Moorhouse also quoted from Lawson's diary, which remained unpublished during his lifetime, in which Lawson reflects that as a young boy he:

> . . . began to be haunted by the dread of 'growing up to be a man' . . . I confided in Father and these ideas seemed to trouble him a lot. I slept in a cot beside the bed and I used to hold his horney [sic] hand until I went to sleep. And Id [sic] often say to him: 'Father! it'll be a long time before I grow up to be a man won't it' . . . But I grew up to be a man in spite of lying awake worrying about it.

Moorhouse was not suggesting that 'effeminacy' is an unambiguous sign of homosexuality. Rather, using a series of sources, he proposes that Lawson was both ambivalent about his masculinity, as framed by the norms of the day, and potentially bisexual. In regard to the latter, Moorhouse explores a long and very close relationship Lawson had with a man called Jim Gordon, whom Lawson met when he travelled to Bourke for *The Bulletin*. Gordon was 17 and Lawson was 25. Gordon described their meeting this way:

I had noticed this long-necked, flat-chested stripling eyeing me off, each time we passed and I noticed too that he had the most beautiful and remarkable eyes I have ever seen on a human being . . . soft as velvet and of a depth of brownness that is indescribable.

Gordon was running low on food, and he writes that Lawson 'gripped' his hand and said, 'Come camp with me.' Lawson and Gordon spent eighteen months together, wandering the outback to find work, sharing their earnings and their food, and sleeping under the stars or in huts when they found them.

Moorhouse surmised, based on his reading of Gordon's and Lawson's accounts: 'I imagine that it was for Lawson and Jim, perhaps emotionally, the most important times in their lives. From what I know of male life, I would imagine that their personal romance grew, even if the romance of the bush did not.'

After they parted ways, Lawson wrote a poem about Gordon. They reunited 23 years later in Leeton, after both had married and fathered children. According to Moorhouse:

They bonded again as mates—Lawson used the expression 're-mated'. Each day they spent more and more time with each other, camping together for days on the Murrumbidgee River. 'Fishing' was their cover; the image recalls the two married closeted cowboys in *Brokeback Mountain*. Jim records that they spent their time talking and drinking. Jim's wife Daisy became jealous . . .

Moorhouse also noted that Lawson wrote that the name he called Gordon 'surprised and disturbed' Daisy and caused her 'distress and pain'. Gordon also writes of walking 'hand-in-hand' with Lawson. Whether their relationship was ever consummated is, of course, a matter of speculation, and open to the charge that contemporary interpretations have been overlaid on a simple story of mateship. Moorhouse himself was alive to that possibility. He wrote that he was 'resistant to Manning Clark's view of mateship as a form of "sublimated homosexuality"'. He rejected the term 'suppressed homosexuality' as something that can be 'confidently discerned by observation'.

Moorhouse also wrote about his strong identification with Lawson. 'I should at this point declare a bias in the trace of my research, something of an undertow: I discovered, and I feel, other personality empathies with Lawson through parallels with my own life,' he acknowledged. The parallels he referred to are 'the apartness he felt from becoming a writer'; an alcohol dependency, 'although not one as unmanageable or destructive as Lawson's'; trouble maintaining long-term domestic relationships with women; and trouble managing money. He wrote: 'But more curiously, as with Lawson, I know the feeling of apartness, if not alienation, from some of the mainstream masculine cultures.'

One of the striking things about Lawson's iconic story *The Drover's Wife* is the author's capacity to inhabit the mind of a woman in a spare, yet nuanced way. Moorhouse reflected on whether Lawson's own apparently androgynous nature influenced his ability to write the story through the eyes of a woman. 'Many writers have contemplated the role of androgyny and gender fluidity in the arts; I have myself,' he said. 'But what does the androgynous personality know—both conventional genders? Or neither fully. Does androgyny open up insights, or does it close off the writer in an ungendered no-person's land?' Moorhouse too, of course, had an uncanny ability to write from the perspective of a central female character.

As a number of Lawson commentators and literary critics have noted, it's an open question about how much Lawson's portrait of the drover's wife was influenced by his mother Louisa Lawson's 1889 essay 'The Australian Bush-Woman', published three years before her son's story. Louisa Lawson was a formidable woman—a suffragist, feminist, writer and publisher. In 1891, Louisa and other members of the Women's Literary Society became founding members of the Womanhood Suffrage League of New South Wales. As Janette Joy Prichard writes:

Lawson was a great fighter and regarded resignation as a crime. In an editorial in *The Dawn* [a newspaper for women she founded] in January 1902, she wrote: 'Resignation is selfishness under another name, it is cowardice under a white veil of goodness. The patient endurance of wrong leaves wrong free to attack elsewhere; to spread itself in this generation and to transmit its widened influence to the next.'

As a teenager, Lawson lived with his mother in a bohemian feminist household in Sydney, after Louisa left his father and the bush. In 1887, she bought *The Republican* magazine and she and Henry, then aged twenty, wrote most of its copy and edited it. Moorhouse points out that they created a merged authorial identity, writing under the pseudonym 'Archie Lawson'.

Her essay on the bush-woman, which was first published in the *Boston Woman's Journal*, describes the type this way:

She is utterly self-neglectful. The white plump women of the city seem soft to her. They cannot walk a mile without fatigue, while she will tramp five miles with a heavy child on her hip, do a day's washing and tramp back again at night. She works harder than a man. You may see her with her sons putting up a fence, or with the shearers, whistling and working as well as any. She has a fine, hard patient character; she is not emotional, nor very susceptive, but she has no conception of the little jealousies, the spite and petty meannesses of city women. Her generosity to any sort of stranger is natural . . .

There can be little doubt that Louisa Lawson's description of the bush-woman was the model for her son's story. Not simply in the physical descriptions of her appearance and life, but in his attention to the threats that lurk in the shadows of her existence. There are, of course, the challenges she and her children face from natural forces: drought, illness, venomous snakes, bushfire and flood. But Lawson's story also conjures with the hovering potential of male violence: 'Occasionally a bushman in the horrors, or a villainous-looking sundowner, comes and nearly scares the life out of her.' He writes about a swagman who throws his swag down on the verandah and demands food. As night closes in, he announces his intention to stay. She gets a batten from the sofa, lets the dog loose and confronts him. He eventually leaves. Louisa Lawson, as those familiar with her life and work know well, was a tireless advocate on the scourge of domestic violence, among other feminist causes.

Moorhouse believed that part of the success of Henry Lawson's story was his capacity to 'successfully empathise with the drover's wife's sense of herself as a lone, threatened female coping with significant difficulties in a hostile bush'. He cites Lawson's poem 'Ruth', in which he writes: 'I am shamed for Australia and haunted by the face of the haggard bush wife—/She who fights her grim battle undaunted because she knows nothing of life.'

In essence, Moorhouse sees Lawson's capacity to empathise with the central female character in his short story as founded on his own sense of alienation from the dominant masculine culture, and by the profound influence of his feminist mother. 'In writing "The Drover's Wife",' Moorhouse says, 'he, too, became girl-woman-wife-mother and, while he did not merge into the landscape, he became, instead, a writer.'

———

Despite his love for the bush and his careful preparations to ward off disaster, Moorhouse did have some bad experiences on his treks. 'Over the years,' he writes, 'I've had minor injuries— I have fallen into a creek and cracked a rib or two, I have stubbed my toe seriously and I have had to drug up and limp out—but together with minor burns, scratches, cuts and bites, that's about it.' At least, it was until the summer when he almost lost his life on a solo trek in 2007.

Moorhouse was in Bourke, hoping to walk to a geological oddity called Mount Gunderbooka, about 60 kilometres south-west of the town. He drove to the Dry Tank campground in the National Park, and set off on a sortie to see if there was surface water in one of the closer creeks. He didn't find any, so he struck camp, confident he had enough water for the following day. He rose and headed to Gunderbooka, which was only two hours from his car. He reached the base of the mountain, found a small waterhole and again set up camp.

The next day he climbed to the summit early in the morning and made his descent as the day was warming up. It grew increasingly hot, and he retreated to his tent to escape the swarming insects and read, of all things, Kenneth Clark's *Civilisation*. As night fell, he was feeling unwell and somewhat breathless.

He rose early the next morning and broke camp, planning to head back to his car.

When the sun rose, the day was even hotter than the one before—he was later to discover it reached 42 degrees. Moorhouse decided to follow a fence line rather than his compass, and ultimately lost his bearings.

> I was now conscious of the risk of hyperthermia . . . The heat was hitting down through the thin canopy of trees, perhaps cypress pine, and beating back up from the red clay. Radiant heat . . . I was shocked to realise that I had been walking for nearly five hours—not good. I had been walking for far too long. I should be at the car by now . . . I tried to recalculate the route. The heat was becoming agonising.

He realised that he had been staring at the compass without comprehension, his legs gave way and what he calls his 'emergency mind' told him he was in serious trouble. Moorhouse crawled to some open ground and let off his EPIRB—an 'emergency position-indicating radio beacon'. He was eventually rescued by police officers, who took him to a waiting ambulance. He spent a week at Bourke Hospital in the acute care ward.

It is a mark of Moorhouse's persistence, or perhaps stubbornness, that three months later, in winter, he returned to Dry Tank with a friend and retraced the trip. 'The insects were not angry; the weather was benign,' he reports. 'It went like a textbook exercise in Australian bush trekking. I am not finished with Mount Gunderbooka and I intend to go there again.'

He had another traumatising experience related to the bush. But this one involved people rather than nature. Moorhouse once took a visiting American, Elliott Anderson, an academic and editor from Northwestern University, into the bush. They went way off the beaten track—as evidenced by a long exchange of letters with the Budget car rental company about damage to the car. There are also photos of them hunting and shooting kangaroos.

When it became known that Moorhouse had shot roos, he faced a strong reaction from a group who claimed to represent animal rights. Moorhouse, who was always open about owning a gun, and who occasionally went kangaroo shooting, like many people who grew up in rural Australia, was shocked by the reaction. He understood the arguments put forward by animal rights activists, even if he disagreed with some of their positions. What he wasn't prepared for was a campaign that involved years of abusive and threatening postcards from all around the world.

From whom and from where these came is unclear. They all have photos of kangaroos on them, and the messages purport to be from the 'Animal Welfare Committee of the Society of Australian Deltiologists'. There are postcards from Sydney, the United States, Indonesia, London and Papua New Guinea, among other places. One reads: 'We're looking for you Frank'. There is no question that the postcards were intended to threaten and unsettle him.

Moorhouse talked to very few people about this episode in his life, but he did ask his archivist and friend Nicholas Pounder to keep the material and only release it after his death. Pounder duly shared the material with me after Moorhouse passed.

Moorhouse's relationship with the bush and his rural past was, like everything else in his life, complicated. But it was rich and thoughtful and fully formed. In his later years, Moorhouse reflected that he had made his peace with the bush; now he went trekking for different reasons from the ones that propelled him on difficult and solitary walks earlier in his life. Feeling initially embarrassed about having to be rescued in the bush outside Bourke, he wrote:

> I have absorbed this don't-quit attitude from my family, especially my brothers, and from the masculine country town culture of toughness in which I grew up, and all the leadership training I went through in scouting and in the army . . . I have had a lifelong quarrel with the negative parts of my masculinity, maybe with all crude masculinity. My personality, as I discovered it, at a deep level, was strongly inclined to androgyny, to the femme side of androgyny. I no longer go trekking to perform the primitive 'ordeal rituals' of masculinity, to prove myself as a man.

Moorhouse's making peace with the bush was also part of him making peace with himself, or more specifically with his struggles with his ambivalence about his gender. His personality was, he wrote, 'under the command of a more placid androgyny these days'. Half of his ashes were scattered near the Budawang Range in the Sassafras National Park, on a track where he so often started his hikes.

CONCLUSION

On 26 June 2022, Frank Moorhouse passed away in his sleep overnight. His close friends Nick and Carol Dettmann and Sandra Levy were with him in the hours before his death. Moorhouse wrote eighteen books, numerous screenplays and countless essays. He was a lifelong activist who helped change restrictive censorship laws, advocated for writers' rights, including the reform of copyright law, and supported gay liberation and women's liberation.

In her book *The Year of Magical Thinking*, Joan Didion writes about being told of her husband's death:

'He's dead, isn't he,' I heard myself say to the doctor. The doctor looked at the social worker. 'It's okay,' the social worker said. 'She's a pretty cool customer.' . . .

When I walked into the apartment and saw John's jacket and scarf still lying on the chair where he had dropped them . . . I wondered what an uncool customer would be allowed to do? Break down? Require sedation? Scream?

Didion is sketching here the unfinished sentence which marks the death of a significant other. It's the ones who knew the person who are left to finish that sentence.

When I heard about Moorhouse's death, my immediate thought was: 'What would Frank say?' He would no doubt have had a lot to say. Searching his writings, I can't find any extended reflection on death. As a person, he was both intensely private and yet very public. Death was something he talked about with friends but shied away from addressing in his work. He was guarded about showing open vulnerability, despite being someone who constantly wrestled with the subject of human frailty.

A characteristic of Moorhouse which has not been publicly remarked on but which became abundantly clear to me after his death, both on social media and in conversations with people who knew him, was how many people felt they had a special connection with him. His extensive network of friends was, to a very large extent, compartmentalised. Indeed, a number of them commented at his memorial on how surprised they were to learn that they each had their own friendship with Moorhouse without their paths having crossed through him. A lot of people have, generously, called me to share their memories of him subsequent to his death. A surprising number used the word 'soulmate' to describe their relationship. Moorhouse had the gift of making anyone he had taken an interest in feel like the most fascinating person in the room. And they were, when he was with them. He kept his friendship circles largely separate because he knew who he needed to see and when he needed to see them. He very carefully curated most of his social relationships.

In the days that followed his death, I wrote an obituary for *The Sydney Morning Herald* and spoke to some of his closest friends.

Without exception, the first thing they mentioned was his personal and professional generosity. The second thing they mentioned was his sense of humour. Matt Condon, who like Moorhouse was a journalist as well as an author, said: 'He was a loyal and generous friend and one of the funniest human beings I have ever known. In his final phone texts, he wrote that he no longer had an interest in Police Rounds, as he did in his younger years, but had moved onto Existential Rounds.'

Fiona Giles, on whom he based *Forty-Seventeen*, said: 'Despite the complicated shape of our relationship, Frank was always incredibly generous, always protective and a wonderfully intellectual adventurer.'

During the League of Nations trilogy and subsequent books, Moorhouse worked closely with publishers Jane Palfreyman and Meredith Curnow at Random House Australia. It is worth quoting Palfreyman at length, given that their editing/writing partnership was central to three of his finest works, *Grand Days*, *Dark Palace* and *Martini*. On learning of his death, she told me:

Frank Moorhouse was an astonishing talent, a true original and one of our finest writers. Working with him on those momentous League of Nations novels *Grand Days* and *Dark Palace* and his quirky and intoxicating *Martini: A Memoir* were huge life highlights for me. I was quite young and completely dazzled by Frank and his writing and what could have been an overwhelming and intimidating experience for me was made to seem like the greatest fun in the world as well as a thrilling intellectual experience because of his warmth, respect and generosity of spirit. He was both utterly fearless in the way he would give free rein to his imagination and where it would take him and also meticulous and even pernickety when it came to research.

How many conversations can be had about the right way to make a martini? An immeasurable number—but, as he loved to joke, if you are lost in the bush, just make a martini and someone will come along to tell you you're doing it wrong.

Frank cared as much about the laciest details of Edith Campbell Berry's lingerie as he did the arcane and obscure areas of League of Nations protocols. He loved the intricacies of bureaucracy as much as the untethered intimacies of the human heart; and he brought both to vivid and astonishing life. To work with Frank was to be wholeheartedly welcomed into his mind and world: hard work in the morning, then an excellent lunch followed by looser, more instinctive work in the afternoon, and then the inevitable martini or many. We would spend hours and hours (over years) talking about Edith and Ambrose as though they were close friends; and many readers say that is how they feel about these indelible characters when they meet them on the page. Frank is a true and singular genius of Australian Literature and his books will live forever and be a perpetual measure of his brilliance and originality. We were so lucky to have him. Feeling heartbroken and bereft, as are all who knew and loved him.

Literary critic and journalist Susan Wyndham first met Frank Moorhouse in her mother's living room in 1974. Moorhouse had written the screenplay for *Between Wars* and her mother was working for the Australian Film Development Corporation, which financed the film. Wyndham's mother was also in a 'passionately tempestuous relationship' with Mike Thornhill, who directed the film.

'At sixteen, I knew I was on the edge of an exciting cultural wave and an unfamiliar bohemian lifestyle,' she says.

Frank in corduroys and horn-rimmed glasses was diffident and polite to me that day. I met him on my own terms more than twenty years later when I was literary editor of *The Sydney Morning Herald* and he was the admired author of numerous books, scathing about powerful institutions, insightful about human foibles, and hilariously funny . . . Frank lived between hedonism and hard work, joie de vivre and melancholy, grandeur and poverty . . . Frank leaves us with some extra-ordinary books and I look forward to reading them again.

Leading copyright advocate Virginia Gordon recalls first meeting Moorhouse in 'the darkened warmth of our beloved Bayswater Brasserie'.

He was sitting with a fine red wine, observing, back to the wall, an angled vantage of all the comings and goings and darkened pairings and adventurers. Writing on the 3 x 5 note cards to which he was introduced by Michele Field, with the pocket wallet in which they were placed sitting next to them . . . If the Bayswater Brasserie were still open we would be there now, everyone who ever knew him. There would have been a week of mourning. We would have a blue plaque outside the door and a plaque above his two tables and a bar stool.

The author Julia Leigh said: 'I think of cher F as a man of many darlings,' she says. 'Intimate conspiracy was his metier. He did not shy from discussing his transsexuality or the erotic life in general. I'm quite impressed that he kept that flame going in his own life for so long.'

Writer Angelo Loukakis said:

Over the past half century, few writers in this country have
mattered as much as Frank. He mattered to the many thousands of readers who understood and enjoyed his writing—and
he also mattered to other writers who, while they appreciated
his work, also learned from him . . . I came to know Frank in
the late 1970s when he and Richard [Dick] Hall, myself and
a couple [of] others were among the first clients of [the] then
new literary agent Rose Creswell, another important figure in
the growth of local writing at the time. As with Rose, Frank
too became a friend and colleague. Like other writers who will
doubtless speak in days to come of what he meant to them,
I can say Frank greatly encouraged and supported me in my
work. From its earliest days, he was also a great supporter
of the Australian Society of Authors, indeed was instrumental in its development. When I eventually came to head up
that organisation he again gave me his encouragement and
support, contributing to various events and offering his experienced counsel in dealing with rights issues and politicians of
all stripes.

Tim Herbert met Moorhouse when the latter was Writer in
Residence at Sydney University. Like Moorhouse, Herbert was
interested in writing about sexuality and erotic pleasures. 'Frank
had his detractors,' he acknowledges.

Many in the gay community figured him evasive, a reactionary.
A closet queen. I remember thinking myself, back in 1980, just
three pages into *The Everlasting Secret Family*, with its raw gutter
sex carnality, 'Surely this can't be written by a straight man'.

Eventually I'd realised that when it comes to writing desire, perversity and erotic pleasure, Frank had a rare sensibility. Not straight or gay. Not even bisexual, unless corralled by a journalist into making a declaration. He was a ground breaker in fiction and in his own sexuality. To quote *Forty-Seventeen*: 'Sexuality did seem to be infinite in its variations.'

Photojournalist and writer Tony Maniaty, who worked with Moorhouse at the ABC, reflected:

Frank was part of an early 80s group centred on our literary agent Rose Creswell, at a time when Australian literature was finding a fresh voice, along with the Australian film industry. Frank was at the heart of that movement, as a strikingly innovative writer, a tireless representative of authors' rights, and—most devilishly—as the instigator, over late night drinks, of robust discussions marked by his incisive commentary and very droll humour. Frank had been, like me, an editor on the ABC News international desk, a role we both agreed helped in our fiction writing—the world observed large. But Frank's equal specialty was in the nuanced observation of human nature, not least the foibles of the social circles he moved in.

As so many will attest, he was a complex and generous being and a literary professional who imposed high standards on everything he wrote.

Moorhouse's niece Karin Moorhouse reached out after his death with the following anecdote:

One of the last people to visit Frank was his niece Ingrid Aysu on a home visit from Turkey, where she lives. She arrived at his room masked up, making it difficult for her uncle to recognise her. She had interrupted him fumbling to send a text to his doctor about his impending cataract operation. Visibly frustrated, his demeanour was transformed when she presented him with a dozen fresh, plump oysters. The plastic tray hardly mattered. Even if he couldn't see them, he could anticipate them. He promptly pulled out his Swiss Army knife and proceeded to savour each one, methodically turning over the empty shells. It was classic Frank, and those were his last oysters.

Nick Horne inherited Moorhouse as a lunch companion after the death of his father, Donald. 'Frank called me his reality checker,' he says, 'but it was Frank who had the greater appreciation of the complexity and nuance of human reality; the conflicting and sometimes contradictory emotions, thoughts and physical needs that make up a person and affect how people interact. He appreciated it and he felt it and it wasn't always easy but it helped him produce great art.'

On an afternoon I spent with his friend the late poet Robert Adamson and his wife, the photographer Juno Gemes, in their home on the Hawkesbury River, Adamson vividly recalled Moorhouse's generosity when he arrived in Balmain. Adamson had spent a lot of his young life in jail for petty offences. Moorhouse helped bring him into the circle of writers living there at the time, and Adamson ended up living in a house Moorhouse had previously occupied in Church Street. Adamson was also friends with Michael Wilding, and observed how influenced both were by American writers. For Moorhouse the major influences were Hunter S. Thompson and William Faulkner, while 'Michael was more influenced by Jack Kerouac'.

'I think the most amazing thing about Frank's writing is how readable it is,' Adamson said. 'You want to keep reading it. A lot of good writers—you read a few pages and you think, that's good but I'll have a break. With Frank, I want to finish the whole book.'

In a documentary on Moorhouse called *A Writer's Camp*, Moorhouse jokes about his Balmain poet friends. When asked why the side passage to the house is so overgrown, he tells Rose Creswell: 'The poets have been doing the gardening again.'

Moorhouse had an extraordinarily wide circle of friends and ex-lovers, as well as devoted readers. I interviewed 45 people for this biography. I have not been able to include quotes from all of them, but their insights and careful reflection on the man and his work have been invaluable.

I think it fitting to end by quoting Fiona Giles, who published a piece on Moorhouse after his death in *The Monthly*. In it she describes the extraordinary combination of whimsy, intensity and delight in pleasure that he brought to his life, his work and his friendships:

> Frank identified as Freudian, and often accused me of express-
> ing displaced anger for my father instead of a problem, for
> example, with the washing up . . .
>
> This is not to say that our grand passion did not bequeath me
> countless vivid memories: visiting strip clubs and porn cinemas
> in the Cross on my first visit to Sydney as an 18-year-old; suggest-
> ing I put fresh apricots in a bowl at Ewenton Street, so as not
> to miss out on the aesthetic pleasure they afforded . . . Gifting
> me a subscription to *The New Yorker*, which I still subscribe to
> 46 years later; showing me how to fire his Luger pistol, which
> he took with him to the bush, 'just in case'. His kindness when

I accidentally spilled a bottle of Krug champagne during lunch in the south of France; punting on the River Cherwell drinking champagne from crystal glasses he'd purchased with my scholarship money; his cooking pigeon and peas, while I wept on the floor of my Wolfson College rooms for the loss of another man, for the loss of my brother, and all the nameless losses; Frank and I deciding to leave his semen in my hair where it landed while making love one afternoon. His love of piano bars, and the song 'Moon River'; Frank and I lunching with his friends Gough and Margaret Whitlam in their flat in Double Bay.

Moorhouse's life encompassed many passions and spanned many worlds. His ultimate legacy is there in his work. He was fittingly farewelled at the State Library of New South Wales on 13 July 2022, at an event organised by Carol Dettmann. His brother Arthur, his friends and fellow writers and publishers Don Anderson, Meredith Curnow, Jane Palfreyman, Helen Lewis, Julia Leigh (speaking for Tim Herbert), Nick Horne, and Sam and Jessie Dettmann all spoke. One of Australia's finest writers, Tom Keneally, was the last speaker and bade him a final farewell, pausing to note: 'Above all, Frank was cool.'

AFTERWORD:
IN THE MOORHOUSE ARCHIVE

Frank Moorhouse was a writer who thought deeply about ethics: about the ethics of writing and the ethics of being human. He questioned the ethics of writing about the self and the ethics of writing about others. His writing gnawed at a fundamental question: what do we owe ourselves and what do we owe others— as humans but equally, in his case, as a writer?

It seemed impossible to write a biography of Frank Moorhouse without asking myself the same questions. What are the ethics of biography? And what do I owe the subject of this biography, his readers, and those who knew him and who are described in its pages? Moorhouse and I discussed this question many times in the interviews I did with him for this book. In this Afterword, for those readers who are curious, I will explain how I approached these questions and conducted the research which underpins this book.

I came to know Moorhouse in the early 1990s, when we were both invited to what I recall as an improbably titled 'Festival of

Australian Ideas' in Washington D.C. We caught up for lunch when he came through New York, where I was living at the time, and continued a friendship back in Sydney. I popped the biography question after writing a profile of him for *The Bulletin* magazine which he told me was one of the few profiles of him where he felt someone really 'got' him. Or perhaps he just found it flattering. We agreed on the terms of engagement: Moorhouse would give me full access to his archive and answer any questions I had. He would read all the chapters in the book for the purposes of fact checking. He would not ask for any substantive changes. He kept to his side of the bargain and read everything except the conclusion, which I wrote after his death.

When I embarked on the biography, a new relationship formed which tempered our friendship: the biographical relationship. Over the course of a decade, I interviewed Moorhouse more than twenty times for the book and we talked about the purpose of biography and what a life can tell you—and what it can't—about a writer's creative work. I also interviewed 45 people who were connected with Moorhouse personally or professionally. Biography is a genre that creeps up on the biographer. Each biographer slightly recasts the form. Some spend years searching for small clues that will allow them to add fresh insights to lives that have been comprehensively mined by earlier authors. Others contend with subjects who have ordered their executors to destroy all their papers.

Moorhouse offered his biographers no such obstacle. He kept every significant letter he ever received, and a copy of every significant letter he ever wrote. His archive is a map of his life as much as of his work. There is an enormous volume of material to mine, including 158 boxes of personal papers in the main archive at the Fryer Library at the University of Queensland. Simon Farley and his expert team at the Fryer showed me extraordinary generosity during my research. And the archive kept growing, as I discovered over the decade I spent researching this book.

His detailed archive reflects his strong intellectual and political reservations about the cultural and political value of privacy. He questioned the prevailing moral insistence on it. 'We would all be better off and healthier if we moved away from most of our positions on privacy, which are often just an endorsement of stigma,' he told me. As a person, though, I found him at times more selectively vigilant about his personal life than this statement suggests.

I once asked Moorhouse to give me a timeline of where he had lived in his life, what he was doing at the time and who he was living with. The results were unexpected—alarming even. Moorhouse presented me with a list, starting when he was in primary school, of everywhere he had ever lived, the jobs or roles he had at the time, who he was living with and the erotic acts he was engaged in at the time. But if we take Moorhouse at his word on his own disavowal of privacy, where does that leave the people whose lives are also laid out in his archive? Where does it leave his biographers? What ethical duties do we owe the people whose relationships with Moorhouse are documented there?

Some years ago, I was working in the Fryer with archivist Nicholas Pounder. The Fryer is housed in a building that abuts the University of Queensland's honey-hued sandstone quadrangle and holds an impressive collection of published and unpublished material in Australian literature. As Moorhouse's archivist, Pounder understands more about the subject of the archive than anyone else. Or as Moorhouse once joked, Pounder may well know more, given the human tendency to efface unwanted memories. Pounder accompanied me on a number of my journeys to the Fryer, advising me on which boxes to trawl, pointing out key material and diagnosing scrawled signatures.

Just after lunch one Friday, he placed a large box on my desk containing a series of fat manila folders. 'I think you'll find these of some interest,' he said a little archly.

I opened the box. One of the first letters in the folders began innocently enough: 'Dear Fiona, Yes I remember you . . .' The letter was dated 14 April 1976. Moorhouse was 37 at the time, and the well-known author of four works of fiction. He was writing to a seventeen-year-old Perth schoolgirl he'd met at a Fellowship of Australian Authors seminar in Perth. A spontaneous trip to Kalgoorlie with her had ensued. The first line of her letter to him—'Do you remember me?'—was teasing. She knew there was no way he could have forgotten her.

The correspondence in the file traced the emotional, intellectual and sexual contours of a relationship that had spanned thirteen years and ended with an undated and unsent suicide letter from Moorhouse to Fiona Giles after their relationship ended. The file contained the story of one of the longest and most intimate relationships in the author's life. She was, perhaps, his *amour fou*. Their letters were by turns passionate, playful, literary and erotic. To read them was to trespass on the most intimate of exchanges.

In my case, it was a double trespass: Fiona, an academic and writer, had been one of my closest friends for 30 years. Yet I found myself sitting in the hushed respectability of a university library, slipping between the covers of her sexual, academic and romantic life, and taking notes. Halfway through reading the file, I found myself standing in the university quadrangle crying, gulping for air and calling my friend to tell her what I was reading. She drew her own deep breath and said: 'Darling, it's okay. You're the biographer. You *have* to read everything. Better you than some horny old Marxist.'

So what of the third parties caught up in Moorhouse's life, who didn't ask to be part of the biography? The choice I made was to keep much of what I read in their letters private and opt instead to interview as many key people in Moorhouse's life as I was able so they could give their own account. I have erred on the side of caution when it comes to revealing intimate relationships documented in the archive which are not public knowledge.

The Code of Ethics for Archivists adopted by the Council of the Society of American Archivists in 1992 requires those dealing with archives to respect the privacy of individuals 'who created, or are the subjects of, documentary materials of long-term value'. The code offers no advice on how to determine what should remain private. Some libraries make all material available to researchers; others limit access. At least one, the Bodleian Library at Oxford University, seals all letters by living people and refuses access even to the donor.

Protecting the privacy of those who did not ask to be part of a biography is clearly a key ethical principle that any responsible biographer must at the very least consider. Yet it's a principle that, equally, needs to be weighed against the public and scholarly interest in significant cultural figures. And sometimes the writer does not get the final say. There are many instances of family members burning the private papers of writers who may have wanted their archives to be available for study. James Joyce's grandson Stephen Joyce burned letters by Samuel Beckett and Joyce's daughter, Lucia, that Joyce scholars regarded as critical in the field.

In writing this biography, I have constantly balanced my desire to include a quote from a letter that would add genuine shade or light to this biography with my concern about the potential harm that might be done to others by an unexpected disclosure. And, in the case of the Moorhouse archive 'disclosure' seems an excessively polite word for some of the material that implicates other people.

The politics, sexuality and ethics that marked Moorhouse's work and his approach to living have always been confronting for fans of the status quo. Yet Moorhouse didn't set out to provoke. He found political grandstanding abhorrent when it slid into moral vanity (now known as 'virtue signalling'), and had no interest in proselytising. He was always entirely open about his politics, and eventually with his sexuality (in his younger days he had to contend with criminal laws). Naturally, not everyone who was part of his life shared his ethos. Or, perhaps they may have shared his ethos when they considered themselves part of a bohemian set, but later have come to see things differently. Or, of course, perhaps Moorhouse remembered things differently from the way they did—memory being unreliable, as we all know.

To return to my discussion of what a biographer should do with abundant archival material that discloses the private lives of individuals who didn't expect or ask to be written about and how I respond to that issue in this book. In some cases, I only name people who were important in Moorhouse's life—particularly his intimate life—if there is little risk of damage or if I have contacted them and they have given me permission. In all cases I have tried to be guided by a concern to honestly reflect the deeper patterns that structured Moorhouse's life, his relationships and his oeuvre.

ACKNOWLEDGEMENTS

My first acknowledgement is to Jane Palfreyman, the most patient publisher on the planet. Thank you for accepting the challenge of publishing this book, and for sharing your deep insights into Frank Moorhouse and his work. I owe you and your wonderful team at Allen & Unwin a round of martinis.

Thanks also to Nicholas Pounder, Moorhouse's archivist, who carefully sourced and curated the photographs for this book, and who guided my journey through his archive and read parts of the manuscript.

Huge thanks to Simon Farley and his remarkable team at the Fryer Library at the University of Queensland. They are the keepers of multiple archives which define Australian literary and artistic culture. It was a privilege to work there.

Laura Robins assisted me throughout the book, organising interviews and keeping the voluminous research materials in order.

I also thank a number of wonderful research assistants who worked on edits and footnotes for me: Dr Ann Hine, Judith Ireland, Emily Baulch, Jose Borghino and Dr Joseph Brennan.

I interviewed the following people, who graciously gave me their time and shared their insights: Christine Allsop, Don Anderson, Wendy Bacon, Peter Banki, Tony Bilson, Richard Brennan, Susie Carleton, Lenore Coltheart, Paul Coombes, Matt Condon, Annabel Crabb, Nick and Carol Dettmann, Sarah Ducker, André Frankovits, Zoe Fraser, Fiona Giles, Rohan Haslam, Xavier Hennekinne, Tim Herbert, Tom Keneally, Brian Kiernan, Wendy James, Matthew Lamb, Helen Lewis, Robert Macklin, David Marr, Fay and Peter Martin, Jane Messer, Tony Moore, Meaghan Morris, Craig Munro, John Newton, Jane Palfreyman, Nicholas Pounder, David Roe, Tim Rowse, Meg Stewart, Errol Sullivan, David Williamson.

And a final special thanks to my amazing husband, Larry, for his unfailing encouragement and for tolerating me talking about this book in my sleep.

ENDNOTES

CHAPTER 1: LEAVING NOWRA

p. 3   'This memoir is not a comprehensive overview . . .' Frank Moorhouse, *Martini: A Memoir*, Sydney: Random House, 2006, p. 205.

p. 8   'Writers sometimes talk of the mother novel and the father novel . . .' Steger, J., 'Interview: Frank Moorhouse', *The Sydney Morning Herald*, 12 November 2011.

p. 10   'I think Mr Moorhouse is one of . . .' Moorhouse Family Archive.

p. 11   'In those days, the problem in the dairying industry . . .' Commonwealth, *Parliamentary Debates*, Senate, 21 Sept. 1994, p. 1145 (Michael Baume Senator) (Aust.).

p. 11   'the greatest contribution to good quality milk . . .' Commonwealth, Parliamentary Debates, p. 1145.

p. 12   'Therefore, it shall be my purpose . . .' Moorhouse Family Archive.

p. 14   'CWA social occasions, such as a branch opening . . .' Jones, J., *Country Women and the Colour Bar: Grassroots Activism and the Country Women's Association*, Canberra: Aboriginal Studies Press, 2015, p. 100.

p. 14   'CWA was an organisation that reinforced existing class hierarchies . . .' Jones, *Country Women and the Colour Bar*, p. 98.

p. 14   'wished "bon voyage" as they embarked on overseas trips . . .' Jones, *Women and the Colour Bar*, p. 107.

p. 24   'T. George McDowell was a man who believed . . .' Moorhouse, F., *The Electrical Experience*, Sydney: Angus & Robertson, 1988, p. 8.

p. 24   '[t]he South Coast produced a better sort of person . . .' Moorhouse, *The Electrical Experience*, p. 7.

p. 25   'He said to Margoulis that freedom of enterprise . . .' Moorhouse, *The Electrical Experience*, p. 37.

p. 25   'I believe in shirt-sleeve words . . .' Moorhouse, *The Electrical Experience*, p. 8.

p. 25   'He rather thought, self-control slipping . . .' Moorhouse, *The Electrical Experience*, p. 16.

p. 25   'To say, drink alcohol, like some of the others . . .' Moorhouse, *The Electrical Experience*, p. 38.

p. 26　'Being in Geneva had permitted her to behave . . .' Moorhouse, *Grand Days*, Chippendale: Pan Macmillan, 1994, p. 282.

p. 27　'The Christmas feast of my childhood . . .' Moorhouse, F., 'Road to Nowra', *The Monthly*, December 2012–January 2013, p. 56.

p. 47　'[I]t was about as shocking for my family . . .' Moorhouse, 'Road to Nowra', p. 57.

p. 28　'I remember vividly the day in my early 30s . . .' Moorhouse, 'Road to Nowra', p. 58.

p. 32　'In the 50s I was in total confusion about my sexuality . . .' Guilliatt, R., 'His Dark Material', *The Australian Magazine*, 1 December 2007, p. 24.

p. 33　'For months I'd resisted his advances . . .' Moorhouse, *Martini*, p. 181.

p. 34　'What of the young wife from the martini story . . .' Moorhouse, *Martini*, p. 181.

p. 34　'where I'd first kissed Margaret my girlfriend . . .' Moorhouse, *Martini*, p. 183.

p. 35　'The sentence about the teacher . . .' Moorhouse, *Martini*, p. 190.

p. 35　'Frank Moorhouse, my husband a long time ago . . .' Porter, J., 'Martini stirs Moorhouse ex's fury', *The Australian*, 31 March 2007.

p. 35　'It wasn't about Wendy, it wasn't an attempt to depict her . . .' Guilliatt, 'His Dark Material', p. 26.

p. 37　'Although he was a few years younger . . .' Moorhouse, *Grand Days*, pp. 279–80.

p. 38　'It wasn't that Australia was not a "real" place . . .' Moorhouse, *Grand Days*, p. 281.

CHAPTER 2: LIVING IN THE '70S: SEX, GENDER AND POLITICS

p. 40　'They rolled hard with the knife between them . . .' Moorhouse, F., 'The Story of the Knife', in *Futility and Other Animals*, Sydney: Picador, 1969, pp. 7–8.

p. 43　'By the early seventies, friends had drifted into Balmain . . .' Moorhouse, F., *Days of Wine and Rage*, Melbourne: Penguin, 1980, p. 117.

p. 44　'began as a gathering of young writers and friends . . .' Moorhouse, *Days of Wine and Rage*, p. 129.

p. 44　'What they're spending on alcohol and drugs . . .' Moorhouse, *Days of Wine and Rage*, p. 117.

p. 44　'We had the Balmain Pub Crawl . . .' Moorhouse, *Days of Wine and Rage*, p. 117.

p. 45　'I can see that you're not interested . . .' Moorhouse, 'The Story of the Knife', p. 11.

p. 46　'The Myth of the Vaginal Orgasm . . .' Koedt, A. 'The Myth of the Vaginal Orgasm', *Notes from the Second Year*, 1970.

p. 46　'With my limited sexual experience . . .' Le Masurier, M., 'Photograph: Germaine Greer', in Alison Bartlett and Margaret Henderson (eds), *Things That Liberate: An Australian feminist wunderkammer*, Newcastle, England: Cambridge Scholars Publishing, p. 123.

p. 46　'The Myth of the Male Orgasm . . .' Moorhouse, *Days of Wine and Rage*, pp. 31–36.

p. 47　'Men created this myth to deny the sexuality of women . . .' Moorhouse, F. 'The Myth of the Male Orgasm', *Sex*, 1971, pp. 8–10. Moorhouse's response also appeared in *Days of Wine and Rage*, pp. 31–36.

p. 47　'Got a young man yet? . . .' Moorhouse, F., 'Dell Goes into Politics', in *The Americans, Baby*, Sydney: Angus & Robertson, 1973, p. 1.

p. 48　'They had not moved from the settee . . .' Moorhouse, 'The American, Paul Jonson', in *The Americans, Baby*, p. 12.

p. 49   'Jimmy changed my ideas about sex . . .' Moorhouse, F., 'What Can You Say?', in *Futility and Other Animals*, Sydney: Picador, 1969, p. 18.

p. 49   'When he drinks he sometimes relaxes . . .' Moorhouse, F., 'The Alter Ego Interpretation', in *Tales of Mystery and Romance*, Sydney: Angus & Robertson, 1977, pp. 2–14.

p. 50   'a significant turning point in the representation . . .' Murrie, L., 'The Australian legend: Writing Australian masculinity/writing "Australian" masculine', *Journal of Australian Studies*, 1998, vol. 22, no. 56, pp. 68–77.

p. 50   'Moorhouse subverts patriarchal constructions . . .' Murrie, 'The Australian legend', p. 69.

p. 50   'We talked about keeping it . . .' Moorhouse, F., 'Anderson, How Can There Be a Baby and No Crying?', in *Futility and Other Animals*, p. 38.

p. 51   'intelligence, courage, curiosity and determined idealism . . .' Coltheart, L., 'Who is Edith Campbell Berry', *Island*, 2013, vol. 132, Autumn, p. 8.

p. 52   'a residual culture of Australian middle class ockerism . . .' Henderson, M., 'The girl who met Simone de Beauvoir in Brisbane, or, must we burn Beauvoir?', *Hecate*, 2000, vol. 26, no. 1, p. 113.

p. 52   'The creation of one's self as a work of art . . .' Moore, T., *Dancing with Empty Pockets: Australia's Bohemians*, Sydney: Pier 9, 2012, p. 23.

p. 52   'While [Anderson] himself preferred a life of thinking . . .' Moore, *Dancing with Empty Pockets*, p. 23.

p. 53   'They were not like the Bloomsbury set . . .' Coombs, A., *Sex and Anarchy: The Life and Death of the Sydney Push*, Melbourne: Penguin, 1996, p. viii.

p. 54   'It was a social dance choreographed . . .' Farrelly, E., 'When push came to shove', *The Sydney Morning Herald*, 4 April 2009.

p. 54   'We met and drank most nights . . .' Moorhouse, *Days of Wine and Rage*, p. 134.

p. 55   'We were being guided by Darcy Waters . . .' Moorhouse, F., *Loose Living*, Sydney: Vintage Books, 2009, p. 133.

p. 56   'We went to this renowned Carlton restaurant . . .' Moorhouse, *Loose Living*, p. 134.

p. 56   'These new movements were fundamentally different . . .' Docker, J., *Australian Cultural Elites: Intellectual traditions in Sydney and Melbourne*, Sydney: Angus & Robertson, 1974, p. 159.

p. 57   'destructive and mechanical in their sense . . .' Docker, *Australian Cultural Elites*, p. 162.

p. 57   'Where Norman Lindsay . . .' Docker, *Australian Cultural Elites*, p. 161.

p. 58   'Really, they were romantics . . .' Coombs, *Sex and Anarchy*, cover blurb.

p. 58   'Libertarians did not use condoms . . .' Coombs, *Sex and Anarchy*, p. 37.

p. 58   'Coombs recounts the story of a young woman . . .' Coombs, *Sex and Anarchy*, p. 39.

p. 59   'If Anderson saw a parallel between sexual repression and servility . . .' Wark, M., *The Virtual Republic: Australia's culture wars of the 1990s*, Sydney: Allen & Unwin, 1997, p. 69.

p. 59   'The outside world had rules to hedge you . . .' Coombs, *Sex and Anarchy*, p. 68.

p. 60   'Above all, the average woman is a mother . . .' George Patterson Pty Ltd, *The Patterson Report: Or, 'Wooing the Australian woman'*, Sydney: George Patterson, 1972.

p. 61   'the ideas behind sexual liberation . . .' Le Masurier, M., 'Resurrecting Germaine's theory of cuntpower', *Australian Feminist Studies*, 2016, vol. 31, no. 87, p. 30.

ENDNOTES

p. 61　'consciousness-raising sessions . . .' Le Masurier, 'Resurrecting Germaine's theory of cuntpower', p. 31.

p. 62　'When I first entered the dingy back room . . .' Coombs, *Sex and Anarchy*, p. 114.

p. 62　'*The Female Eunuch* is unabashedly libertarian . . .' Gleeson, K., 'From *Suck* magazine to *Corporate Paedophilia*. Feminism and pornography – remembering the Australian way', *Women's Studies International Forum*, 2013, vol. 38, May–June, p. 86.

p. 63　'refused to settle for the clitoral orgasms of Masters and Johnson . . .' Le Masurier, 'Resurrecting Germaine's theory of cuntpower', p. 33.

p. 63　'The response in the early years was . . .' Coombs, *Sex and Anarchy*, p. 258.

p. 63　'The libertarian strand in Sydney feminism remained strong in some quarters . . .' Lumby, C., *Bad Girls: The media, sex and feminism in the 90s*, Sydney: Allen & Unwin, 1997.

p. 63　'I wasn't a person who had never been . . .' Coombs, *Sex and Anarchy*, p. 256.

p. 64　'Women's Lib was different in Sydney . . .' Coombs, *Sex and Anarchy*, p. 264.

p. 64　'We found the victory celebration party . . .' Moorhouse, *Days of Wine and Rage*, p. 44.

p. 65　'If Asked in a Survey . . .' Moorhouse, F., 'If asked in a survey, yes, I'd say I was a liberated lady', *The Bulletin*, 3 June 1972, pp. 67–70.

p. 65　'My gosh, it's all very well for young girls . . .' Moorhouse, *Days of Wine and Rage*, p. 38.

p. 65　'Oh, she could have been a lot worse off . . .' Moorhouse, 'If asked in a survey, yes', p. 70.

p. 68　'instrumental in transforming a celebration of homosexuality . . .' Kanaganayakan, C., 'Form and meaning in the short stories of Frank Moorhouse', *Journal of Postcolonial Writing*, 1985, vol. 25, no. 1, p. 72.

p. 68　'the question of self-censorship within . . .' Kirby, S., 'Homosocial desire and homosexual panic in the fiction of David Malouf and Frank Moorhouse', *Meanjin*, 1997, vol. 46, no. 3, pp. 385–93.

p. 69　'To speak of "lesbian/gay" writing . . .' Altman, D., 'A closet of one's own', *Island*, 1991, vol. 48, Spring, p. 31.

p. 69　'The men of the Push delighted in his stories . . .' Coombs, *Sex and Anarchy*, p. 124.

p. 70　'differed most strongly from the later gay community . . .' Willett, G., *Living Out Loud: A history of Gay and Lesbian activism in Australia*, Sydney: Allen & Unwin, 2000, p. 9.

p. 71　'From 1970 to 1973, the first generation of CAMP activists . . .' Reynolds, R., 'CAMP Inc. and the creation of the open homosexual' in *Australia's Homosexual Histories: Gay and Lesbian Perspectives V*, Phillips, D.L. and Willett, G. (eds), Sydney: Australian Centre for Lesbian and Gay Research, 2000, p. 134.

p. 71　'This time they went to Paul's bed . . .' Moorhouse, *The Americans, Baby*, p. 21.

p. 72　'There in the alcove of the pub . . .' Moorhouse, *Futility and Other Animals*, p. 44.

p. 72　'Frank's homosexuality was something . . .' Wilding, M., *Growing Wild*, Arcadia, Melbourne, 2016, p. 172.

p. 73　'I climbed into his bed . . .' Wilding, M., *Growing Wild*, p. 173.

p. 74　'When Sasha Soldatow first began visiting Sydney . . .' Coombs, *Sex and Anarchy*, p. 277.

CHAPTER 3: THE WRITING LIFE

p. 77   'Separated from Gillian and from the ABC . . .' Moorhouse, *Days of Wine and Rage*, p. 3.

p. 77   'I had used the good reviews for *Futility and Other Animals* . . .' Moorhouse, *Days of Wine and Rage*, p. 3.

p. 78   'What had really pulled the curtain up . . .' Horne, D., *Into the Open: Memoirs 1958–1999*, Sydney: HarperCollins, 2000, p. 169.

p. 78   'I took to Frank's writing as an antidote . . .' Horne, *Into the Open*, p. 169.

p. 79   'They handled each other's pens . . .' Moorhouse, F., *Forty-Seventeen*, Ringwood: Viking, 1988, pp. 1–2.

p. 80   'whether the average householder would accept . . .' Lumby, *Bad Girls*, p. 28.

p. 80   'I have found that people who go into parks . . .' Coleman, P., *Obscenity, Blasphemy and Sedition: 100 years of censorship in Australia*, Sydney: Angus & Robertson, 1974, p. 32.

p. 81   'an urgent public feeling . . .' Dutton, G. & Harris, M., *Australia's Censorship Crisis*, Melbourne: Sun Books, 1970, p. 6.

p. 82   'It was my first experience of illegal . . .' Moorhouse, *Days of Wine and Rage*, p. 5.

p. 82   'was to be the most significant activity . . .' Moorhouse, *Days of Wine and Rage*, p. 5.

p. 83   'student pornographic movement . . .' Moorhouse, F., 'Porno Politics', in Wendy Bacon et al. (eds), *Uni Sex: A Study of Sexual Attitudes and Behaviour at Australian Universities*, Melbourne: Eclipse Books, 1972, p. 31.

p. 83   'Australia, partly in the drag-stream . . .' Moorhouse, *Days of Wine and Rage*, p. 8.

p. 84   'I said that it was not legal for them . . .' Moorhouse, *Days of Wine and Rage*, p. 21.

p. 85   'It was as if we had been in a deep . . .' Moorhouse, F., 'The Urge to Censor', in *The Inspector-General of Misconception: The ultimate compendium to sorting things out*, Milsons Point: Vintage, 2002, pp. 265–66.

p. 86   'the single mythic line of the outback story . . .' Wilding, *The Tabloid Story Pocket Book*, Sydney: Wild & Woolley, 1978, p. 303.

p. 87   'We knew there was good prose around . . .' Wilding, *The Tabloid Story Pocket Book*, p. 302.

p. 87   'The host magazine taking *Tabloid Story* . . .' Wilding, *The Tabloid Story Pocket Book*, p. 299.

p. 88   'once *Tabloid Story* had publicised the issue . . .' Wilding, *The Tabloid Story Pocket Book*, p. 300.

p. 88   'We didn't require them to type . . .' Wilding, *The Tabloid Story Pocket Book*, pp. 299–300.

p. 89   'To us at that time the girlie magazines . . .' Wilding, *The Tabloid Story Pocket Book*, p. 296.

p. 90   'a country that is ninety per cent uninhabited . . .' Moorhouse, F., *Cold Light*, Random House: Sydney, 2011, p. 148.

p. 91   'A capitol is not only the place of governance . . .' Moorhouse, *Cold Light*, p. 148.

p. 92   'It may not have been illegal . . .' Moorhouse, F., *Australia Under Surveillance: How should we act?*, Sydney: Random House, 2014, p. 11.

p. 92   'Protection of the young by suppressing . . .' Moorhouse, *The Inspector-General of Misconception*, pp. 275–76.

p. 93 'We all know how ugly hate speech can be . . .' Moorhouse, *Australia Under Surveillance*, p. 117.

p. 94 'It boils down to four basic principles . . .' Moorhouse, *Australia Under Surveillance*, p. 118.

p. 94 'a group of fundamentalist moderates . . .' Moorhouse, *Australia Under Surveillance*, p. 119.

p. 94 'why is the artistic imagination treated . . .' Moorhouse, F., 'Manifesto for the Imagination', *Griffith Review*, Autumn 2009.

p. 95 'The artistic imagination sometimes draws . . .' Moorhouse, 'Manifesto for the Imagination', p. 52.

p. 96 'These cards were what I needed . . .' Moorhouse, F. 'The Survival of Australian Writing: The Role and Authority of the Literary Imagination', Fryer Lecture in Australian Literature, University of Queensland, 5 December 2015, https://espace.library.uq.edu.au/view/UQ:729012

p. 97 'I've carried these index cards . . .' Quoted in Judy Rymer (dir.), *A Writer's Camp*, Iguana Films, 1987.

p. 102 '"Hold on," I said, "isn't setting up an infringement an illegal act?" . . .' Moorhouse, F., Unpublished Address to the Copyright Society, Sydney, 5 December 2011.

p. 102 'The recent dramatic advance in techniques of reprography . . .' Nase, P., 'Case Notes', Patterson Report, George Patterson, *Federal Law Review*, 1976, vol. 7, no. 2, pp. 227–31.

p. 103 'Copyright protection and the meeting . . .' Meredith, P., *Realising the Vision: A history of Copyright Agency Limited 1974-2004*, Sydney: Copyright Agency Limited, 2004, p. 10.

p. 104 'We all walked out and went to Customs House . . .' Meredith, *Realising the Vision*, p. 19.

p. 104 'This was a much more satisfactory . . .' Meredith, *Realising the Vision*, p. 20.

p. 104 'Despite his great admiration and personal fondness . . .' Meredith, *Realising the Vision*, p. 24.

p. 105 'I tell new writers that the literary writer . . .' Moorhouse, F., 'The First Negotiation, Amorality, and Temerity', *Westerly*, vol. 57, no. 2, 2012, p. 48.

p. 105 'In the case of shared domesticity . . .' Moorhouse, 'The First Negotiation, Amorality, and Temerity', pp. 48–49.

p. 107 'During one mixing he misremembered . . .' Moorhouse, *Martini*, p. 87.

p. 108 '[A]s a storyteller, I coined an expression . . .' Moorhouse, 'The First Negotiation, Amorality, and Temerity', p. 51.

p. 110 'In the early nineteen-sixties . . .' Wood, J., 'Helen Garner's savage self-scrutiny', *The New Yorker*, 5 December 2016.

p. 110 'above all, a savage self-scrutineer . . .' Wood, 'Helen Garner's savage self-scrutiny'.

p. 112 'After Jane [Palfreyman] called me . . .' Gill, R. and Wyndham, S., 'Portrait of the Angry Author Whose $20,000 Prize Went the Way of the Kelly Gang', *The Age*, 4 October 2001, p. 1.

p. 113 'This is an appalling way to treat a person . . .' Gill, R. and Wyndham, S., 'Portrait of the Angry Author Whose $20,000 Prize Went the Way of the Kelly Gang', *The Age*, p. 1.

p. 113 'Who won the Miles Franklin? Frank Moorhouse . . .' Gill, R. and Wyndham, S., 'Portrait of the Angry Author Whose $20,000 Prize Went the Way of the Kelly Gang', *The Age*, p. 1.

p. 114 'There was the impression of a new sensibility . . .' Kiernan, B., 'Introduction', in Brian Kiernan (ed.), *The Most Beautiful Lies*, Sydney: Angus & Robertson, 1977, p. x.

p. 114 'There is no homogenous "new" fiction . . .' Kiernan, *The Most Beautiful Lies*, p. xiii.

p. 114 'My euphoria about Sydney was soon tempered . . .' Williamson, *Home Truths*, Sydney: HarperCollins, 2021, p. 212.

p. 115 'Sydney had different networks of cultural power . . .' Williamson, *Home Truths*, pp. 212–13.

p. 118 'I cable Makavejev's agent . . .' Moorhouse, F., *Lateshows*, North Sydney: Vintage Books, 1990, p. 94.

CHAPTER 4: THE MOORHOUSE METHOD: RULES FOR LIVING

p. 122 'I realised that our family meals lacked something . . .' Moorhouse, *Loose Living*, p. 169.

p. 123 'On his return to Nowra . . .' Moorhouse, *Loose Living*, p. 171.

p. 123 'It is not to do so much with the soup . . .' Moorhouse, *Grand Days*, p. 8.

p. 124 'I could become really hooked on martinis . . .' Moorhouse, *Forty-Seventeen*, p. 116.

p. 125 'You do not panic. You do not walk aimlessly . . .' Moorhouse, *Martini*, p. 179.

p. 126 'This martini is not cold enough . . .' Moorhouse, *Martini*, p. 179.

p. 127 'what is interesting about people . . .' Wilde, O., 'The Decay of Lying', *The Complete Works of Oscar Wilde*, London & Glasgow: Collins, 1971.

p. 127 'for those eating out in Australia in the 1950s . . .' Symons, M., *One Continuous Picnic: A gastronomic history of Australia*, Melbourne: Melbourne University Press, 2007.

p. 128 'Up the steps to old Diethnes . . .' Moorhouse, 'A Change of Restaurant', in *Days of Wine and Rage*, p. 277.

p. 129 'Up the stairs we would come . . .' Moorhouse, 'A Change of Restaurant', p. 277.

p. 129 'Do you like Greek food? . . .' Moorhouse, 'A Change of Restaurant', p. 277.

p. 130 'Reading at random from 1975 . . .' Bilson, G., *Plenty: Digressions on Food*, Ringwood: Penguin/Lantern, 2004, p. 21.

p. 131 'People swapped tables bringing their bottle . . .' Symons, *One Continuous Picnic*, pp. 275–76.

p. 131 'Bon Gout nourished a portion of that generation . . .' Bilson, *Plenty*, p. 25.

p. 133 'It was about now that Friedman . . .' Moorhouse, F., *Conference-ville*, Sydney: Angus & Robertson, 1976, p. 121.

p. 135 'Somehow Moorhouse has married this asceticism . . .' Guilliatt, 'His Dark Material', p. 26.

p. 137 'which the Swedes have established to create living arrangements . . .' Moorhouse, *Loose Living*, p. 31.

p. 137 'A political litany is where the host . . .' Moorhouse, *Lateshows*, p. 28.

p. 138 'The Late Parents had been gone fifteen minutes . . .' Moorhouse, *Lateshows*, pp. 23–24.

p. 139 'At around the age of eight or nine . . .' Moorhouse, *Martini*, p. 96.

p. 140 'We were interested in first getting to know vermouth . . .' Moorhouse, *Martini*, pp. 58–59.

p. 141 'I know that the bell captain has swiftly . . .' Frank Moorhouse, 'The New York Bell Captain', in *Room Service*, Sydney: Viking, 1985, p. 3.

p. 141 'What the bell captain has done . . .' Moorhouse, *Room Service*, p. 4.

p. 142 'my window looked out on my house . . .' Moorhouse, F., 'Hiltonia', in *Room Service*, p. 22.

p. 142 'I myself have a fondness for chain motels . . .' Moorhouse, *Room Service*, p. 23.

p. 142 'I wanted to write a sequel called . . .' Moorhouse, *Room Service*, p. 23.

p. 143 'Here in Cairo at the Rameses Hilton . . .' Moorhouse, *Room Service*, pp. 25–26.

p. 143 'I have begun to think that it is important . . .' Moorhouse, F., 'Oyster Love', *Gourmet Traveller*, June 2011, pp. 77–78.

p. 144 'which trigger, ever so slightly . . .' Moorhouse, 'Oyster Love', p. 78.

p. 145 'We discovered that using a small spoon . . .' Moorhouse, 'Oyster Love', p. 78.

p. 145 'I am not by inclination a spiritual person . . .' Moorhouse, 'Oyster Love', p. 78.

p. 145 'Conversation is a wide spectrum of intercourse . . .' Moorhouse, *The Inspector-General of Misconception*, p. 111.

p. 146 'We concede that alcohol enhances very few activities . . .' Moorhouse, *The Inspector-General of Misconception*, p. 113.

p. 148 'Dim, calm, a place where you should . . .' Moorhouse, *Conference-ville*, pp. 109–10.

p. 150 'None of us were under the protection . . .' Moorhouse, *The Inspector-General of Misconception*, p. 51.

CHAPTER 5: BORDER CROSSINGS

p. 151 'insufficiently Australian . . .' Steger, J. 'Everyone recognises it: The life-changing impact of a Miles Franklin nod', *The Sydney Morning Herald*, 14 July 2022.

p. 151 'Grumblings that an Australian writer . . .' Moorhouse, F., 'The Cringe – new variants of the virus', *The Sydney Morning Herald*, 28 September 1995.

p. 152 '"Cultural cringe" is a term coined . . .' Hesketh, R., 'A.A. Phillips and the cultural cringe: creating an Australian tradition', *Meanjin*, 2013, vol. 72, no. 3, pp. 92–103.

p. 152 'The term was linked explicitly . . .' Hesketh, 'A.A. Phillips and the cultural cringe', p. 94.

p. 152 'Naturally, the Miles Franklin judges had this picture . . .' Moorhouse, 'The Cringe—new variants of the virus'.

p. 153 'Dissent broke out like spot fires. . . .' Condon, M., 'Out to lunch', *The Sun-Herald*, 1 October 1995, p. 115.

p. 153 'I have never met Frank Moorhouse . . .' Carlton, M., 'Cliches trip on fairy wings', *The Sydney Morning Herald*, 30 September 1995, p. 30.

p. 153 'Far from a personal whinge . . .' Collins, P., 'Moorhouse in the minefield', *The Sydney Morning Herald*, 29 September 1995, p. 17.

p. 154 'Australian writing cannot spurn the cosmopolitan . . .' Holgate, B., 'A Culture Still Trying to Cure Its Pimples', *The Sydney Morning Herald*, 29 September 1995, p. 17.

p. 154 'The fact that we've got to congratulate ourselves . . .' Holgate, B., 'A Culture Still Trying to Cure Its Pimples', p. 17.

p. 155 'Phillips should be alive today to smell the corpse now . . .' Moorhouse, *The Inspector-General of Misconception*, p. 217.

p. 156 'As she said this, she thought . . .' Moorhouse, *Grand Days*, p. 660.

p. 156 'As she stared out of the railway carriage . . .' Moorhouse, F., *Dark Palace*, Sydney: Picador, 2000, pp. 261–63.

p. 157   'Together with this disconcerting idea . . .' Moorhouse, *Dark Palace*, pp. 390–91.

p. 157   'She had a vocation and . . .' Moorhouse, *Dark Palace*, p. 25.

p. 160   'The book embodies a lot of my own personal preoccupations . . .' Lumby, C., 'Frank Moorhouse', *The Bulletin*, 25 July 2000, p. 50.

p. 160   'Moorhouse published a section of the working manuscript . . .' Moorhouse, F., 'Schooling', in P. Blazey, V. Dawson and T. Herbert (eds), *Love Cries*, Sydney: Angus & Robertson, 1995.

p. 161   'Not all taboos are nonsense . . .' Moorhouse, 'Manifesto for the Imagination', p. 54.

p. 162   'A Shakespearean play—say, *Romeo and Juliet* . . .' Moorhouse, 'Manifesto for the Imagination', p. 56.

p. 163   'In his memoir *Things I Didn't Know* . . .' Hughes, R., *Things I Didn't Know: A memoir*, New York: Alfred A. Knopf, 2005.

p. 163   'In a book about his passion for fishing . . .' Hughes, R., *A Jerk on One End: Reflections of a mediocre fisherman*, New York: Ballantine Books, 1999.

p. 163   'Perhaps pornography can be most usefully understood . . .' Lumby, *Bad Girls*, p. 97.

p. 164   'Despite all appearances to the contrary . . .' Kendrick, W., *The Secret Museum: Pornography in modern culture*, New York: Viking, 1987, p. 9.

p. 166   'Pornography, like rape, is a male invention . . .' Brownmiller, S., *Against Our Will*, New York: Ballantine Books, 1975, p. 376.

p. 166   'The latest phase of the pornography debate . . .' Kendrick, *The Secret Museum*, p. 236.

p. 167   'He had, glancing at their faces . . .' Moorhouse, F., *The Everlasting Secret Family*, Sydney: Angus & Robertson, 1980, p. 6.

p. 169   'she could not tell whether there was . . .' Moorhouse, *Grand Days*, p. 28.

p. 169   'He then came to her as a woman . . .' Moorhouse, *Grand Days*, p. 113.

p. 170   'As she undressed herself before him . . .' Moorhouse, *Dark Palace*, p. 145.

p. 170   'she'd always told herself that Ambrose . . .' Moorhouse, *Dark Palace*, p. 136.

p. 171   'analyses the way cross-dressing directs the viewer . . .' Garber, M., *Vested Interests: Cross-Dressing and Cultural Anxiety*, New York: HarperCollins, 1992.

p. 171   'it was conventional to dress boys in pink and girls in blue . . .' Garber, *Vested Interests*, p. 1.

p. 172   'easy notions of binarity, putting into question . . .' Garber, *Vested Interests*, pp. 9–10.

p. 172   'The "third" is a mode of articulation . . .' Garber, *Vested Interests*, p. 11.

p. 174   'We should all have another self . . .' Moorhouse, *Grand Days*, p. 290.

p. 174   'Time and movement then became slippery . . .' Moorhouse, *Grand Days*, p. 198.

p. 175   'she felt that she'd had a private insight . . .' Moorhouse, *Grand Days*, p. 204.

CHAPTER 6: GRAND SCHEMES

p. 180   'There was something intoxicating . . .' Moorhouse quoted in Hicks, I., 'Full House Hears Written Words', *The Sydney Morning Herald*, 7 March 1994, p. 9.

p. 182   '*Grand Days* and its stand-alone sequel . . .' Kiernan, B., 'Libertarian Rules', *The Australian*, 14 February 2001.

p. 183   'Mary McGeachy was sitting in a chair . . .' Moorhouse, F., 'A league of her own', *The Sydney Morning Herald*, 4 September 1993, p. 4.

p. 184 'My role as a researching fiction writer on this matter . . .' Moorhouse, 'A league of her own', p. 4.

p. 185 'Frankly, she didn't care one way or another . . .' Moorhouse, *Grand Days*, pp. 247–48.

p. 186 'She's like a living person . . .' Crabb, A., 'What would Edith do?', Sydney Writers' Festival, 19 May 2012.

p. 186 'At least since Samuel Richardson . . .' Indyk, I., 'Bureaucrats as Bohemians? Yes, Yes, Yes', *The Sunday Age*, 31 October 1993.

p. 187 'She thought of committees as parlour games . . .' Moorhouse, *Grand Days*, p. 44.

p. 187 'And that, dear Cooper . . .' Moorhouse, *Grand Days*, p. 396.

p. 188 'Half seriously, Horne's Rule of commitment-to-the-total-experience . . .' Moorhouse, *Conference-ville*, p. 21.

p. 188 'She moved, in what she felt was a gathered-together way . . .' Moorhouse, *Grand Days*, p. 3.

p. 189 'right down to the furniture . . .' Kiernan, 'Libertarian Rules'.

p. 189 'the league is a grand metaphor . . .' Indyk, 'Bureaucrats as Bohemians'.

p. 190 'We have come to Geneva to aid the League . . .' Moorhouse, *Grand Days*, p. 80.

p. 190 'You think there are people who would try to harm us? . . .' Moorhouse, *Grand Days*, p. 82.

p. 191 'Wilson, along with many other internationalists . . .' Ostrower, G., 'The United States and the League of Nations, 1919–1939', in *The League of Nations in Retrospect*, Berlin & New York: Walter de Gruyter, 1983, pp. 128–43.

p. 192 'While on leave, I saw an invention . . .' Moorhouse, *Grand Days*, pp. 563–64.

p. 197 'Local fascist youths burst in . . .' Kiernan, 'Libertarian Rules'.

p. 198 'the seating arrangements might shake them . . .' Moorhouse, *Dark Palace*, p. 119.

p. 199 'Such disruption of the codes . . .' Kiernan, 'Libertarian Rules'.

CHAPTER 7: DESIGNING A NATION

p. 202 'What are you guys doing . . .' Moorhouse, *The Americans, Baby*, p. 66.

p. 203 'She knew that if you were . . .' Moorhouse, *Cold Light*, p. 92.

p. 203 'A Greek male refuses . . .' Nussbaum, M., *The Cosmopolitan Tradition: A Noble but Flawed Ideal*, Cambridge, Massachusetts: Harvard University Press, 2019, p. 1.

p. 204 'But didn't you do the same, Edith? . . .' Moorhouse, *Cold Light*, p. 17.

p. 205 'What should we do about us? . . .' Moorhouse, *Cold Light*, p. 30.

p. 205 'Over the years . . .' Moorhouse, *Cold Light*, p. 523.

p. 206 'Being dumped here . . .' Moorhouse, *Cold Light*, p. 54.

p. 206 'the lobby included . . .' Coleman, *Obscenity, Blasphemy and Sedition*, pp. 106–11.

p. 207 'The negro and his African jungle . . .' Coleman, *Obscenity, Blasphemy and Sedition*, p. 109.

p. 207 'I suppose I lean more towards Fabian socialism . . .' Moorhouse, *Cold Light*, p. 57.

p. 208 'She had laughingly refused . . .' Moorhouse, *Forty-Seventeen*, p. 8.

p. 209 'She was a married woman . . .' Moorhouse, *Cold Light*, p. 79.

p. 209 'There are those who want us to be as British as can be . . .' Moorhouse, *Cold Light*, p. 93.

p. 209 'Here we are in this diplomatically insignificant country . . .' Moorhouse, *Cold Light*, p. 113.

p. 210 'There is no history . . .' Moorhouse, *Cold Light*, p. 148.

p. 210 'made a virtue of the Australian fear . . .' Taylor, Paul (ed.). *Anything Goes: Art in Australia 1970–1980*, Melbourne: Art & Text, 1984.

p. 211 'luxuriate in your . . .' Mann, S., 'Confessions of a Reluctant Expatriate', *The Sydney Morning Herald*, 1 November 2000, p. 14.

p. 212 'These capitalist enterprises . . .' Penfold, H., *Indigenous Geographies of Home at Orient Point, NSW*, Human Geography (Honours), SGSC, University of Wollongong, 2017, p. 19.

p. 212 'The site has a long running historical significance . . .' Penfold, *Indigenous Geographies of Home at Orient Point*, p. 22.

p. 213 'nearly 30 concerned white citizens . . .' Jones, *Country Women and the Colour Bar*, p. 90.

p. 213 'Mrs Moorhouse, she was a beautiful old lady . . .' Jones, *Country Women and the Colour Bar*, pp. 98–99.

p. 214 'not to be a charity organisation . . .' Jones, *Country Women and the Colour Bar*, p. 91.

p. 214 'In our tin shack, we only had . . .' Jones, *Country Women and the Colour Bar*, p. 213.

p. 215 'as the first thing that ever happened that was good . . .' Jones, *Country Women and the Colour Bar*, p. 96.

p. 215 'Mrs Bate said . . .' Jones, *Country Women and the Colour Bar*, p. 94.

p. 216 'Aboriginal CWA members like Belle McCleod . . .' Jones, *Country Women and the Colour Bar*, pp. 103–7.

p. 217 'A city is more than bricks and mortar . . .' The National Capital Development Commission, *The Future of Canberra*, Sydney: Angus & Robertson, 1965, p. 37.

p. 218 'Canberra could be a stunningly distinctive city . . .' Moorhouse, *Cold Light*, pp. 200–1.

p. 219 'She mostly felt she saw it all so clearly . . .' Moorhouse, *Cold Light*, pp. 201–2.

p. 220 'to betray a political party . . .' Moorhouse, *Cold Light*, pp. 253–55.

p. 221 'Back then ASIO had been in existence . . .' Moorhouse, *Australia Under Surveillance*, p. xiii.

p. 221 'I was a seventeen-year-old cadet journalist . . .' Moorhouse, *Australia Under Surveillance*, p. 7.

p. 222 'In many ways, as a result, ASIO . . .' Moorhouse, *Australia Under Surveillance*, p. 7.

p. 222 'Those writers thought to be connected . . .' Moorhouse, *Australia Under Surveillance*, p. 13.

p. 223 'I was hurt that Australian intelligence . . .' Moorhouse, *Australia Under Surveillance*, pp. 13–14.

p. 223 'Although recorded as a person interested . . .' Moorhouse, *Australia Under Surveillance*, p. 17.

p. 223 'The current suppressions of freedom of expression . . .' Moorhouse, *Australia Under Surveillance*, p. 62.

p. 224 'He added, 'It's an important city . . .' Moorhouse, *Cold Light*, p. 559.

p. 224 'She thought that there was an opportunity . . .' Moorhouse, *Cold Light*, p. 202.

p. 225 'Paths to the front door would curve . . .' Moorhouse, *Cold Light*, p. 560.

p. 225 'The city would be our Chartres Cathedral . . .' Moorhouse, *Cold Light*, p. 563.

ENDNOTES

CHAPTER 8: THE BUSH

p. 226 'The Australian bush is both real and imaginary . . .' Watson, D., *The Bush*, Melbourne: Penguin Random House, 2014, p. 66.

p. 227 'At the age of eight as a cub scout . . .' Moorhouse, F., 'I, Initiation', *Southerly*, vol. 74, no. 2, 2014, p. 43.

p. 227 'A crucially important experience . . .' de Berg, H. 'Excerpts From An Oral History Interview', recorded by Hazel de Berg, 29 June 1974 in *Frank Moorhouse: A Celebration*, National Library of Australia, Canberra, 2004.

p. 228 'I was expelled from the Scouts . . .' de Berg, 'Excerpts from an Oral History Interview'.

p. 229 'Although it was never stated explicitly . . .' Moorhouse, F., 'I, Initiation', p. 46.

p. 230 'I called to one of the scout leaders . . .' Moorhouse, 'I, Initiation', p. 49.

p. 230 'On the night of my fall . . .' Moorhouse, 'I, Initiation', p. 51.

p. 231 'Whatever we make of it . . .' Moorhouse, 'I, Initiation', p. 53.

p. 231 'As they walked deeper into the bush . . .' Moorhouse, F., 'From a Bush Log Book 1', *in Forty-Seventeen*, p. 36.

p. 231 'I don't go into the bush for views . . .' Moorhouse, 'From a Bush Log Book 1', p. 36.

p. 232 'because he liked to leave the tent . . .' Moorhouse, 'From a Bush Log Book 1', p. 42.

p. 232 'The disquiet came because Belle . . .' Moorhouse, 'From a Bush Log Book 1', p. 49.

p. 233 'Moorhouse is the lachrymosely joking chronicler . . .' Pierce, P., *The Country of Lost Children: An Australian anxiety*, New York: Cambridge University Press, 1999, p. 121.

p. 233 'Moorhouse's lost children are not rural waifs . . .' Pierce, *The Country of Lost Children*, p. 126.

p. 234 'What he didn't say to his mother and father . . .' Moorhouse, F., 'From a Bush Log Book 2', in *Forty-Seventeen*, p. 49.

p. 234 'What are you going to eat out there? . . .' Moorhouse, 'From a Bush Log Book 2', p. 51.

p. 235 'He told them he was going to the upper reaches . . .' Moorhouse, 'From a Bush Log Book 2', p. 53.

p. 235 'I'd like to go into the bush without a plan . . .' Moorhouse, 'From a Bush Log Book 2', p. 54.

p. 236 'From the moment you left the car behind you . . .' Moorhouse, 'From a Bush Log Book 2', p. 58.

p. 239 'The paper purports to analyse Lawson's "The Drover's Wife" . . .' Moorhouse, F., *The Drover's Wife: A Celebration of a Great Australian Love Affair*, Sydney: Random House, 2017, p. 269.

p. 240 'Each of these works has the status of an Australian classic . . .' Moorhouse, *The Drover's Wife*, p. 269.

p. 240 'All cultures have a need for artworks . . .' Moorhouse, *The Drover's Wife*, p. 270.

p. 240 'What historians have not been able to incorporate . . .' Moorhouse, *The Drover's Wife*, p. 272.

p. 241 'In the story, in the absence of her drover husband . . .' Moorhouse, *The Drover's Wife*, p. 275.

p. 241 'I think I should tell you . . .' Moorhouse, *The Drover's Wife*, p. 290.

p. 242 'that transformed Australian fiction . . .' King, B., '*The Faber Book of Contemporary Australian Short Stories* by Murray Bail' [review], *World Literature Today*, vol. 62, no. 4, 1988, p. 724.

p. 242 'The writers of the 1970s such as Moorhouse . . .' Bail, M., *The Faber Book of Contemporary Australian Short Stories*, London: Faber & Faber, 1988.

p. 242 'ironic, masculine voices, parodying themselves . . .' Sallay, A., 'Virgin Sock-Washers and Tweed Jackets', *Southerly*, vol. 68, no. 2, 2008, p. 184.

p. 243 'So there is the nationalist cult of the short story . . .' Wilding, *The Tabloid Story Pocket Book*, p. 303.

p. 244 '[I]t could be said that both the Lawson story . . .' Moorhouse, *The Drover's Wife*, pp. 18–19.

p. 245 'Lawson knew intimately . . .' Moorhouse, *The Drover's Wife*, pp. 15–16.

p. 245 'Contemporary descriptions of the personality . . .' Moorhouse, *The Drover's Wife*, pp. 26–27.

p. 246 'began to be haunted by the dread . . .' Lawson quoted in Moorhouse, *The Drover's Wife*, pp. 26–27.

p. 247 'I had noticed this long-necked . . .' Gordon quoted in Moorhouse, *The Drover's Wife*, p. 56.

p. 247 'I imagine that it was for Lawson and Jim . . .' Moorhouse, *The Drover's Wife*, p. 59.

p. 247 'They bonded again as mates . . .' Jim in Moorhouse, *The Drover's Wife*, pp. 61–62.

p. 248 'resistant to Manning Clark's view . . .' Moorhouse, *The Drover's Wife*, p. 64.

p. 248 'I should at this point declare . . .' Moorhouse, *The Drover's Wife*, p. 57.

p. 248 'But more curiously . . .' Moorhouse, *The Drover's Wife*, pp. 57–58.

p. 248 'Many writers have contemplated . . .' Moorhouse, *The Drover's Wife*, p. 39.

p. 249 'Lawson was a great fighter . . .' Prichard, J.J. 'Louisa Lawson' in Caine, B. (ed), *Australian Feminism: A Companion*, Melbourne: Oxford University Press, 1998, p. 446.

p. 249 'She is utterly self-neglectful . . .' Moorhouse, *The Drover's Wife*, p. 84.

p. 250 'successfully empathise with the drover's wife's . . .' Moorhouse, *The Drover's Wife*, p. 41.

p. 251 'In writing "The Drover's Wife" . . .' Moorhouse, *The Drover's Wife*, p. 42.

p. 251 'Over the years . . .' Moorhouse, F., 'If you know Bourke you know Australia: Walpurgis Night on Mount Gunderbooka', *Griffith Review*, no. 36, 2012, p. 13.

p. 252 'I was now conscious of the risk . . .' Moorhouse, F., 'If you know Bourke you know Australia', p. 19.

p. 252 'The insects were not angry . . .' Moorhouse, 'If you know Bourke you know Australia', p. 25.

p. 254 'I have absorbed this don't-quit attitude from my family . . .' Moorhouse, 'If you know Bourke you know Australia', p. 21.

CONCLUSION

p. 255 'He's dead, isn't he . . .' Joan Didion, *The Year of Magical Thinking*, New York: Knopf, 2005, p. 15

p. 263 'Frank identified as Freudian . . .' Fiona Giles, 'Frank Recollections', *The Monthly*, August 2022, p. 49.

IMAGE CREDITS

INSERT A

Page 1

i   Contemporary family records, Moorhouse Papers, Fryer Library, University of Queensland

ii Contemporary family records, Moorhouse Papers, Fryer Library, University of Queensland

Page 2

i   Contemporary family records, Moorhouse Papers, Fryer Library, University of Queensland

ii Contemporary family records, Moorhouse Papers, Fryer Library, University of Queensland

Page 3

Contemporary family records, Moorhouse Papers, Fryer Library, University of Queensland

Page 4

i   Photo provided by Wendy (Halloway) James

ii Contemporary family records, Moorhouse Papers, Fryer Library, University of Queensland

Page 5

i   Contemporary family records, Moorhouse Papers, Fryer Library, University of Queensland

ii Photo provided by Wendy (Halloway) James

Page 6

i   Moorhouse Papers, Fryer Library, University of Queensland

ii *Riverina Express* (1958–63), proprietors David E. Gyger & Edwin Cross, Moorhouse Papers, Fryer Library, University of Queensland

Page 7

Riverina Express (1958–63), proprietors David E. Gyger & Edwin Cross, Moorhouse Papers, Fryer Library, University of Queensland

Page 8

i   Photograph provided by Wendy (Halloway) James

ii Moorhouse Papers, Fryer Library, University of Queensland

INSERT B

Page 1
i   Photograph by Frank Moorhouse
ii Photograph provided by Sandra Levy

Page 2
i   Photograph provided by Carl Harrison-Ford
ii Photographer unknown

Page 3
i   Moorhouse Papers, Fryer Library, University of Queensland
ii Photographer unknown

Page 4
i   Photographer unknown
ii Production still, photographer unknown, Moorhouse Papers, Fryer Library, University of Queensland

Page 5
i   Photograph provided by Sandra Levy
ii Itinerant photographer

Page 6
i   Moorhouse Papers, Fryer Library, University of Queensland
ii Photographer unknown

Page 7
i   Itinerant photographer
ii Photographer unknown

Page 8
i   Photographer unknown
ii Photographer unknown

INSERT C

Page 1
i   Photograph by Rita Scharf
ii Itinerant photographer (Polaroid)

Page 2
i   Photograph by staff waiter
ii Photograph by staff waiter

Page 3
i   Photograph by Anthony Stones (deceased)
ii Photograph by Kristen Williamson

Page 4
i   Photograph by Guibourg Delamotte
ii Cinema Enterprises/David Roe

Page 5
i   Still
ii Photographer unknown

Page 6
i   Photograph provided by Xavier Hennekinne
ii Photograph provided by Xavier Hennekinne

Page 7
i   Photograph by Jill White
ii Photographer unknown, image licensed under the Creative Commons Attribution-Share Alike 4.0 International license

Page 8
i   Photographer unknown, portrait is made available under the Creative Commons CC0 1.0 Universal Public Domain Dedication
ii Moorhouse Papers, Fryer Library, University of Queensland

INDEX

INDEX

INDEX